T0313737

The
Living
Trust Advisor

The Living Trust Advisor

Second Edition

EVERYTHING YOU (AND YOUR FINANCIAL PLANNER) NEED TO KNOW ABOUT YOUR LIVING TRUST

Jeffrey L. Condon, Esq.

WILEY

Cover design: Wiley

Published by John Wiley & Sons, Inc., Hoboken, New Jersey.
The first edition was published by Wiley in 2008.
Published simultaneously in Canada.

For general information on our other products and services or for technical support, please
contact our Customer Care Department within the United States at (800) 762-2974, outside
the United States at (317) 572-3993 or fax (317) 572-4002.

Wiley publishes in a variety of print and electronic formats and by print-on-demand. Some
material included with standard print versions of this book may not be included in e-books
or in print-on-demand. If this book refers to media such as a CD or DVD that is not included
in the version you purchased, you may download this material at http://booksupport.wiley
.com. For more information about Wiley products, visit www.wiley.com.

Library of Congress Cataloging-in-Publication Data:
Condon, Jeffrey L., author.
  The living trust advisor : everything you (and your financial planner) need to know about
your living trust / Jeffrey L. Condon. — Second edition.
      pages cm
  Includes index.
  ISBN 978-1-119-07394-9 (cloth); ISBN 978-1-119-09328-2 (ePDF);
ISBN 978-1-119-09331-2 (ePub)
  1. Living trusts—United States—Popular works. 2. Estate planning—United States—
Popular works. I. Title.
  KF734.C66 2016
  346.7305'2—dc23
                                                                    2015029526

Printed in the United States of America

10 9 8 7 6 5 4 3 2 1

For Kyle Collins. For my family and I, your name shall hereinafter be synonymous with resilience, courage, and strength of spirit.

Contents

Pregame Warm-Up

OR,

READ THIS BEFORE YOU READ THIS BOOK

If this book is in your hands, you are probably thinking about putting together a Living Trust, which is the primary tool in the United States for the transfer of your assets after the deaths of both you and your spouse to your children, grandchildren, or other heirs. Or perhaps you already have your Living Trust, which has collected dust on your bookshelf or in your safe-deposit box, and you somehow have been prompted into revisiting it.

For a combined 70 years, my late father, teacher, and mentor, Gerald Condon, and I set up thousands of Living Trusts for our clients. After all those years of advising clients on their inheritance instructions, I am left with this one conclusion: **You really don't know much about the Living Trust . . . or how it works . . . or what it should say or do . . . even if you have one!**

Actually, perhaps that assessment is too broad to be of practical use. I do tend to speak in sweeping generalizations. Let me be more specific by lumping you into one of four categories of Living Trust clients:

1. You do not have a Living Trust, and you don't really know much about the Living Trust other than it is some kind of inheritance document.
2. You already have a Living Trust, but you have no real or meaningful understanding of what it is or how it works beyond the basic function of transferring your assets to your

children after your death without probate. In other words, you just signed it where your attorney told you to sign, threw it into your car, and have not thought about it since.

3. You have a Living Trust and you initially made a real and earnest effort to decipher its form and function. But many years have passed since you established it, and all you really recall is (a) you have a Living Trust and (b) it contains your inheritance instructions.

4. You have a Living Trust, and you refused to sign it until your lawyer explained every single paragraph and provision to your satisfaction. If you are such a person, I say to you: Your kind is so rare that you qualify as an urban legend.

Whether you are a Living Trust rookie or veteran, welcome to this revised edition of *The Living Trust Advisor,* and congratulations on dealing with the often unpleasant task of facing your mortality!

Now, for you readers who are in the financial planning and advising profession, I also extend my heartiest welcome. At first blush, you may say to yourself, "Self, why do you need an education in the nuts and bolts of the Living Trust? You're not a lawyer. Your job description is to make as much money for your clients as safely possible. If your clients have any estate planning needs, you'll simply advise them to see an estate planning attorney. Have a nice day, Self!"

That's what I used to think as well. You financial people come up with a plan to make your clients money, and I'll come up with a plan to leave your clients' money to their children, grandchildren, and other heirs. And never the twain shall meet.

Let me tell you how I learned otherwise with the tale of the comeuppance that I received from a 300-plus group of your colleagues. It wasn't pretty. But if it wasn't for that experience, I would never have come to know about the importance of the financial advisor in my professional life.

About 10 years ago, I was invited to speak on "The Right Way and the Wrong Way of Leaving Money to Your Children (& Others)" before a national conference of the Financial Planning Association (FPA) in Colorado Springs. I gave this talk at a few previous regional

FPA conferences (including Providence, Rhode Island, where I met an FPA member named . . . Jeff Condon. What are the odds?). I assume I was a big enough hit at those prior gigs to justify the FPA paying my speaking fee and travel expenses for the national gathering. Using baseball parlance, it was like going from the minor leagues to the Show.

When I am introduced at my talks, my "credits" never fail to strike a chord with the attendees. Although there are numerous estate planning attorneys with more impressive professional credentials than mine, none can claim that they wrote the best-selling inheritance-related book in American publishing history that the *Wall Street Journal* called the "best estate planning book in America" . . . or can say they have appeared on dozens of well-known television, radio, and Internet shows and outlets. As the conference's program coordinator ran through my accomplishments, I heard the usual mutters of "Wow!" "Really?" "Impressive." "Gee." "This should be good." Before I uttered word one, I had won over the 300 or so attendees—and I knew for certain that my presentation would leave them entertained and edified.

Yes, I was all full of myself. But that feeling was relatively short-lived.

After the (yet another successful) presentation, a standing microphone was placed on the floor near the dais for those who wanted to ask questions. The line quickly formed and snaked to the ballroom entrance. I believe it was the fourth person in line who asked me this: "Mr. Condon. I just want to say that was a terrific talk, and I learned a lot. Can you tell me how you use the financial planner in your practice?"

And this was my exact word-for-word response: "Ummm . . . I . . . uhhh . . . I don't really use the financial planner at all. Why would I?"

Have you ever had the experience of being ostracized by a large gathering of people? You don't want it. It's the initial silence of incredulousness. Then the sounds of notebooks shutting, chairs backing away, barely disguised mutterings, and feet walking in a direction other than yours. The sight of faces who were moments before enraptured, now revealing disdain and disgust. The sudden feeling of warm sweat permeating throughout the body. I take great pride in making a great impression on my audience. Not just good, but great. But now I was doing the polar opposite.

This was one of those times when the truth—that bringing the financial planner into the estate planning process had never before crossed my mind—was not the best response. The financial planner helps the client make money; the estate planning lawyer helps the client transfer that money to their children, grandchildren, and other heirs. Two separate worlds. And I assumed that financial planners believed likewise. But at that nightmarish moment—where I undid in 3 seconds the goodwill I had established in the previous 90 minutes with my inadvertent diminishment of the entire financial planning industry—I discovered that such an assumption was erroneous.

There was no pulling up from this nosedive. The program ended with the en masse walkout. As I was about to trudge from the dais, the program coordinator stood in front of me, put his hands on my shoulders, and said, "Jeff, I can see you are about to go into a deep funk. But try to hear me. Instead of castigating you, I think they should be thanking you. You woke us up to the fact that your industry is totally in the dark about what we do and how we can be of service. What you said about not needing us—that should be our rallying cry to find ways to explain to you why and how you need us. Not as a reason to get out the tar and feathers."

Those words talked me off the ledge. But more important, they were the impetus for my awakening to the fact that the financial planner is integral to the estate-planning process. While the estate-planning lawyer rarely sees or communicates with his Living Trust clients, you, the financial planner, are on the front line of your clients' lives. You are in touch with them at least every few months with calls, statements, emails, and invitations to seminars. You make, at least, annual inquires about their financial health and status, which, typically, beget a discussion of their latest family goings-on. Births of grandchildren. Graduations. Deaths. Children's employment status. What's going on with the "problem" child. As part of that discussion, you invariably bring up their estate planning—because you recognize that a sound plan to leave their wealth after death is just as important as the investment strategy that creates that wealth.

So you ask the usual questions about your clients' estate plan. Do they have one? If so, is it a Living Trust or a will? Was it prepared by an attorney? How old is it? When did they last have it reviewed? Does it speak to any of their current family dynamics and circumstances? And after this brief discussion, you advise them to see an attorney, which, most likely, will not be an easy sell. Why? Because your clients, like most people, are not accustomed to seeing lawyers. Most people go through almost their entire lives without anything "legal" happening to them. No divorces, arrests, lawsuits, or entity formations. Or, if your clients have had previous brushes with lawyers, those experiences may have been less than pleasant. Well, whether your clients go willingly or reluctantly, you, the financial planner, must strongly advise them to see an estate planning attorney about establishing or amending their Living Trust.

Is that it? Do I think you are just the shill for the estate planning attorney? Absolutely not. You are part of the estate planning *team*. While the attorney sits at his desk, you sit in front of your clients. You're there with them . . . and their Living Trust. With the Financial Alerts peppered throughout this book, you will be able to confidently sift through your clients' Living Trust and zero in on certain sections that could inadvertently cause harm to your clients' children and their relationships with each other. These alerts will give you the knowledge you need to engage in a productive conversation about the effect and ramifications of certain provisions that they may have never before considered.

Your clients don't know what they don't know. They don't know whether their Living Trust will solve inheritance problems . . . or create them. However, after you read this book—and after your clients regale you with their current family circumstances—you will have the ability to recognize whether certain provisions in their Living Trust should be changed or removed to ensure that your clients' Living Trust applies to those family conditions.

These Financial Alerts do not ask you to practice law. They are educating you on recognizing problems. As my father taught me, 95 percent of the solution to any problem is recognizing the problem in the first place. Once you are able to point out the unwanted or unintended ramifications of certain provisions of your clients' Living Trust, then your advice for them to see the lawyer is not just lip service to make you look good or protect your back.

Without you first reviewing your clients' Living Trust . . . and without you first having taken the tour of your clients' financial and family lives . . . and without you looking at important provisions in your clients' Living Trust in the context of their present circumstances, it is highly unlikely they will ever see a lawyer for a Living Trust review and fix.

Maybe this isn't a traditional part of the financial advisor job description; still, it's an important function that helps to maintain family harmony in the inheritance arena, which can only enhance the valuable services you bring to your clients.

The Big Game: Living and Dying with Your Living Trust

The purpose of this book is quite simple. I want you to think of me as your Living Trust coach. Like any coach, I want to train you so you will be ready to play the big game, which, in this case, is living with your Living Trust with no financial, emotional, or practical upheaval in your life, and dying with a Living Trust that will adequately and effectively provide for your spouse, children, charities, and other heirs and beneficiaries with a minimum of conflict, diversion, tax, and expense.

- Like any football or basketball game, this big game takes place in a special arena . . . the inheritance arena. The players are you, your spouse, your Living Trust lawyer, your assets, your children, your other beneficiaries, and, perhaps, the Internal Revenue Service (IRS). And like any game, there is a warm-up period (which is where you are right now), four quarters of play, and a cool-down period. Think of *The Living*

Trust Advisor as your playbook that describes how to play the big game during those different periods, which are: The First Quarter: Establishing Your Living Trust.

- The Second Quarter: Living with Your Living Trust during the Lifetimes of You and Your Spouse.
- The Third Quarter: Living with Your Living Trust after the Death of Your Spouse.
- The Fourth Quarter: Dying with Your Living Trust.
- Postgame: Review and Lessons Learned.

The big game begins the moment the concept of doing your Living Trust pops in your mind. That is when the whistle blows to start play. It ends when both you and your spouse have died and your Living Trust assets are in the hands of your children or other beneficiaries.

Between the beginning and end of the big game, though, there is a lot that happens.

- There is the selection of the Living Trust lawyer.
- There is the understanding of the nuts and bolts of the Living Trust document.
- There is the allocation of the assets—real estate, stocks, bank accounts, brokerage assets, businesses, personal effects—to the Living Trust.
- There is the operation and management of the Living Trust during the lifetimes of both you and your spouse.
- There is dealing with your Living Trust real estate when you sell or refinance that property.
- There is the selection of key players—the managers, agents, and protectors—upon which depends the success or failure of your Living Trust and your inheritance instructions.
- There is the operation and management of the Living Trust when the first spouse dies (the deceased spouse).
- There is the protection of the surviving spouse's ownership and control of the Living Trust assets during that spouse's incapacity or incompetence.
- There is the operation and management of the Living Trust when the last spouse (the surviving spouse) dies.

- There is the filing of the last spouse's estate tax return and payment of estate taxes.
- There is the distribution of the Living Trust assets to your children without creating conflict and chaos between them.
- And there is the protection of your children's Living Trust inheritance from the winds of their fates: their addictions, divorces, remarriages, mental disabilities, financial immaturity, and creditors.

It does not matter whether you have played the big game before or whether you already have your Living Trust. After you read *The Living Trust Advisor* playbook, you will know how to play the big game the way it should be played. If you follow my training and listen to my advice, I believe you will walk away from the big game a winner. In my book, winning means:

- Having a clearer understanding of your Living Trust.
- Opening your eyes to the numerous problems and issues in the inheritance arena that you must consider before your first meeting with your Living Trust lawyer.
- Maintaining ownership and control of your Living Trust assets while you and your spouse are both alive, and then after the death of one spouse.
- Facilitating the smooth transfer of your Living Trust assets to your children, grandchildren, and other heirs after your death.
- Identifying potential inheritance problem areas now so you have the opportunity to build solutions into your Living Trust in order to prevent those problems from arising during your life and after your death.

A Few Things You Should Know about My Coaching Style

Before I say something trite right now like "Let the big game begin!" I must first convey a few things you should know about my style of coaching in order to help you follow the instructions in this playbook.

Bringing You into My Personal Life

Throughout this book, I will pepper you with numerous examples that illustrate a key point or demonstrate how you can do something. While many of these examples may be drawn from experiences with clients, others may provide you with an occasional glimpse into my personal life. Whether I allude to my business history, divorce, girlfriend, or likes and dislikes, I use these personal anecdotes as a device to support certain issues or emphasize particular concepts that arise in this book.

While I understand the viewpoint that divulging one's personal anecdotes and professional experiences may be unprofessional, I have always disagreed with it. I believe that providing examples and sharing details that have arisen in my personal life and law practice bring this nonfiction book about estate planning alive and make the advice offered applicable to your life, too.

Therefore, you are not getting a technical lecture filled with charts, graphs, and PowerPoint slides within this book. Instead, you are receiving the advice and opinions of one attorney based on his observations and experiences—both professional and personal. With such a subjective approach, it is near impossible to convey effective lessons by keeping the private life out of the process.

Making Sweeping Generalizations

I am fond of broad and superlative statements that appear to be intended to apply universally to every reader of this book. Of course, I know that for every person who embodies such an absolute, there is another person for whom that absolute does not apply. Nonetheless, in order to help convey information and emphasize a particular point, a statement must come across as somewhat dogmatic without reference to exceptions. Therefore, the sweeping generalization is a literary device I often employ in *The Living Trust Advisor.*

Using Everyday Language to Explain Technical Ideas

The Living Trust, family inheritance planning, and estate taxes involve complex personal and financial issues. But discussing these issues in a legal manner would ensure this book's quick demise and bargain-basement status, as it would render the book a somewhat lackluster and uninteresting read. Moreover, if I used fancy legal jargon, I fear that many readers might not understand what I was saying. Therefore, I use nontechnical language to explain many technical concepts throughout this book. For example, the person whom you appoint to carry out your instructions after your death is called the *successor trustee*. In this book, I refer to that person as the *after-death agent*. Since your attorney might wonder what you are talking about if you mention appointing your after-death agent, I also supply the technical term.

Getting My Sense of Humor

At my seminars, there are two compliments that I can never get enough of. The first: "Gee, Mr. Condon, are you sure you're a lawyer? I understood every word you said." The second: "Mr. Condon, I never thought I would find myself laughing at a seminar on death and taxes. I was really entertained."

I'm not using these comments to wow you into buying this book or attending my seminars. I'm just trying to show you that I have found success in using humor as the medicine to help folks digest this material more easily, and that this book follows suit with my usual comedic approach.

I have an absurd sense of humor, and this book is riddled with it. With a title like *The Living Trust Advisor*, you probably would not expect to find such a quality in an inheritance planning book. I am aware that some readers may not find it appropriate to address death-and-taxes-type matters with a comedic approach. However, I could not restrain myself, for two reasons. First, I just gotta be me. Second, approaching such a tedious subject as the Living Trust with humor simply makes that matter less tedious and, if I have my way, even entertaining.

Consulting Your Own Living Trust Lawyer

This book is designed to identify situations, problems, and conflicts that arise in the establishment, maintenance, and distribution of your Living Trust. However, because your set of circumstances may differ from the scenarios I describe, it is critical that you do not include any of my suggestions in your own Living Trust without first consulting your own Living Trust attorney.

Your Final Locker Room Pep Talk Before Training Begins

I was on water polo and swim teams throughout high school and college. I remember some amazing locker room pep talks made by my coaches that took us from lackadaisical ("What are we doing here?") to motivated and focused on the mission ("Let's go get 'em!"). Inspired by those sessions in those days of yore, I now want to give you my pep talk to motivate you throughout your training.

You are about to embark on a process that is more than just dollars and cents. Your Living Trust is the last great lesson you will give to your spouse, children, and other beneficiaries. It is the vehicle by which you transfer your lifetime of accumulations to them. If your Living Trust lesson goes sour—by leaving your beneficiaries in conflict, or by causing your assets to be depleted by taxes and expenses, or by requiring that your beneficiaries go through probate to obtain ownership of your Living Trust assets, or by causing your Living Trust assets to become depleted once they are in the hands of your beneficiaries—so too will the memory of you be impaired.

But it does not have to be that way. That's what I—your Living Trust coach—am here for. That's why you have this *Living Trust Advisor* playbook in your hands. With this book, you will learn all you ever need to know about how to play the Living Trust game—from the time the concept of the Living Trust enters your head to the time its inheritance instructions are carried out after you and your spouse are gone.

Here it comes: Let the big game begin!

Acknowledgments

Writing can be a very rewarding experience. But, when the writing involves trying to turn a subject as complex and tedious as the Living Trust into (one hopes) a lighthearted and entertaining romp, it can also be exasperating. No one thinks of the estate planning attorney as a tortured artist; but, after multiple occasions of spending hours on a single paragraph attempting to be informative *and* witty, I felt I was Van Gogh.

With the three editions of my other book and this second edition of the *Living Trust Advisor,* this is the fifth opportunity I've had to publicly acknowledge *in a real book* the important persons in my life and the ones who were integral in producing this book. Such mentions just don't seem as special and permanent in social media, do they? On the Internet, anyone can acknowledge anyone for anything. Just the other day on Facebook I posted my congratulations to my mother's dog, Molly, for successfully jumping off the couch. Just too easy (both the posting and the couch-jumping)! But when folks see their name in print in a real, old-fashioned book that they can see and feel, that must be a thrill for them, yes? Well, at least it's still a thrill for me to have this platform.

In keeping with my lawyer-like penchant to compartmentalize, I shall break my acknowledgments into three separate and distinct categories.

For Those without Whom This Revised Edition Wouldn't Exist

Stacey Rivera and Tula Batanchiev. Stacey is my manuscript editor at Wiley, and Tula is the acquiring editor who originated and championed the idea of this revised edition of *Living Trust Advisor*. Both are not only brilliant and industrious, they are masters of the lost art of editor-author diplomacy. Painful cuts and edits in my precious manuscript and rejections of my inspired cover design ideas (such as a Pomeranian sitting on a wad of cash) were almost a pleasure with their pleasant and engaging manner. From now on, whenever bad news about anything has to be delivered to me, I want Stacey and Tula to be the messengers.

For Those Who Happen to Be My Children

I have previously used my acknowledgments to impart awesome and incredible fatherly advice to my three children, Bradley, Hayley, and Carly. Why should this one be any different? So if you happen to be a child of Jeffrey Condon, listen up (read up?) to this Top Ten List of Things You Need to Do, Not Do or Know:

1. A gift is for the giver.
2. In any non-life-threatening heated discussion or argument with anyone, think before you speak and stay on point.
3. Don't text and drive.
4. Conduct all your interactions and interpersonal relations with the Golden Rule in mind.
5. Although it was really cool to see Han Solo and Chewbacca back in action, *Star Trek* STILL RULES over *Star Wars*.
6. Do not loan money to a friend, and do not borrow money from a friend. The money relationship will end the friendship.
7. When I die, *don't* sell my comic book collection. It's worth more than the three of you combined. Preserve and protect it.
8. As Coach used to say: If you can't do what you want, do what you can.

9. Do some kind of athletic activity every day. Getting the blood pumping energizes you and makes a tangible difference in how you approach and handle the day. Don't wait until you feel like it because no one ever feels like it.
10. I love you all.

For Those Who Made the Cut

In all of my prior acknowledgments, I had fun mentioning everyone with some connection to me. It was fun to see their reactions to their names in my book, especially when they had no reason to expect to ever see their names in my book. Distant relatives. Friends. Acquaintances. My children's friends. My children's friends' parents. My children's coaches and teachers. If I saw somebody once a week who had even a small role in my existence or the lives of my children, they made it in.

Now with my children grown and gone, those old social spheres have disappeared, and I have practically no connection to most of those people. Which leaves the ones who remain whom I am fortunate to have. These are the most meaningful and important people in my life . . . and who made me a happy (or at least, pacified) camper during the arduous process of writing this revision. So if you happen to see your name here, congrats! You made the cut!

My fun, beautiful, charismatic, cookie-pushing, and just plain nice girlfriend, Kimberly Klaskin, and her daughter, Jenna. Best of luck to both of you in your next adventure—life with Jessie!

My closest buddies since elementary and middle school: Bret Donnelly, Brad Wheeler, Mark Beede, Milton Stumpus, Eric Fonkalsrud, and Paul Cooke.

My old law school buddies: Kenneth Aslan and Anthony Caronna.

My secretary, Marbelis Garcia.

My Atlanta cousins: Phillip and Gilda Franklyn, and the majority of their four reasonably well-behaved daughters, Stephanie, Rachel, Sarah, and Julia. I'll leave it up to them to figure out which one did not make the cut. And with regard to Stephanie's and Rachel's upcoming nuptials, please inform your respective fiancés that your top wedding-day priority shall be the care and comfort of your Uncle/Cousin Frizz.

My lovely, venerable, and age-defying mother Esther Condon.

ESTABLISHING YOUR LIVING TRUST

If you have picked up this book, my hope is that you are finally at the point where the concept of actually establishing your Living Trust has entered the combined minds of you and your spouse. No more procrastination or excuses for not getting to it. You're here! You can't get more here than right here.

This is the beginning of your Living Trust training. Do you want to cross the goal line, spike that football, and revel in the roar of the crowd? Well, you know the drill. You first have to learn what a football is. To get to point Z, you must get to—and through—point A, which is getting you to understand what the Living Trust is, what it does, and how it works.

I wish I had the ability to get you through your Living Trust training in a 30-second workout montage, à la *Rocky*. But with this being real life, I can only offer you this mundane instruction: Turn the page and introduce yourself to the various components and players that make up your Living Trust.

1

How You Established Your Living Trust Without a Clear Understanding of What It Is and How It Works

OR,

YOU DON'T KNOW WHAT YOU DON'T KNOW ABOUT YOUR LIVING TRUST

Before your real Living Trust training begins in Chapter 2, I feel the need to address a point that is somewhat obvious, which I will state in your first person: "I already have a Living Trust. Why do I need your training session on the Living Trust when I have already received that information?"

In the Pregame Warm-Up, I made the bold and very broad assumption that you do not know much about your Living Trust, even if you have one. How did you react to such a presumptive assertion? Did you nod your head in recognition? Or did you fling this book across the room (or the bookstore) in disbelief and anger?

Let me tell you how I came to the assumption that you know very little, if anything at all, about your Living Trust, the document that your lawyer prepared, or you drafted yourself with LegalZoom and that you believe you already know all about.

What Does It All Mean?

I am an estate planning attorney. I am in the business of putting together inheritance plans. In the old days, you would have set forth your inheritance instructions in a will. Nowadays, those instructions will be set forth in a Living Trust. In effect, this makes me a Living Trust lawyer.

I learned this business from my father, Gerald M. Condon, who, in the early 1970s, was perhaps the first lawyer in the United States to conduct Living Trust seminars. This was a real homespun family operation. I manned the check-in table, my father gave the talk, and my mother made the brownies that the attendees devoured during the break.

About a decade after my father conducted his first seminar, Living Trust seminars became ubiquitous. They were seemingly everywhere, offered by attorneys, insurance companies, real estate firms, banks, and brokerage firms. You could not open your newspaper or mailbox without receiving a solicitation to attend one.

In the 1990s, the market for the Living Trust business had become farmed out. It was dog-eat-dog for the same potential pool of clients. Living Trusts became so cheap that reputable attorneys advertised their Living Trust services for as low as $499.

You get what you pay for in this world of ours, and the Living Trust consumer often experienced firsthand that old adage. Some Living Trust attorneys offered a good price, but at the expense of customer service. Practices became about volume. People never met the attorney who purportedly prepared their document. Instead, they saw paralegals who rushed them through the draft reviews. People felt like numbers instead of clients, and were too cowed by the manic process to ask questions. Ultimately, they signed their Living Trust without any meaningful understanding of the effect and function of the document and were politely shown the door. Next!

At his seminars, my father consistently gave what I believe, in my less-than-objective opinion, was the best presentation on the Living Trust since the world was a ball of molten lava. But the Living Trust world had changed, and we had to change with it.

The client base for Living Trust business had been tapped out, and people were weary of being bombarded with flyers, advertisements, and seminar invitations for low-cost Living Trusts.

As a result, our Living Trust seminars became "Family Inheritance Planning" seminars. Instead of talking about Living Trust mechanics, we focused on the human side of inheritances, such as how your children can share an inheritance when they could not even share their toys, and how you can prevent your surviving spouse from losing control of her money and property if the children are grasping for an early inheritance. Eventually, this new emphasis on the human and personal element in the inheritance arena comprised the theme of the first book my father and I co-wrote in 1996, *Beyond the Grave: The Right Way and the Wrong Way of Leaving Money to Your Children (and Others)*, which has since become the most widely distributed inheritance planning book in American publishing history.

Financial Advisor Alert

In connection with the marketing of the book, my father and I appeared on more than 100 radio talk shows throughout the United States, where we answered hundreds of questions from listeners about a wide range of inheritance planning issues—from succession of the family business, to protecting a widow from her own children grasping for an early inheritance, to leaving money to the family dog. Yet, of all the questions asked by callers, 90 percent of them were about the basics of the Living Trust. What is it? How does it work? What does it do? Why should I have one? What happens to it after I die? Where should I keep it? Why does it have so many pages? Moreover, these questions were asked by callers who informed us that they have Living Trusts that were prepared by lawyers!

So . . . consider presenting an inheritance planning seminar for your present and prospective clients with an experienced trusts and estates attorney as the guest speaker. By doing so, you will provide yourself with the opportunity to press the flesh and enhance your reputation as one who takes the time to make available information that the attendees will find absolutely invaluable.

I have been conducting Family Inheritance Planning seminars on my own for about 15 years. Although my style is certainly more freewheeling than my father's horse-sense suffer-no-fools approach, I proudly walk in his footsteps to offer invaluable information about family inheritance planning to audiences around the country. And as they did years ago, folks come up to me after my talks with their Living Trusts in hand, pointing to certain pages and asking me, "What the hell does this mean?"

And if you think there is a lot of ignorance out there with lawyer-drafted Living Trusts, don't get me started on the misconceptions and misinformation that arise in Living Trusts that are prepared without lawyers.

Too late! You got me started!

The Self-Drafted Living Trust—Don't Do It!

This book's title may have given you the impression that I am going to tell you how to establish your Living Trust on your own—without having to pay for a lawyer.

I hope I did not get your hopes up. This is not a "how to become your own lawyer" book. You would never consider being your own doctor. Why would you even think about being your own lawyer?

Certainly, taking the lawyer out of the process probably sounds pretty good to you. After all, if you are like most people, you have never before met with a lawyer, because, quite simply, you never had to. You have never been sued or divorced. You have never sued anyone. You have never been charged with a crime. You have not set up a corporation or partnership or engaged in a complex business transaction.

Indeed, you may have gone almost your entire life without the need to consult with a lawyer. I said "almost," because now you face the prospect of an inheritance document that, while simple in concept, can be quite daunting to construct. If you have seen a Living Trust before, you have found that they are somewhat lengthy. In my office, the typical Living Trust is 50 pages long.

But even though your head says you need a lawyer to help you through the minefield, your heart may be urging you to do it alone. Why? Because you have heard the lawyer horror stories from your family, friends, and co-workers. "My lawyer charges too much." "My lawyer never returns my calls." "I paid my lawyer a retainer months ago, and I haven't seen any documents yet." And on and on . . .

Of course, there is nothing to stop you from giving it the old college try. In fact, you will find a lot of help. There are a host of how-to books, software programs, and stationery forms, replete with terms and provisions that you can pick and choose to incorporate into your own Living Trust.

In all my years as an inheritance-planning lawyer, I have met with hundreds of do-it-yourselfers who have paid me a fee to review their efforts. Yes, that does sound inconsistent. Why would they want to pay me a fee to review their self-drafted Living Trusts when their main goal was to avoid paying me a fee in the first place? Their answers were universally the same: "I just wanted to be sure that everything is legal."

Let me tell you something, and please consider this your first piece of my advice. If you prepare your own Living Trust, it will be wrong in some way, shape, or form.

Maybe it will be a harmless error, such as explaining estate tax concepts with outdated language. Does your Living Trust use the term *A-B Trust* to incorporate the plan of preserving the deceased spouse's applicable exclusion amount? That is the right concept, but the wrong words. The use of the wrong language will not be fatal to that tax-saving plan, but the Living Trust is, technically, still wrong.

Maybe the mistake will be overkill. Several times a year, I review self-drafted Living Trusts that contain complex tax-reduction plans that would be appropriate only for the heads of Fortune 500 companies. But the persons who drafted those Living Trusts are nowhere near that wealth category. If those persons die with those plans in place, their beneficiaries will be stuck in a morass of expensive and unnecessary processes.

Maybe the mistake will be fatal to your children. One man came into my office explaining that his son was a drug addict. After reviewing the Living Trust he prepared with the help of the Trustmaker software program, I said to him with all the sarcasm I could muster: "Why does your Living Trust leave your drug-addicted son his inheritance share outright and under his full control? The second he gets his inheritance, he's going to turn it over to his pusher!"

After having reviewed hundreds of self-attempted Living Trusts, I have never seen one that has been correct, complete, or appropriate for the circumstances. It doesn't matter how smart you are, and what you do for a living is irrelevant (unless you are an inheritance planning attorney). There are too many subtleties and intricacies concerning your inheritance instructions in the Living Trust that the how-to books just don't pick up. You don't realize this because, in a circular bit of reasoning, the how-to books have not made you aware of them. In other words, you don't know what you don't know.

Financial Advisor Alert

When your clients tell you that they have a Living Trust, your follow-up question should always be, "Did an attorney prepare that Living Trust?" If the answer is no, tell them that out of an abundance of caution, they should have it reviewed by an attorney. Expect the response to be of the "We did this on our own to avoid attorney fees" variety. To that you say, "No matter how much energy you poured into your self-drafted Living Trust, you just don't know if you drafted it correctly. One mistake could lead your family into post-death chaos. One meeting with an attorney to review your Living Trust will give you the peace of mind that you didn't miss anything."

The only true way to learn about the dos and don'ts of the Living Trust is the hard way—from on-the-job training. That is why my profession is called the "practice" of law. We get to practice this stuff until we get it right.

For example, when I was a young attorney, I was innocent in my approach to drafting my clients' inheritance instructions in the Living Trust. When my clients told me there would never be any inheritance conflicts between their children, I believed them. After all, who was I to dispute my clients' conclusions about their children?

Nothing, however, prepared me for the harsh reality of human conflict when my clients' perfect children divided their inheritance. Lawyers are not taught to recognize inheritance conflicts in law school. There are no advice books or classes on this subject. The only way I learned about inheritance conflicts was from having a number of clients die and then dealing with their children when they divided the family money. Having observed what happens between children following their parents' deaths, I have arrived at this indelible conclusion: Your children might seem perfect—but you really don't know them until they divide your money.

You Might Have Living Trust Training, but You Haven't Been Trained My Way!

These experiences with both lawyer-prepared and self-drafted Living Trusts caused me to arrive at the sweeping generalization about how little you know about the Living Trust, even if you have one. A ton of people have been to Living Trust seminars, read Living Trust books, downloaded Living Trust software, and attended complimentary Living Trust consultations. Another ton of people have Living Trusts. But, those same tons of people still possess a definite and palpable thirst for knowledge about Living Trust basics.

In order to answer the questions of these many bewildered, misinformed, and mistaken people, I'm back with this, the revised edition of my second book, which is about living and dying with a Living Trust. I like to refer to it as "The Living Trust's Greatest Hits." In other words, this book presents everything you need to know about the establishment, maintenance, and management of a Living Trust at all stages of the game. Why should you pay thousands of dollars for a Living Trust just to have no meaningful and practical understanding of what may be the most important document of your life?

If you think you know everything about your Living Trust because your lawyer explained it to you—or you read the guidebook that came with the software—you don't!

If you think you don't need training on your Living Trust because you've already received that training—you do!

You have not been trained in your Living Trust my way. My way is to show you what you need to know before your Living Trust is set in stone. It will follow the flow of your money and property in the Living Trust at all stages of the game: while both you and your spouse are alive, then after the first spouse dies, and then when the last spouse dies and distribution is made to your children and grandchildren. The chapters that lie ahead explore aspects about your Living Trust that your lawyer—or software—never or inadequately explained to you.

So, just when you thought you were done with all matters Living Trust, I've pulled you back in. The Living Trust is back, baby! And I, your Living Trust advisor, will help you get through it.

CHAPTER

2

What Does the Living Trust Do, and How Does It Do It?

OR,

THE BEST EXPLANATION OF THE LIVING TRUST YOU WILL EVER GET

I have attended (snuck into?) some of the Living Trust seminars conducted by my colleagues. I have heard them take more than an hour to describe what the Living Trust is and how it works. Maybe you have been to one and wondered why you are sitting in a hot room for over an hour, listening to someone talk and talk about the purpose of a Living Trust. In this chapter, I will tell you—in three to five minutes—what a Living Trust is and what it does.

As you listen to my advice, I would ask that you forget everything you have ever heard about the basic mechanics of the Living Trust, even if you have one. If you focus on my explanation of the Living Trust—that it is simply an after-death power of attorney—you will guide yourself out of the legal haze thrust upon you by the Living Trust's multiple pages filled with legal words that we lawyers have to use so the document can qualify as a legally correct trust.

A Simple Explanation

The Living Trust is not a true trust arrangement. Oh, yes—it looks like a trust, reads like a trust, smells like a trust, and tastes like a trust. It has all the complex words and phrases that a trust is supposed to have. But still, it is not a true trust arrangement.

A true trust arrangement takes place when you take your money and property to a money manager and say, "I want you to manage these assets. I want you to take care of all the transactions—the buying, selling, leasing, exchanging, investing, wheeling and dealing—and send me a check for the income on the first of each month. I also want you to dip into the assets and give me principal or send it to someone else when I so instruct."

But that's not how it goes with a Living Trust. You don't transfer your assets to a third-party money manager. You transfer it to yourself. When you set up a Living Trust, you are saying to yourself, "Self, I want you to manage these assets—all the buying, selling, leasing, exchanging, investing, wheeling and dealing. And, Self, I want you to send me a monthly check for the income. And furthermore, Self, I want you to give me the principal whenever I want it or pay it to whomever I want."

You may think, "What an absurd and silly proposition! Why would any sane person set this up?"

Here is why:

The main purpose of the Living Trust is to provide you with the power to appoint the person or persons of your choice to sign your name to the title-transferring documents after you die. In short, the Living Trust is your after-death power of attorney.

In order to better understand this concept, there are some important questions that need to be answered.

- **Do you know what a power of attorney means?** A power of attorney is a document that you sign in which you—as the principal—give someone else—as the agent—the power to sign your name to documents and bind you to legal transactions. For example, let's say you are selling your house, but will be vacationing in Liechtenstein when the transaction will take place. Since you are unable to sign the legal documents yourself, you designate your sister to have power of attorney to sign your name to the deed and escrow documents. This is a quite common arrangement, and perfectly valid and legal.

That example is identical to your Living Trust, with an additional caveat. It is a power of attorney that you sign in which you—as the principal—give someone else—as the agent—the power to sign your name *after your death* to documents that transfer your lifetime of accumulations to your designated beneficiaries, such as your spouse, children, charities, and so forth. Documents that may be signed by the agent include the deed to your house, bank account forms, brokerage account forms, partnership and limited liability company assignments, and automobile transfer forms provided by the Department of Motor Vehicles.

- **What are the assets that are to be transferred?** Your after-death agent has the power to sign the title-transferring documents for any assets that you transferred to your Living Trust during your lifetime and that are still in your Living Trust at the time of your death—your house and other real estate, bank accounts, brokerage accounts, insurance policies, partnerships, corporations, cars, silverware, fancy dogs and cats—pretty much everything you own.

- **How did your assets get into your Living Trust in the first place?** You transferred them to your Living Trust after you established it. For your house and other real estate, you signed a deed that your lawyer prepared, which transferred title from you to you as trustee of your Living Trust. For your bank and brokerage accounts, you visited your account representatives and told them that you wanted to transfer your assets to your Living Trust. The representatives then presented you with documents for you to complete to establish new accounts in the name of you as trustee of your Living Trust.

Financial Advisor Alert

The only assets that your clients transfer to their Living Trust are those that are NOT self-executing. Self-executing assets are those that already have existing beneficiary designations, such as insurance policies, IRA accounts, annuities, and bank and brokerage accounts with an existing pay-on-death (POD) designation.

- **How does your after-death agent know what assets are in your Living Trust after your death?** Perhaps you have made a list of all of your Living Trust assets and inserted that list with your Living Trust documents. However, the most common method that an after-death agent uses to discover your Living Trust assets is to rummage through your business desk and look for your most recent account statements.

Financial Advisor Alert

Discovering what assets your clients owned at death shouldn't be akin to embarking on a treasure hunt. Advise your clients to make an updated list of assets annually and to send that list to you. When your clients' after-death agents notify you of their deaths, you can provide them with the latest asset information that you have.

- **Who are the persons to whom the after-death agent transfers the Living Trust assets after your death?** Your after-death agent will transfer your Living Trust assets after you die to whomever you have designated.
- **Where do you list who gets your Living Trust assets after you die?** You describe who gets what, when they get it, and how they get it in your Living Trust document. After you die, your after-death agent opens up your Living Trust, reads the inheritance instructions, and transfers the Living Trust assets to the persons—and in the manner—described in those instructions.

- **Who will be your after-death agent?** Your after-death agent will be the person(s) you name in your Living Trust as your after-death agent.

Putting this all together—the Living Trust is a signed document in which you authorize an agent to transfer your Living Trust assets to the persons whom you have named as beneficiaries after your death.

Financial Advisor Alert

You can also describe the Living Trust as a bucket into which your clients transfer their assets. Your clients own and manage the assets in that bucket as the "settlors" (owners) and "trustees" (managers). This bucket comes with a set of instructions that state that the assets in the bucket are held, managed, and used for your clients' (the settlors and the trustees) benefit during their lifetime—and who will receive those assets in the bucket after your clients die. I have found this to be a pretty good way to inject the use of the technical and alien words "settlor" and "trustee" into the conversation about explaining the concept of the Living Trust.

It's an After-Death Power of Attorney, but It's Not

Do not take my simplistic explanation the wrong way. In my seminars, many people ask, "Mr. Condon, if an after-death power of attorney will do the job of transferring my assets after I die, why can't I just sign one of those and forget about the Living Trust?"

It's a good question. Here's the answer: There is no such thing as an after-death power of attorney. It does not exist. Any power of attorney that you sign dies when you die. It does not live on after your death.

But we lawyers, not to be daunted, developed the Living Trust so that it would have the same effect as the nonexistent after-death power of attorney; all we did was change the language and terminology. Instead of using language found in a power of attorney (principal, agent), we used the language found in a trust (settlor, trustee). Whereas you would be considered the "principal" authorizing the power of attorney, you are labeled a "settlor" in the Living Trust document. Instead of you appointing a power of attorney "agent," you appoint a Living Trust "successor trustee." Now, here is where we introduce a completely new term—the *trust estate*. After you—the settlor—die, your successor trustee distributes the assets in your Living Trust. These assets, referred to as the *trust estate*, are dispersed among the persons whom you have named in your Living Trust as your beneficiaries.

Now that you know everything you need to know about what the Living Trust is and how it works, the big question becomes: Do you need one? The last thing you want is to be sold something you don't need. To help you make this decision, I refer you to the next chapter.

3

Do You Really Need a Living Trust?

OR,

DON'T LET SOMEONE SELL YOU SOMETHING YOU DON'T NEED

In Chapter 2, I presented you with the best explanation of the Living Trust you have ever heard in your life. By having the Living Trust described as an "after-death power of attorney," you now understand that the Living Trust appoints someone—your after-death agent—to sign documents after your death to transfer your assets to the beneficiaries you named in your Living Trust. Lovely!

Okay. So where do we go from here? We continue with a series of questions: So what? Who cares about appointing an after-death agent? Why is that fun? Answering those questions in the order in which they just appeared may give you a better sense of the next steps.

- **So what?** The Living Trust process will save your beneficiaries thousands of dollars after your death because it prevents them from having to probate your assets.
- **Who cares?** The beneficiaries you named in your Living Trust care.
- **Why is that fun?** The money you saved for your beneficiaries by avoiding the probate process will provide them with the additional funds they need for that shopping spree, car purchase, dream trip, or whatever else floats their boats.

The Reasons Why a Living Trust Is a No-Brainer

You may have heard—or you know—that the Living Trust keeps your children (and your assets) from having to go through the probate process after you die. That is the number one reason why people establish their Living Trusts. Without the desire to avoid probate, there would be no such thing as a Living Trust.

Probate is the court-supervised process of transferring your assets to the beneficiaries of your estate. Actually, that is a fairly boring legal explanation of probate, and I promised you that I would avoid legal jargon as much as possible. Let me state it in a more accessible fashion.

The purpose of probate is to get the judge to do something. And that something is to sign an order that authorizes someone to jump in after you die and transfer title of all of your assets from "dead you" to your spouse, children, or other heirs.

The someone who transfers your assets is the person you have named as the executor in your will. I sometimes call the executor the judge's helper. After all, the judge is certainly not going to do the down-and-dirty work of managing and distributing your assets after you die. That's not what the judge does. Instead, the judge is merely a voice box that gives your executor permission to do what needs to be done: marshal your assets, inventory them, pay off your creditors (if any), and distribute your assets to your beneficiaries, who are the designated people you have named in your will.

Is that it? Is that all probate is—just getting the judge to sign an order distributing your assets? That sounds pretty simple. After you die, maybe your executor can go to the courthouse on his or her lunch hour, flag the judge down in the hallway, show the judge your will, and say, "Please sign this order right here."

Obviously, this facetious statement is designed to make a point: It is not easy. In fact, probate is time-consuming, with most normal, garden-variety, noncontested probates taking a minimum of six months to complete; and it is expensive because of filing fees and court costs that can run into the thousands of dollars. Perhaps most daunting, probate is a lawsuit. In other words, whenever you try to get a judge to do something, even if it is just signing a distribution order, you have to bring a lawsuit. Therefore, probate is litigation that your beneficiaries bring to obtain an order of the court to transfer your assets—to them!

Financial Advisor Alert

Check if your state has a "Small Estate Law" that prevents full-blown probate administration of, well, small assets.

In California, where I practice, a deceased person's probate assets (meaning, bank or brokerage assets in that deceased person's sole name) that total less than $150,000 can be distributed to that deceased person's legal heirs *without any court involvement whatsoever* when those heirs present the account holders with a one-page "Small Estate Affidavit." After the account holders receive that Affidavit, they are required by law to turn over those accounts to the heirs. It's that simple.

But now the question becomes, who are the heirs so entitled to those accounts? Although it's not your function to make that determination, here is a helpful tip you can give when you are presented with this situation: "If that deceased person has a Living Trust, he will also have an *I forgot will*, which states, in essence, that his Living Trust is the sole beneficiary of all assets that are in his sole name. As a result, that Living Trust is the heir . . . and the ones who sign and present the Small Estate Affidavit are the Successor Trustees of that Living Trust." For more about the *I forgot will*, see Chapter 4.

Like any lawsuit, probate involves attorneys. And where you have attorneys, you have fees. There are two types of fees. First, there is a fee for ordinary legal services, such as filing the court petitions, preparing the distribution order, inventorying the assets, and preparing the accounting. These ordinary fees are usually based on the value of the assets that are going through the probate process. For example, in California, attorneys get 4 percent of the first $100,000 of the assets going through probate, then 3 percent of the next $100,000, then 2 percent of the next $800,000. An estate of $1 million will cost the beneficiaries $23,000!

For us attorneys, this is great! It's a lot of money for what is not especially a lot of legal work. No wonder my father called probate "the lawyer's retirement fund."

But it gets better . . . at least, for my colleagues and me. The other fee is for services that the court considers extraordinary, and it is paid *on top of* the fee we already get for ordinary services! So, if there are legal services rendered to deal with matters "beyond the ordinary," such as selling real estate, defending against a will contest brought by a disgruntled heir, or filing a lawsuit against a person who has an asset that should be brought back into the estate, the attorney gets to bill the usual hourly rate.

The delays and fees associated with probate are outrageous, and you should go out of your way to prevent them from befalling your family. In order to avoid these problems, you should establish a Living Trust. With the Living Trust, you appoint someone other than the judge—your successor trustee (whom I refer to in Chapter 2 and throughout this book as the "after-death agent"—to do what the judge usually does, which is to transfer your assets to your live beneficiaries after your death. The Living Trust has several advantages:

- A Living Trust is less expensive and more time efficient.
- The fees for a Living Trust transfer are significantly less than the probate fees, perhaps 0.5 percent of the value of Living Trust assets.
- The transfer of the Living Trust assets can take place as soon as your successor trustee wants it to take place . . . perhaps as soon as 20 minutes after your funeral. That situation has actually occurred during my practice, but it was borne out of efficiency (as opposed to greed and selfishness). My client's Living Trust appointed her four children as her successor trustees. After she died, her children came together for the first time in many years for her funeral. Thinking they might never gather again in the same city for the rest of their lives, they came directly to my office after the service, where I prepared a deed that transferred my client's house from her Living Trust to her children, which they signed on the spot.

So, What's Not to Like?

It sounds like having a Living Trust, as opposed to a will, is a no-brainer. I agree. Use a will—go to probate. Use a Living Trust—avoid probate and save thousands of dollars for your family. But still, you may believe you need a Living Trust when, in fact, you really could do without.

My basic rule about whether you need a Living Trust is this: If you own real estate of any value, whether $10,000 or $10 million, you need a Living Trust. It's that simple. If you own any real estate, you should establish your Living Trust and transfer title of your real estate to yourself as trustee of your Living Trust. This vesting is accomplished with a deed, which will read as follows:

> Grantor:
> **Mr. and Mrs. Bookbuyer, Husband and Wife**
> Hereby transfers, conveys, and quitclaims to:
> Grantee:
> **Mr. and Mrs. Bookbuyer, Trustees of the Bookbuyer Living Trust**

When both of you have died, the person or persons you appoint as your successor trustee—probably your children—will transfer the property to the persons whom you have named in your Living Trust as the beneficiaries of your house. No mess. No fuss. No muss.

If you do not own real estate, and your estate consists of, say, cash or brokerage assets, you could prevent those assets from going through probate after your death, and without the Living Trust, by simply revesting the accounts so that they are "pay over on death" accounts. These are accounts that keep the cash or stock in your name during your lifetime and, on your death, are automatically transferred (without probate) to the persons whom you have named as beneficiaries on the account.

In order to establish this type of account, you have to schlep to your bank or brokerage house and tell the account representative, "I want to change my account so that it becomes a 'pay over on death' account like Mr. Condon said in his amazing Living

Trust book." The representative will then have you complete some paperwork in which you name the people whom you want to receive the account after you die. For example, if you want your daughter to be the beneficiary of that account, the account will then be vested as: Mr. and Mrs. Bookbuyer ATF the Bookbuyers' Daughter." The term *ATF* means "as trustee for," which expressly states that you are now holding the account as trustees for your daughter.

The "pay over on death" account is kind of like establishing a separate Living Trust for that asset. I say "kind of" because there is no separate inheritance instrument for that account other than the account itself. But during your lifetime, you have complete control and ownership of the account as if it were in a Living Trust, and your daughter has no access to that account during your lifetime. When you die, your daughter takes over the account as if she were the successor trustee and transfers it to herself as the beneficiary.

Financial Advisor Alert

If your client sets up this "pay over on death" account and the beneficiary dies before your client, then the account becomes a probate asset and must undergo the probate processes. Instruct your client that if the beneficiary dies during your client's life, the client must either (a) transfer the account to the Living Trust or (b) name a new beneficiary on that account.

This sounds like a pretty good arrangement. So you think, "I will just perform the 'pay over on death' arrangement on my house and prevent it from going through probate. Why do I need an expensive Living Trust to avoid probate on my house when I can just put it in the 'pay over on death' format?"

I will tell you why! Because that method of holding title to real estate does not exist in the United States. There is no form of real estate ownership in which you can put real property in an "ATF" manner and still have the full use of your house while you are alive.

There is, however, one method of holding title to real estate in which you can avoid probate of your house without a Living Trust: joint ownership. As you are reading this very sentence, you have the perfect legal right to put your children on title to your house as joint tenants. When you die, your share of the house will automatically transfer to your children (with the preparation and recording of a document that states that you, a co-joint tenant, have died). It is as simple as that.

There! Like a magician who has disclosed the secret of an ancient illusion, I have told you how to beat the system. Actually, I am probably not revealing anything new to you, so I don't have to worry about my colleagues hunting me down for disclosing a trade secret that can cost them some fees. Most likely, you hold title to your house jointly with your spouse. It is a logical extension to consider putting your children's names on the title as well—especially if that trick can prevent your assets from being diminished by the probate process after you die.

So, if you can prevent your house from going through probate after your death by putting your children's names on the deed, why have a Living Trust at all? Why not just use that device and forget the Living Trust altogether? The answer is hinted at in the next heading.

Putting Your House in Joint Tenancy with Your Child Is This Side of Insanity

You have to be mad, or manipulatively persuaded by a self-serving beneficiary, to put your children's names on the title to your house or any other real property that you own, because when you put your house in your child's name, you now subject your house to their financial burdens and risks in life. For example:

- **Divorce:** What if your daughter gets a divorce? Your son-in-law will claim that he has an ownership interest in the portion of your house in your daughter's name. He may not succeed, but your house becomes part of your daughter's divorce settlement. And as we lawyers say, who knows what some crazy judge will do?

Or perhaps your son puts his share into the joint names of himself and his wife. Love today is a divorce tomorrow, and your ex-daughter-in-law walks away with a portion of your house.

- **Bankruptcy:** What if your son files for bankruptcy? The bankruptcy trustee will attempt to attach your house as an asset that can be used—that is, *sold*—to pay off your son's creditors.

- **The Internal Revenue Service (IRS):** What if your daughter gets into a tussle with the IRS over income taxes? The IRS will attempt to place a tax lien against your house to ensure that she, someday, pays all her back taxes. With that lien in place, you will have an unbelievably difficult time selling or refinancing your house.

- **Other creditors:** What if your son gets into an accident and does not have sufficient insurance? Or what if your daughter is a physician and runs into a big malpractice action? In either case, your house may be sold to pay off their creditors.

Certainly, you do not have these thoughts in mind when you consider placing your house in joint tenancy with your child in order to avoid probate. But this is the Law of Unintended Consequences; that is, these are the events that are never supposed to happen—and they happen notwithstanding our best intentions to the contrary. I have seen numerous situations where clients have co-owned their houses with their children to save their families the costs and hassles of probate, only to lose all or portions of them to their children's spouses and creditors.

And for those who were fortunate enough not to be divested of their homes, they nonetheless suffered extreme distress and anguish from living under the cloud of uncertainty brought about by the litigation in their children's lives.

Financial Advisor Alert

Obviously, the dangers posed by joint tenancy home ownership between parents and children apply as well to such personal assets as bank and brokerage accounts. The Law of Unintended Consequences can subject your clients' years of cash and stock accumulations to their children's' problems and risks of life. As a result, you should raise your clients' awareness of these potential losses if your clients ever instruct you to place their children on their bank and brokerage assets as joint owners.

In Summary

All of this brings me back to my main tenet about whether you need a Living Trust.

Again, if you have real estate, use a Living Trust to transfer it to your beneficiaries after you die, as well as your bank and brokerage assets.

If you don't have real estate, you can use joint ownership or ATF accounts to transfer your assets to your beneficiaries without a Living Trust. However, you must be advised that the assets you place in joint ownership with your beneficiary will be subject to your beneficiary's problems and risks of loss.

To avoid ending up as a cautionary tale of what not to do, I still advise you to use a Living Trust for the after-death transfer of your assets to your beneficiaries.

CHAPTER 4

Establishing Your Living Trust

OR,

NO BETTER WAY TO GET STARTED . . . THAN TO GET STARTED

The Living Trust, as a concept, is actually easily comprehensible. As I explained in Chapter 2, it is just like an after-death power of attorney in which you authorize a living person to sign your name to documents that transfer your assets to designated beneficiaries after your death.

Although the concept of a Living Trust sounds fairly simplistic, you have to prepare yourself for the process of establishing the actual document. Before you retain the services of an attorney to prepare it for you, you must do your homework.

Yes, I said *homework*—a word that may, for you, still ring with the negative connotation of sitting down at a desk and reading, writing, and researching while you would rather be doing something else that you consider more fun. At least, that's the first thing that comes to mind when I hear that word. Even though being an adult means having to work for a living and being a slave to a mortgage, you know what compensates for that? No school tomorrow—and no homework!

But now, your Living Trust advisor is telling you to do your homework. It's part of your Living Trust training. It's what you need to do before you set your Living Trust in stone. And this homework involves picking the right attorney and familiarizing yourself with certain basic words and concepts that your Living Trust must contain in order for it to be a valid and effective document.

Your First Homework Assignment: Selecting Your Living Trust Attorney

There are many fine Living Trust lawyers in the area in which you live. How do you find the one that you will hire? Certainly, you can randomly select one from Internet or yellow pages listings. I encounter such left-field reasoning almost daily, such as the lady who hired me because she liked the font I used in my yellow pages ad, or the gentleman who based his decision on the fact that my last name is the same as that of his favorite pub in Ireland.

But if you want an informed opinion, ask your friends who have Living Trusts whether they would recommend their attorneys. If you have no friends, or none who have Living Trusts, then contact the trust department of the bank at which you do business and ask to speak to one of the trust officers. The trust department has officers who deal with Living Trust attorneys on a daily basis, and they will be happy to share their opinions on who they like to deal with and how they have arrived at those opinions.

But no matter how you reach your decision, there is one universal factor of which you must be certain before you book your appointment with the chosen attorney: **The first consultation must be free.** Why? Because it is only during that first meeting that the lawyer learns about you, your family, and your assets, and he or she needs that information in order to determine whether you need a Living Trust and, if so, what kinds of bells and whistles it should contain. Once so informed, the lawyer can assess the amount of work that will be involved and arrive at an opinion on the fee that will be charged.

In other words, the lawyer should not charge you a fee just to tell you what the fee will be.

Furthermore, the fee should be a flat fee, not an hourly rate. The flat fee should include all meetings and conferences with the attorney. The Living Trust is a process in which the lawyer gets to know you, understand your inheritance desires, and draft a carefully constructed plan to achieve those goals. The lawyer's function is to review those drafts with you and spend as much time as it takes to make you comfortable with the documents. This is a time-consuming process to which the ticking billing clock should not apply.

You do not want to have to look at your watch every time you speak or meet with your Living Trust attorney.

Your Second Homework Assignment: Making Sure Your Living Trust Document Contains the Bare Minimum of Requirements

In order for your Living Trust to be what you would call legal—valid, operative, and effective—your lawyer is going to toss in a plethora of terms, legal jargon, and provisions that will exponentially increase its length and complexity. You may look at its girth and run screaming from the room (which I have actually witnessed). In my office, the minimum number of pages is 50. I wish I could charge by the word!

Your Living Trust will contain an entire new vocabulary that you may have never before heard or encountered. As your Living Trust coach, my function is to give you some tools that can help you decipher that foreign language. Yes, this is part of your homework!

Living Trusts are a creature of state law, meaning that each state has its own set of rules (trust law) that must be followed in order for a Living Trust to be legal. However, there are six declarations that are so basic and essential to the validity and effectiveness of a Living Trust that they must be incorporated into every Living Trust made in the United States.

These are the "Six Greatest Hits of the Living Trust."

Financial Advisor Alert

Don't shy away from reviewing your clients' Living Trust to see if these elements are present. That's not legal work. It's simply ascertaining whether certain language is present and certain steps have been taken.

1. Declaration That the Living Trust Is Your Trust

The first section is the Declaration of Trust, often called the Introduction. This is the second most important part of the document, because this is where you declare that you are establishing your Living Trust. As obvious as that is, if you don't declare your intention to establish your Living Trust, you have not established a trust, even if your Living Trust has all of the other components.

Financial Advisor Alert

The "Declaration of Trust" will invariably be found on the first page of the Living Trust instrument.

2. Declaration That You Have Transferred Your Assets to the Living Trust

A Living Trust is not valid unless you transfer assets to it—even though those assets can be as little as a single dollar. Therefore, there has to be a provision that says that you "hereby transfer" your assets to it. Think of your Living Trust as a bucket in which you deposit your house, bank and brokerage accounts, personal property, and all else that you own.

Does your Living Trust have to describe every asset that you are delivering to the bucket? No. There should be a provision that states, in effect, that all assets described in an attachment to the Living Trust, which I call Exhibit A, are transferred to the Living Trust. This attachment (Exhibit A) is a catchall that functions as a general assignment of everything you own, and assets that you accumulate in the future, into the bucket.

But this Exhibit A is not the be-all and end-all. You still need to physically retitle all of your substantial assets to the bucket. This requires a deed to your house, a visit to your bank and brokerage representatives to open new accounts, and preparation of assignments of your shares and interests in your partnerships, corporations, and limited liability companies. You are required to make these efforts to ensure that your substantial assets are in the bucket, because the Living Trust is operative only to the extent of its assets.

Financial Advisor Alert

Have your clients show you the most recent statements for accounts that are not self-executing. (Remember, a self-executing asset such as an insurance policy or retirement account will not be "tossed" into the Living Trust bucket.) Those statements will show whether those accounts have been transferred to your clients' Living Trust.

Also, contact the customer service department of a title insurance company and ask for a copy of the latest vesting deed of your clients' real property. The copies of the deeds you receive will confirm whether title is properly vested in the name of your clients' Living Trust. That extra effort might not be something you ordinarily perform, but your clients will truly appreciate that you went above and beyond the norm for them.

What happens if you forget to put a bank or brokerage account into the bucket and then you die? If the account is held jointly between you and another person who outlives you, that person will receive the entire account. That would not be a problem—unless the surviving joint tenant is someone you do not want to receive the entire asset.

If the account has an already-designated beneficiary who takes that account automatically on your death, such as an individual retirement account (IRA), a 401(k), or a "pay over on death" account, that beneficiary automatically becomes the owner of that account.

However, if the account is in your individual name, and you forgot to put that account into the bucket, then you, or actually your heirs, have a bit of a dilemma. That account needs to be part of the bucket in order for it to be subject to your Living Trust's inheritance instructions. But it is not in the bucket, and it is left swinging in the breeze . . . directionless and alone.

But wait! We lawyers have already anticipated the possibility that you could die with an asset that is not in your Living Trust. When you sign your Living Trust, you will also sign a will. It is not the typical will that contains your inheritance instructions—those are already in your Living Trust. Rather, your will has only *one* inheritance instruction, which is this: Any asset in your individual name at your death that is not part of your Living Trust shall be added to your Living Trust.

In legal parlance, this document is called a *pour-over will,* because it pours assets that are out of the bucket . . . into the bucket. Personally, I prefer the moniker my father bestowed on this document: the *I forgot will*—as in "I forgot to put this asset into my bucket during my lifetime, so I leave it to my bucket after my death."

If you and I do our jobs correctly and place all of your individual assets into the bucket, your "I forgot will" will never be used. In my 20 years of practice, I have had to resort to the "I forgot will" only three times. On each of those occasions, a client transferred real estate out of the bucket as required by a lender for refinancing purposes, but forgot to put it back. When each of those clients died, the "I forgot will" put the properties back into the Living Trust. But, as with any after-death transfer of property with a will, the properties had to go through probate.

Very ironic. The clients paid me large amounts to set up Living Trusts so their houses could avoid probate, but their houses wound up in probate anyway because of the inadvertent failure to put the houses back into the bucket.

Don't let this happen to you. If you refinance your property and your lender forces you to take it out of the bucket as a loan requirement, make a mental note that it needs to be put back into the bucket after the property has been successfully refinanced. As incongruous as it may seem, you are perfectly within your rights as a property owner to transfer your property back to your Living Trust after you have refinanced it.

With regard to the transfer of your personal property to the bucket, you don't have to be so concerned. In Exhibit A, there will be a provision that states, in essence, that all of your personal property, such as your furniture, clothes, jewelry, antiques, coin and stamp collections, safes, automobiles, silverware, pictures, and photographs, are declared to be in your Living Trust. You do not have to face the arduous and difficult task of affixing "Living Trust" labels on everything inside your house. Exhibit A does that for you. You may now breathe a sigh of relief.

3. Declaration That You Are the Owner and Manager of the Living Trust Assets

Your Living Trust will refer to you as the "settlor" or "trustor" or "grantor." You will see a thousand repetitions of the chosen word throughout the document. Whenever you see that word, substitute the word *owner* in your mind. Why? Because you are the owner of all the assets in the Living Trust. The assets in the bucket belong to you.

You own them. You receive the income from them. You get to spend them on anything you want. You get to dip into the principal for any purpose you desire. Enjoy!

Your Living Trust will also contain thousands of references to the word *trustee*. This is also you, but in a different capacity.

The word *trustee* means manager. This means you are the manager of the assets in the Living Trust. You manage them. You wheel and deal with them. You can invest however you desire. You can choose not to invest at all. You do as you please with the assets, just as if you did not have a Living Trust at all. Sell them. Refinance them. Exchange them. Insure them. Give them away to whomever you want. Burn them. Throw them into the street.

Of course, you are not going to treat your assets so randomly and wastefully, but I wanted to make sure you got the point. With you as the owner and manager of the Living Trust assets, do you have any less right to the assets than if they were out of the Living Trust? Is there any diminishment to your ownership interest in the assets now that they are in your Living Trust? To both questions, the answer is . . . nope! Think of it this way: **You are the Living Trust, and the Living Trust is you.**

4. Declaration of Your Powers as Manager

As the trustee, or the manager, of your Living Trust, you have the complete and absolute power and authority to wheel and deal with the Living Trust assets as you please with no restrictions. But in order to have that freedom, you have to include a recitation of all of those powers. As a result, your Living Trust will contain many pages that dutifully list and describe every power that an owner and manager of assets—any assets—could exercise over those assets.

Most likely, you will not engage in 90 percent of the powers enumerated. For example, are you really going to exercise your power to "redeem at less than par obligations of the United States of America that are redeemable at par in payment of any estate tax liability"? Do you even own any of these types of obligations (called *flower bonds*)? For all practical purposes, you are mainly focused on the one paragraph that gives you the power to "manage, control, grant options on, sell, convey, exchange, partition, divide, improve, and repair assets of the trust estate," which about covers all you probably are ever going to do. However, since none of us wants to accidentally foreclose you from performing or engaging in any activity with your Living Trust assets, no matter how obscure or unlikely it is, your Living Trust lists every power under the sun.

Therefore, your Living Trust will include many pages that empower you to engage in activities with your Living Trust assets that you probably will never consider, because of the infinitesimal chance that someday you might need that authorization. We lawyers call this "covering our rear ends."

Financial Advisor Alert

We lawyers could significantly condense the "Trustee Powers" section by simply stating that your clients, as trustees, have all the powers conferred upon them by law—and then make a specific reference to the state statutes that list those powers. But, we lawyers know that people like to have those powers explicitly set forth in the document to serve as tangible and comforting proof that they can still engage in any activities they wish with their Living Trust assets.

5. Declaration of Who Takes Over as Your Successor Trustee If You Die or Become Incapacitated

The probate-avoidance aspect of the Living Trust is predicated upon appointment of the person who will take charge of the Living Trust assets after your death and distribute them to your beneficiaries. As mentioned earlier, this person is your after-death agent, who is referred to in the Living Trust document as your *successor trustee.*

Your successor trustee is called a successor trustee because that person succeeds you as trustee when you are no longer able to serve as trustee. Death is the most common trigger of the successor trustee provisions.

However, you may also become incapable of serving if you become incapacitated—whether mentally, physically, or both—to the extent that you can no longer manage your financial affairs. The determination of whether you are incapacitated to that point is governed by the successor trustee provisions in the Living Trust. For example, if I drafted your Living Trust, I would provide that you are capable of managing the Living Trust assets *unless* two licensed physicians who are not related to each other or to any member of your family prepare written opinions on their letterheads stating that you are not capable of managing your Living Trust assets—not exactly a casually made decision.

If you are deemed to be incapacitated, the successor trustee takes over during your life to manage the Living Trust assets for your benefit, and *only* for your benefit. This does *not* mean your successor trustee can take your assets for a great time in Las Vegas. It does not mean that your successor trustee can distribute the assets to the persons who are named in the Living Trust as your beneficiaries. Quite the contrary—your successor trustee cannot do anything with the Living Trust assets unless the activities are for your benefit.

Who determines what activities are for your benefit? The successor trustee—the same person who is in charge of your Living Trust assets if you become incapacitated. Thus, the selection of the person you appoint as successor trustee who takes over upon your incapacity is critical. If you choose wisely, that person will take all steps necessary to ensure that your Living Trust assets are used for your benefit—your food, medical bills, health care, house payments, utilities, transportation, and all other matters that are necessary to tend to your day-to-day needs. However, if you make the wrong selection, it is fox-in-the-henhouse time, with your successor trustee taking the position that it benefits you for your Living Trust assets to furnish him or her with lovely meals at the most fabulous restaurants in town.

In any event, using your Living Trust assets for your benefit will require the successor trustee to collect income generated by your Living Trust assets, deposit the income in your Living Trust bank accounts, and write checks against those accounts for your health, support, care, comfort, welfare, and maintenance. If the bucket consists of more complex assets (e.g., partnerships, businesses, shares of closely held corporations), the management tasks attended to by the successor trustee will be more intricate and involved.

As you can see, the office of the successor trustee is filled with importance and responsibility. During your incapacity, that person is *legally* responsible for your financial well-being and ensuring that your most basic needs are met and paid for. After your death, that person is *legally* obligated to faithfully carry out your inheritance instructions as you set them forth in your Living Trust, and to make sure the assets are preserved and productive from the date of your death to the time they are distributed to the beneficiaries.

Notice I mentioned, and italicized, the word *legally* twice, before the words *responsible* and *obligated*. I do so because I want to impress upon you that your successor trustee has a legally charged duty to manage and distribute the Living Trust in accordance with its instructions. Perhaps that gives you a sense of confidence that your successor trustee will—in fact, must—do a good job . . . until I remind you that people break laws all the time.

During your incapacity, will your successor trustee skip town with your Living Trust assets? Perhaps she believes that a lovely trip on a Disney cruise ship with the children on your dime is just the pause that refreshes and reenergizes her efforts as your successor trustee.

During your incapacity, will your successor trustee manage the assets more for his benefit than yours? Perhaps your successor trustee believes that a brand-new car—paid for with your money—is just what is needed to schlep you to your doctors. After all, he thinks, he will not allow you to be seen being driven around town in your old junk heap.

Does your Living Trust leave a percentage of assets to your successor trustee after your death? If so, then your successor trustee realizes that the less spent on you leaves more for her. With that in mind, will your successor trustee spend any amount necessary to get you the best health care around, or will she dump you into that infamously awful nursing home that was profiled on *60 Minutes*?

Does your successor trustee have any asset investment or management experience? If not, will your well-intentioned successor trustee inadvertently mismanage your Living Trust assets into the ground?

After your death, will your successor trustee distribute the Living Trust assets in accordance with your inheritance instructions? Perhaps you left some money to your favorite charity. But, he thinks, your wish is not his wish.

These are not just what-if scenarios that exist only in conjecture. I have seen variations of these abuses throughout my practice, and I impart them to you as cautionary tales. Indeed, you can have the most expensive Living Trust in the world or a supercheap one written on a cocktail napkin. However, they are both created equal in that their success or failure is dependent on the fidelity and skill of the person you appoint as your successor trustee.

Financial Advisor Alert

You want to drill your clients on whether the person they have selected as successor trustee is trustworthy. That is, if that person takes over as successor trustee because your clients have become ill or incapacitated, can your clients *really* trust the person to fulfill the legal obligation to use the Living Trust assets *solely* for their benefit? If the answer you get is anything other than an immediate and emphatic yes, you should suggest that your clients name a more trusted person (or a professional fiduciary) as their lifetime successor trustee.

I discuss this issue in more depth in the upcoming chapters.

6. Declaration of Your Inheritance Instructions

This is the most important aspect of your Living Trust. I describe this part to my clients as the "meat and potatoes" section. These are your last words to those who survive you. These are your inheritance instructions, and the last lesson you will ever give to your children. But, if that lesson goes sour, so, too, will your children's memory of you.

Are these the words of a cynical and jaded attorney who needs a vacation? Yes, they are. But they are true nevertheless. The subject of preserving family relationships in the inheritance arena is extraordinarily broad and covers every conceivable family inheritance problem that may arise when people die and the family wealth is divided.

The declaration of your inheritance instructions—when your beneficiaries get their inheritance, where they get it, and how they get it—and the innumerable factors, circumstances, and considerations you must take into account before deciding upon that declaration are discussed at length in the Fourth Quarter of this book, which covers the distribution of your Living Trust assets after the deaths of both you and your spouse.

But for now, it is sufficient to point out that it is a major part of your homework—and the function of your Living Trust attorney—to recognize potential inheritance problems and conflicts that could befall your family, and arrive at solutions so that your plan does no harm to your survivors, and does not result in mismanagement and the diversion of your Living Trust assets from your bloodline. The cautionary tales of Living Trusts gone bad because of ill-conceived and uninformed inheritance declarations and instructions are beyond commonplace, and the training you receive and the lessons you learn in the Fourth Quarter of this book will help you prevent your Living Trust from becoming yet another tale of woe.

After You Have Finished Your Homework

Okay. In this chapter, you learned how to select your Living Trust attorney, and you have become cognizant of the basic requirement that your Living Trust has to possess the six declarations in order to be valid and effective.

Great. Your next assignment is to select the person who can make or break the success of your Living Trust. This is the successor trustee who will serve as your Living Trust's lifetime agent if you become incapacitated, and who becomes your Living Trust's after-death agent who will carry out your Living Trust's inheritance instructions.

These topics are covered in the next two chapters.

5

Who Should You Select as the Lifetime Agent of Your Living Trust?

OR,

IF YOU BECOME INCAPACITATED, WILL YOUR LIFETIME AGENT MANAGE YOUR LIVING TRUST FOR YOUR BENEFIT . . . OR FOR HIS?

A longer life is one of the blessings of our times. However, a longer life capacity brings with it the likelihood—perhaps a near certainty—that one's spouse will become severely injured, incapacitated, or unable to make clear mental decisions before the death of the other spouse.

Financial Advisor Alert

As you are likely aware, many of your married clients' financial and investment decisions are made by the "Man of the House" with the wife knowing nothing about the family finances other than writing checks for daily household expenses. You have to prevail upon that husband to ensure that before he dies, he must set up the proper support system for his wife to protect her from her own financial naïvete—and from those willing to capitalize on an easy mark. And that support system includes a Living Trust in which a trusted third party is appointed as her Living Trust asset manager (whom I refer to in this chapter as the Lifetime Agent) if the husband dies or becomes incapacitated to the extent he can no longer tend to financial matters.

Sound sexist? Yes. But for a couple that includes a wife who may have never even met the CPA, setting up this plan is the most precious and loving gift that the husband can ever bestow upon her.

If you become physically, mentally, or emotionally incapacitated, you are no longer able to effectively and efficiently control and manage your own assets. Therefore, someone must step in and fill that role. This person is known as the court-appointed conservator. A conservator is someone who receives an order from the court, which allows him or her to take over the incapacitated person's medical and financial affairs. Generally, this person is your spouse, your child, your cousin, or even some professional caretaker. Although conservator agreements appear to be a sound option, they are time-consuming and expensive. Moreover, there is the unnerving possibility that someone you don't know or don't like will manage your financial portfolio and, in essence, be your boss!

As an experienced attorney who has seen his fair share of disgruntled conservatorship relationships, I believe that they should be avoided at all costs. On a selfish level, preparing conservatorship documents can be one of the most time-consuming, work-intensive, and tedious tasks that falls on an estate planning attorney's desk. I suppose that is the way it should be. After all, if a court is going to take away your right to make your own medical and financial decisions and then surrender that power to someone else, the court needs a boatload of information about you and the person who has applied to take over. On many occasions, this paperwork has to be done yesterday in order to give the applicant the power to deal with an emergency that could result in harm to you, like revoking the power of attorney you signed while in your haze that gave some predatory fortune hunter unfettered access to your bank accounts. But do not fear. The conservatorship process can be avoided if you appoint someone to be your financial agent in a non–Living Trust document called a *power of attorney for asset management.* In this document, you appoint someone to sign your name to financial documents—deeds, checks, contracts—if you become incapacitated as determined by a licensed physician.

However, the power of attorney is not effective over Living Trust assets. In other words, this financial agent does not have any power to manage or wheel and deal your Living Trust assets.

Financial Advisor Alert

I have seen more than a few powers of attorney that give the "attorney-in-fact" the power to manage and handle transactions with Living Trust assets. This means that two different "offices" have power over the same Living Trust assets—the successor trustee and the attorney-in-fact ... with one office able to override or wipe out the wheeling-and-dealing of the other.

If those two offices are held by the same person or entity, then this conflict is, of course, significantly mitigated. But, if they are held by two different persons or entities, the Big Mess is inevitable.

Ask your client to let you review the power of attorney and take a look at the powers it bestows on the attorney-in-fact. If those powers include handling Living Trust transactions, advise that a new power of attorney be prepared that does not contain that authority.

Therefore, in your Living Trust, you must appoint someone known as the *successor trustee* to act as your lifetime agent over your Living Trust assets. The successor trustee comes into play during your lifetime if you become incapacitated to the point where you can no longer manage your Living Trust assets. Translation: You become so physically or mentally addled that you can no longer write checks or pay bills without someone guiding the pen in your hand.

In addition, your successor trustee can also kick in during your life if you resign as trustee because, for example, you no longer want to be bothered with the seemingly endless details of managing your financial affairs. If your successor trustee takes over during your lifetime for either of these reasons, he or she becomes your lifetime agent. (If your successor trustee kicks in because you have . . . ahem . . . kicked the bucket, he or she becomes your after-death agent.) Because the person who inhabits the role of lifetime agent has tremendous power over your finances, this chapter focuses on selecting your lifetime agent.

Financial Advisor Alert

Your clients and their assets should never have to be subjected to the conservatorship process. Between the two vehicles of a Living Trust and a power of attorney, your clients can easily "farm out" their financial decision making to others in the event of their incapacity and/or incompetency. If your clients do not want a Living Trust for whatever reason ("It's too expensive!" "It's too much of a hassle!" "It's only for rich people!"), then insist that they have a financial power of attorney. It's cheap and will save their families from being deprived of tens of thousands of dollars in conservatorship fees and costs.

Your Lifetime Agent's Duty to Accomplish the Three Ps of Asset Management

Your lifetime agent's major objectives are to manage your Living Trust assets and to pay (or apply) the income and principal for your benefit. From an administrative standpoint, the responsibilities include collecting the income from your Living Trust assets, writing checks for your day-to-day needs, and making sure that none of the assets are used for any purpose other than your support, health, education, comfort, and maintenance. The lifetime agent also has the duty to engage in all steps that are "reasonable and necessary" (lawyer lingo) to accomplish what I call the Three Ps of asset management: preserve your assets, protect them, and make them productive.

Financial Advisor Alert

You will notice that the Three Ps are not conducive to "making a killing." That investment philosophy might be appropriate for the Lifetime Agent . . . but not for your client, who is the person the Three Ps are designed to protect. Underlying the Lifetime Agent's investment and management function are the standards of reasonableness and prudence. So, if your client's lifetime agent comes to you with risky or imaginative investment ideas or opportunities that he claims will likely "hit big," your response should be to hold up those claims to the light of the Three Ps and determine whether they adhere to these goals of wealth protection and preservation.

1. **Preserve your Living Trust assets.** Your lifetime agent cannot allow the assets to be diminished or wasted through diversion, bad management, or inappropriate or risky investments. In other words, your lifetime agent cannot use your Living Trust assets to purchase a vacation home for you when you do not need that property for vacation or investment, and cannot spend your money on that "can't miss" tip on that horse in the third race at Santa Anita that he got from his shady brother-in-law.
2. **Protect your Living Trust assets.** Your lifetime agent must ensure that assets are sheltered from any outside interlopers who may attempt to secure and access the assets for purposes other than those set forth in your Living Trust. For example, say your son-in-law is the type of guy who mentally sizes up the value of your estate every time he comes over to your house. You just know that if you become incapacitated he will somehow worm his way into your money and property. This is where your lifetime agent steps in. During your incapacity, your lifetime agent is on the scene to ensure that your Living Trust assets stay in your Living Trust and are protected from any con job that your son-in-law may muster.
3. **Make your Living Trust assets productive.** Your lifetime agent must invest your Living Trust assets so that their value at least keeps pace with inflation. This is not an exacting standard.

For example, a dollar in your Living Trust today can purchase a dollar item today. Ten years from now, when inflation has jacked up the price of that dollar item, the purchasing power of that Living Trust dollar must be raised to purchase that same item. That lift occurs through simple investment in interest-bearing accounts and conservative blue-chip brokerage assets.

The Not Very Scientific Method of Selecting the Lifetime Agent of Your Living Trust

Okay. So now that I've trained you on the role of the lifetime agent—the successor trustee—the time has come to select the person or persons or entity that will play that role if you, the trustee of your Living Trust, become incapacitated.

First off, the one who automatically takes over as your lifetime agent is your spouse. This is a no-brainer. Your spouse is already a co-trustee of your Living Trust. If your spouse is alive and competent, he or she will assume control as the sole trustee—the sole manager of the Living Trust assets.

As the sole manager, your spouse will have the power to wheel and deal the Living Trust assets all day long, just as your spouse had that power since both of you signed your Living Trust. Nothing has changed. Your spouse can still sell the Living Trust assets, exchange them, buy them, and borrow against them . . . whatever your spouse wants to do.

And just as before your incapacity, your spouse collects the income. As the sole manager, your spouse distributes all income generated by the Living Trust assets to the persons who are the beneficiaries of the Living Trust during your joint lifetimes (that is, to you and your spouse).

And just as before your incapacity, your spouse has control over the principal. As the sole manager, your spouse has the power to dip into the Living Trust assets and distribute funds for the support, health, and comfort of the Living Trust beneficiaries, who, again, are you and your spouse.

It's easy to see how your spouse, as the sole manager, distributes income and principal to you. But here's a head-scratcher: How does your spouse, as the sole manager, distribute income and principal to himself or herself as a beneficiary? Isn't your spouse just one person? Yes, but your Living Trust refers to you and your spouse in two capacities—trustees and beneficiaries. That is a name game that must be played so that your Living Trust can qualify as a true trust under the law of your state. So, even though your Living Trust describes this elaborate procedure of delivering income and principal from the trustee to the beneficiaries during your joint lives, you really do not have to engage in the existential exercise of giving a check from your "trustee hand" to your "beneficiary hand." Remember, you are the Living Trust . . . the Living Trust is you.

Financial Advisor Alert

You will often find that the surviving spouse does *not* want to handle any financial matters. This scenario mostly arises where the wife is the surviving spouse whose deceased husband did all the "money things." Made the investment decisions. Engaged in the wheeling and dealing. Met with the CPA. Wrote all the big checks. All while his wife did little more than write checks for household expenses.

Obviously, this situation demands the involvement and participation of a third party to help the wife own, control, and use the "family money." Hopefully, this couple executed a Living Trust that appointed that third party as the lifetime agent. But if not, then you must advise the wife that she transfer her office of Lifetime Agent to a trusted third party. Or that the wife appoints a *sub-agent* who sets up a system of investments, income collection, and check-writing and submits each transaction to her for her review and signature.

Do You Trust Your Children to Watch Your Back (Financially Speaking)?

However, the plan of your spouse taking over as the sole manager is dependent on several assumptions: that your spouse will be alive when you become incompetent; that your spouse will outlive you;

and that your spouse will remain alive and competent during your entire incapacity.

Of course, we all know that it is entirely likely that your spouse may die before you, or will experience a period of time before death in which she becomes incapacitated herself to the point where she cannot be the sole manager of the Living Trust. Therefore, you now need to engage in the process of selecting the person, persons, or entity that will take over as your lifetime agent—your successor trustee—in the event of your incapacity when your spouse cannot play that role.

Financial Advisor Alert

When I go into nursing homes to get signatures of clients, I notice that most of the residents are women. I know this sounds somewhat crass, but women are not "lucky" like men, who frequently die suddenly, overnight, or after a short illness. Women typically live for many years longer and find themselves in their later years suffering from a long-phase "twilight zone" of mental incapacity. It's our function—the inheritance lawyer and the financial planner—to insist that our clients take the necessary steps to ensure that a vacuum in financial control of their assets is *not* filled by bad guys. And those steps include the establishment of a Living Trust that appoints a trusted lifetime agent to step in and control the Living Trust assets for the wife's *sole* benefit if she enters that twilight zone after the death of her husband.

Before you determine the person who will be responsible for managing your Living Trust, you must figure out whom you *trust* to be your successor trustee. If you are like most of my clients who have children, you will select your children as your lifetime agent. This makes sense since, well, they are your children, and your selection of them to serve is natural and instinctive.

When it comes to your children serving as your lifetime agent, there are two inquiries that must be made: Will they step up and serve when called upon? And do you trust your children with your Living Trust assets?

Will Your Children Serve?

If your children are like the vast majority of those who are appointed as lifetime agent of the Living Trust, they will accept the responsibility of managing your Living Trust assets for your benefit. Perhaps they will not be thrilled with the idea of taking over your financial affairs when they have their own fish to fry, but they will still take the job of being your lifetime agent. Why? Because of blood and instinct. The blood connection between parent and child creates an instinctive moral obligation to help parents when they need help.

I realize this might not be true in all cases. And I know that I do not possess the academic qualifications to bring forth such a psychological explanation. But, after being a percipient witness to hundreds of Living Trust takeovers by the children during my 20-year practice, I can say that not one child has declined to serve as the lifetime agent when the parent became incapacitated. Even children who initially kicked and screamed in resentment wound up serving as lifetime agents.

Let me ask you this rhetorical question: If not for blood and instinct, what else would cause somebody—for no compensation—to spend a considerable amount of time on the often enervating and thankless function of managing the financial affairs of another person? Except for those who wish to capitalize on the opportunity to raid the Living Trust assets for their own use, the only motivation can be that a family member requires assistance.

Do You Trust Your Children?

How dare I ask this question about your precious children, who you might believe can do no wrong? Oh, I dare! If you have seen what I have seen—the financial loss and abuse after children have taken over their parents' Living Trust assets—you would dare, too!

At first blush, selecting your children as your lifetime agent makes sense. After all, your children are your children, and they would never do anything to cause harm to you or loss to your Living Trust assets. As your children, they have a moral obligation to ensure that your Living Trust assets are used entirely for your benefit and that they are protected for you and from any potential risks of loss.

I know I am supposed to sound like a lawyer in order to convey to you a sense of professionalism, but . . . oh yeah?! Moral obligation, my a**! You are not a jaded Living Trust lawyer who has seen happen all the things that were never supposed to happen, including financial abuse from children who just cannot wait to spend their inheritance while you are alive. Check out this dialogue to give you a sense of my take on that so-called moral obligation:

> **Client:** Mr. Condon, I would like to tell you what my husband's last words were to me.
>
> **Me:** Go ahead.
>
> **Client:** He said, "Watch out for the children."
>
> **Me:** Oh, how lovely! He really wanted to make sure that your children are always protected and taken care of.
>
> **Client:** No, no, no.
>
> **Me:** Oh, then you mean he wanted you to be financially generous with them so they never have to worry about money. What a lovely man your husband was.
>
> **Client:** No, no, no. You don't understand. He meant that he wanted me to be on guard against them.
>
> **Me:** Why?
>
> **Client:** Because he knew I would need to protect myself against them.

This brief passion play actually took place in my office, word for word. And yes, I am fond of peppering my sentences with the word "lovely." Not very manly, I admit. But I digress from the point I am making by relating this dialogue. Your children are not getting any younger. They want to use their inheritance to enhance the remaining years of their lives. But the problem is, you are not dead yet. They can see their inheritance. They can touch it and smell it. But if you keep on living, they will be too old to enjoy their inheritance.

Is this the mind-set of your children? You will never know, because they will never tell you, even if the thoughts have crossed their minds. But, it certainly is prevalent among children with elderly parents. In one conversation I had with an attorney in the Los Angeles district attorney's elder abuse unit, I learned that 85 percent of their caseload involves financial elder abuse perpetrated by children of the victims, and many of those cases deal with pressures imposed upon diminished surviving spouses by their children for an early inheritance.

Let me put it another way. Your lifetime agent is supposed to use your Living Trust assets solely for your health and support, but if you select your children as your lifetime agent, they realize that the more of your money spent on you, the less there will be for them when you die.

So, as unpleasant as the task may be, you must ask yourself the same question posed in the preceding chapter: Are your children going to pay for the best home health care or assisted living facility that your Living Trust assets can buy, or are they going to dump you into that nursing home that was profiled on *60 Minutes?*

If you consider the possibilities—however remote—that your children will look at your Living Trust assets as their checkbook during your incapacity, you can make an informed decision on whether your children should serve as your lifetime agent. Most likely, you will dismiss this possibility out of hand, as in, "My children would never steal from me, and I'm going to keep them as my lifetime agent." Fine.

Financial Advisor Alert

This subject can be a bit of a mine field. Your clients may accuse you of (a) casting aspersions on their precious children and (b) attempting to inject yourself into the fee-based office of Lifetime Agent. Still, it's an important topic that you must broach because it's *your* function to raise your clients' awareness of risks. Even if the prospect of that risk becoming reality is very small.

So don't run from this issue. Embrace it! Tell your clients that inherent in appointing their children as Lifetime Agents is a risk that their children will use the Living Trust assets to mainly benefit themselves, If their response is couched in indignity ("How dare you?!"), explain that you are protecting them from the Law of Unintended Consequences. After all, haven't they lived long enough to realize that sometimes things that were never supposed to happen do happen?

Can You Trust Your Friend to Protect You?

However, even if your children are willing to accept the office of your lifetime agent, you might want to consider someone else in that role if:

- Your children are geographically distant from you, making the logistics of taking over impractical.
- Your children are not even capable of managing their own affairs, let alone yours.
- You simply feel uncomfortable with the idea of your children taking over your assets.
- You don't have children.
- You just know or strongly suspect that your children are the type of people who will spend less on your medical care in order to have more of your assets left over after you die.

In these situations, the question becomes: Should you select any other individual to take over as your Living Trust's lifetime agent in the event of your incapacity?

The answer is . . . No! Never let one individual hold and manage money for another individual. (I suppose if I were less dogmatic, the answer would be: If you can possibly help it, do not let one individual hold and manage money for another individual.)

Why such a vituperative and negative response? Actually, there are a bunch of reasons. The individual you have selected might be dead by the time you become incapacitated. Your choice might be a lousy money manager or not be equipped to fulfill the administrative and investment duties necessary to achieve the Three Ps that I discussed earlier in this chapter. Your choice might not have the time or inclination to take over your Living Trust affairs. But the numero uno reason for not selecting a private individual as your lifetime agent is: *There is no police officer looking over that individual's shoulder to ensure that he or she is using your Living Trust funds for your benefit!*

Notice I said, "for *your* benefit." This means that your lifetime agent cannot legally use your Living Trust assets for his or her own benefit. A lifetime agent who uses your Living Trust assets for any purposes other than providing for your needs is committing a breach of trust and becomes subject to civil and criminal prosecution. Of course, in your incapacitated state, you may not have the cognitive ability to become aware of such an illicit activity and will therefore be powerless to protect your Living Trust assets.

For example, your spouse is dead, you become incapacitated, and your best friend is appointed in your Living Trust as your lifetime agent. Your best friend gladly accepts the job. Just as the Living Trust dictates, he adds income to principal and writes checks to pay for your day-to-day expenses.

One day, your buddy is presented with the opportunity to go on that trip he has been dreaming about for a lifetime—a package tour of attending a baseball game at every Major League stadium in the United States. He does not have his own funds, but he notices that your Living Trust assets are just sitting there. So after much hand-wringing, he somehow justifies using your Living Trust assets for that trip. ("He'll never miss it." "I promise to pay it back." "Damn it, I deserve it with all the work I'm doing for him.")

For the baseball purist, it's a little tougher to be a fan these days in light of the rampant use of anabolic steroids and human growth hormones. But for the casual fan like me, it's still nice to go to the occasional Dodgers game with my children and their friends, and a trip around the Major League ballparks sounds like a lot of fun. But I cannot go on your dime, and neither can your lifetime agent.

The baseball trip does not provide for your support or health. It does not provide comfort to you, by any stretch of that word. There is no direct or indirect connection between this expenditure and your well-being. The use of your Living Trust funds for that purpose is a breach of trust. Unless there is some police officer looking over your lifetime agent's shoulder, such as the beneficiaries who will inherit your Living Trust assets after your death, this type of activity can, and probably will, take place on a recurring basis.

The foregoing baseball story is true, as one of my clients unfortunately suffered that fate when I was first starting out in this area of practice. Since this incident took place, I have adjusted my antennae to become intensely sensitive to receive signals that indicate that my clients are being victimized by their lifetime agents, the same persons appointed by my clients in their Living Trusts to protect them during incapacity.

A Good Alternative

As your Living Trust coach, I want you to take notice of this incident. You need to take great care in deciding who will serve as your Living Trust's lifetime agent in the event you become incapacitated after the death of your spouse and your children, for whatever reason, do not, will not, or cannot serve as your lifetime agent. And, in my opinion, the best route you can take is to appoint a professional fiduciary to be your lifetime agent, such as a bank trust department, trust company, fiduciary services business, certified financial planner, or other licensed and bonded third party who is in the business of rendering fiduciary services. In all cases where children do not serve as lifetime agent, I advocate the selection of the professional fiduciary over any other private individual. The professional fiduciary treats asset management as a full-time job with personnel who have the sophistication and experience necessary to manage the assets of others. A private individual, in contrast, probably can give your assets only part-time treatment, and may not have the necessary skills for the job. Also, while there is no police officer looking over the shoulder of the private individual to ensure your funds are being used for proper purposes, the professional fiduciary has multiple levels of internal management review and is subject to audit by state and federal regulators. In addition, the professional fiduciary has facilities to manage all your Living Trust assets, whether real estate, securities, or other assets, while an individual may not be so equipped.

I am not a shill for the professional fiduciary industry. I am, however, an advocate of protecting your ownership and control of your Living Trust assets during your incapacity. I have seen too many situations where even the most well-meaning of individual lifetime agents inadvertently mismanaged and misused my incapacitated clients' Living Trust assets. I have seen the parade of horribles of all those things that were not supposed to happen. As your Living Trust advisor, my function is to give you the training you need, which you can use to ensure that your Living Trust assets will be protected and used for your benefit. Even if that training involves a step you might have never before considered—selecting a professional fiduciary as the lifetime agent in your Living Trust.

6

You Can Select Your Children as Your After-Death Agent, but Will They Carry Out Your Living Trust's Inheritance Instructions?

OR,

"THAT WAS OUR PARENTS' WISH, BUT IT AIN'T OUR WISH"

I t's a wonder anyone would ever voluntarily consent to act as a lifetime agent of a Living Trust. As you see from Chapter 5, that role can become a high-pressure gig. Imagine that you are in charge of the financial affairs of another who is completely dependent on you for his existence. He is counting on you and relying on you to meet his daily needs. And on top of that, this person can sue you if he even merely perceives you are not doing your job properly.

In comparison, the role of your successor trustee as after-death agent is a relative piece of cake. The heavy lifting of managing and controlling the Living Trust assets for your benefit is gone. After your death, the chief purpose of the after-death agent is to distribute your Living Trust assets to the beneficiaries you have named in your Living Trust.

Well, perhaps the allusion to cake is a bit misleading. In carrying out the function of the after-death transfer of your Living Trust assets, the after-death agent must make many determinations that directly impact the distribution process, such as when the distribution will be made, which assets shall comprise each beneficiary's share, which assets will be sold to pay the estate tax, which attorney to use, which accountant to use, which appraiser to use, whether fees will be charged for the distribution efforts, and the like.

Selecting Your Children as Your After-Death Agent

If you are like 95 percent of my clients, you will appoint your children as the after-death agents of your Living Trust. Since your children are, most likely, the beneficiaries of your Living Trust, it makes perfect sense to appoint them as the persons to carry out those inheritance instructions stipulated in your Trust. In essence, they, as your after-death agents, will transfer the Living Trust assets to themselves, as your beneficiaries. As my mother says, "What's not to like?"

Financial Advisor Alert

I have met more than a few financial planners who insist that their clients should never name their children as their after-death agent. Appointing a neutral third-party after-death agent instead, they say, takes the family baggage and emotions out of the distribution process.

I see that point. But in the vast majority of circumstances with the clients' children as after-death agents, I have found that those children, united in their common goal of getting their inheritance share as quickly as possible, are willing and able to put down that baggage. As Gordon Gekko said in *Wall Street*, "greed works." And in the inheritance context, greed works to ensure that all the after-death agents are on board to do what it takes for the most expeditious and efficient trust administration and distribution process possible.

There are, however, two questions that you must ask yourself before deciding that your children will be the after-death agents of your Living Trust: Are you sure they will carry out your instructions? Should all of them be your after-death agents, or only some of them?

Do You Trust Your Children to Carry Out Your Inheritance Instructions?

The question of whether you trust your children to carry out your inheritance instructions may appear somewhat puzzling. Why wouldn't you trust your children to distribute your Living Trust assets? After all, the assets are going to them. And besides, your after-death agent has a legal duty to carry out the instructions in your Living Trust to the letter. If they deviate from those instructions, they can be sued.

This is what I used to believe. In fact, even without those considerations, I believed that the children of my clients felt a moral obligation to distribute the Living Trust assets in accordance with their parents' last wishes. To go against those wishes would be to sour their parents' memory.

However, as an attorney who for 30 years has borne witness to the inheritance arena after my clients died, I have seen all the problems, conflicts, jealousies, and things that were not supposed to happen.

How could this be? As Elaine said to Jerry in one episode of *Seinfeld*, "Oh, it be!" Allow me to convey the following examples where my clients' children have deviated from their parents' inheritance instructions. While reading these seemingly unbelievable and outlandish tales, please keep in mind that these situations have repeated themselves in different variations during my 20-year practice.

"My Properties . . . My Pyramid"

Mr. and Mrs. Styles made a career of buying apartment buildings. From the end of World War II to their deaths, they had accumulated 17 properties. They told me that keeping the buildings in the family would be their way of preserving their identity to their children and grandchildren. As Mr. Styles told me, "I want these buildings to be my pyramid to my family's future." With this information in mind, I prepared a Living Trust, transferred the properties to the Living Trust, and provided that the properties would be kept intact until the death of their last grandchild. I advised Mr. Styles that an institutional trustee should be their after-death agent to preserve these properties. He said, "Hell, no! The bank will charge fees, and my children will do a better job for free."

Undaunted, I replied, "You don't know that. Maybe your kids will get together and sell the properties. After all, there would be no one around to say no." Mr. Styles said dismissively, "Condon, I know my kids better than you do. They are smart enough to know that these properties will make them a good living for the rest of their lives."

Mr. Styles was right. Who was I to argue with him? I was not their parent. So, I relented, and Mr. and Mrs. Styles named their children as their after-death agents. When Mr. Styles died, Mrs. Styles carried on with the management of the properties until her death. Then, their three children took over as the after-death agents and managed the properties, collected the income, and maintained them so they remained habitable and productive . . . until they sold them! I know this happened, because the eldest son so informed me during the process of preparing Mrs. Styles's federal estate tax return. In light of Mr. Styles's confidence in his children's attitude about keeping the property, I was stunned.

With all the indignation and self-righteousness I could muster, I said, "How dare you! That's not what your parents wanted! They wanted you to keep the properties in the family!"

He calmly replied, "That's what our parents wanted. That's not what we wanted. We were so sick and tired of hearing about the damn properties. My brothers and I don't want to be tied together through these properties. We just want to sell them, divide the money, and go our separate ways."

The pyramids in Egypt have been kept intact for thousands of years. Relatively speaking, Mr. Styles's pyramid lasted maybe 10 minutes after his wife's death.

"Your Money Is Family Money"

In Mr. Deering's Living Trust, he provided that his grandson, Joseph, would get $150,000 on his death if the grandson had reached age 25. He also provided that if his grandson was not 25 at the time of his death, his son, David, would be appointed as the after-death agent to manage the $150,000 and deliver it to Joseph when he reached that age.

Joseph was 19 when his grandfather died. In accordance with his grandfather's Living Trust instructions, his father, David, secured the funds.

Fast-forward to six years later when Joseph finally turned 25. I noticed in my appointment book that Joseph had made an appointment to see me. In reviewing his grandfather's trust, I was reminded about the gift provision to him. Therefore, I assumed that Joseph wanted to meet with me for advice on the transfer of that gift to him. As I met Joseph in my waiting room, I said, "Happy birthday! What's the first thing you are going to do with your gift?"

He responded, "Sue my father!"

In my office, Joseph explained what he had meant by such a shocking statement. Upon turning 25, he approached his father for the money. When he did, his father said, "Hey, son, since my money is family money, your money is family money. You've been receiving your distribution all along in the form of food, clothing, and shelter."

Mr. Deering wanted his grandson to have that bequest to help him get a leg up in life: to start that family, buy that home, establish that business. What his grandson got instead was a lesson in the school of hard knocks. When it comes to money, family loyalty goes out the window.

"That Was Our Parents' Wish . . . Not Our Wish"

Mr. and Mrs. Evans used their Living Trust to leave $100,000 to their church. When they both passed away, their children—their after-death agents—came to see me for advice on the administration of the Living Trust. During that meeting, I said, "Don't forget to cut that check to the church. Since that gift is not reduced by estate tax or any other obligation, there is no reason to wait for the end of the trust administration to deliver that bequest."

One of the children said to me in all seriousness, "Mr. Condon, that was our parents' wish. That's not our wish. We're not going to do it."

You are probably as aghast as I was. How do you decide to blatantly go against the inheritance instructions set forth in a Living Trust? The Evans children just did it, and it was easy for them to do. No regret. No compunction. No vacillation. On some strange level, I admired their ability to make a "damn the consequences" decision and not look back. If the situation were reversed and I had made the decision to disregard my parents' clear inheritance instructions, I would be looking over my shoulder for the rest of my life.

"I Got Robbed—and My Own Kid Is the Bandit"

Mr. and Mrs. MacCallum were blessed with 12 grandchildren whom they considered the lights of their lives. When I met with them, they were very clear on their family priorities when Mr. MacCallum said, "Our children are okay, but we really love our grandchildren."

If the MacCallums had their druthers, they would have left all of their Living Trust assets to their grandchildren. However, after several consultations with me, they realized that such an act would leave their children thinking that they got robbed and the bandits were their own kids. But, still wanting to leave their grandchildren something, they ultimately established their Living Trust, which left each living grandchild $10,000, with any remaining assets going to their four children equally.

When the MacCallums were both deceased, their Living Trust assets consisted of about $500,000, including their home, cash, and brokerage assets. When I met with the MacCallums' after-death agents—their children—I advised them of their obligation to distribute a total of $120,000 to their parents' grandchildren. Their daughter responded this way: "That's $120,000! That will leave only $380,000 for the rest of us to split four ways. That's only $95,000 each. That's like nothing! So, Mr. Condon, you know what we're going to do? My siblings and I talked about it and agreed to table that distribution for now. They'll get it eventually."

At that point, one of the other children muttered aloud, "Maybe." To that, I reminded them that as their parents' after-death agents, they were legally obligated to make that distribution. But I might as well have been talking to a toaster. The daughter said, "Mr. Condon, thanks for your time." They got up and walked out, never to be seen (by me) again. I can only assume that the MacCallums' children handled the Living Trust business on their own without the conscientious lawyer buzzing around and reminding them of the duties they are supposed to fulfill.

Mr. and Mrs. MacCallum were not financial slouches. Although I have many clients who have millions in money and property, $500,000 is not a meager estate. Still, had the MacCallums been wealthier, I doubt that their children would have even considered withholding those distributions. But when the inheritance dollars are fewer, each dollar becomes more precious to the beneficiaries.

The Indelible Conclusion: Money Changes Everything

There are too many other examples of this theme to mention in this short book, but I hope you get my point: Appointing your children as your after-death agents does not guarantee that they will faithfully follow through with your inheritance instructions. Based on scenarios like those just referenced, I have come to two indelible conclusions:

1. You really don't know your children . . . until they get around to dividing their inheritance.

2. When it comes to dividing the inheritance, family loyalty goes out the window . . . and it's a whole new ballgame.

I delve more into the area of behavior in the inheritance arena in later chapters, but for now I make these points in order to help you realize that it is entirely possible that your children, as your after-death agents, could very well disregard the inheritance instructions in your Living Trust—and do it their way.

That said, I don't want to mislead you into thinking these scenarios are the norm. As I stated earlier, I tend to make sweeping generalizations in order to get my point across. Most Living Trusts are fairly garden-variety documents that leave the assets to the children, and the children are not going to cheat themselves. And even if your Living Trust leaves assets to beneficiaries other than your children, your children will most likely comply with those instructions—perhaps because they are legally charged to do so, or because the thought of deviation just does not enter their minds.

However, 95 percent of the solution to any problem is recognizing that the problem exists in the first place. I have pointed out to you a sampling of situations where inheritance instructions fell by the wayside—intentionally. With this potential problem brought to your attention, you can now make an informed decision by considering whether there is a risk that your children will deviate from your Living Trust instructions.

If you are like most of my clients, you will conclude that your children will do a fine job as your after-death agent. Or perhaps you may think, "You know, I never thought about that before. Now I have my doubts. I trust my children with money about as far as I can throw them. Maybe I should consider someone else to be my after-death agent." Or perhaps you have dismissed this issue of inheritance deviation by your children as yet another attempt by a money-grubbing lawyer who is trying to manufacture issues so he can charge more money for your Living Trust.

In either event, I have done my job of raising an issue that you may have never before considered.

Financial Advisor Alert

Most states have a statute in their trust law that provides, in essence, that when a trust becomes irrevocable (which basically means after the deaths of the persons who set it up), the after-death agents *are required to* send a certain "notice" to all the persons and entities who are named as beneficiaries. This notice must, at a minimum, identify the inheritance instructions and the persons/entities who serve as the after-death agent. The purpose? To "arm" the named beneficiaries with knowledge of what they are legally entitled to receive from the Living Trust. With that knowledge comes the power of the beneficiaries to protect themselves from after-death agents who might decide to deviate from the inheritance instructions.

Type "notice of irrevocable trust" in your favorite search engine and see if your state has such a statute. If so, then look for an opportunity to speak with your clients' after-death agent children following your clients' deaths to inform them of this notice obligation and to see an attorney about fulfilling it.

Should You Name All Your Children—or Some of Them—as Your After-Death Agent?

The question of whether you should name all of your children or just some of them as your after-death agent is such an important topic that I generally devote at least 20 minutes to it in my seminars. As it's very difficult to pontificate in a book, I won't beat around the bush. The answer to this question is this: Unless you have a child with a substance abuse problem, or unless you are completely estranged from a child, always . . . *always* . . . name *all* of your children as your after-death agents, because leaving out a child as an after-death agent is the fastest way to create family conflicts and jealousies among your children. Conflict will arise faster than if you had left your children an unequal inheritance.

To illustrate my point, consider the following scenario. Imagine that for no apparent reason, you were forced outside the playground while your siblings could remain in it playing. How would you feel as you watched your brothers or sisters having fun? The emotions you would feel are probably the same emotions felt by your left-out child, who thinks, "Gee, Mom and Dad didn't love me as much, or didn't trust me as much, or didn't think I was smart enough to do the job."

Fanning the flames of this emotion is the fact that your left-out child has no say on all the decisions that must be made with respect to the division of the inheritance. Continuing the playground analogy, your left-out child becomes the kid outside the playground fence who can only watch in despair as his siblings have all the fun playing, running, swinging, and sliding.

When you exclude a child from that process, that left-out child may attempt to assert some influence that, to the siblings-in-power, may be unwanted. If rebuffed, the left-out child might challenge every decision made—to the point of hiring an attorney and filing petitions with the court.

At this point, you say you have a good reason for excluding a child, which may be one of the following:

- You have a child who lives in Alaska or some other distant locale, and the distance is too great for that child to be actively involved in the distribution and administration of the Living Trust assets.
- You believe that naming all your children as after-death agents will create too much chaos and delay. In other words, too many cooks spoil the broth.
- You believe that your professional child—the lawyer, doctor, businessperson, accountant, money manager—is more qualified to perform the work than your nonprofessional children.
- You believe that your children will not get along to make decisions together, and the distribution of the Living Trust assets will be caught up in their disagreements.

While these are all good points about the efficiency of appointing fewer than all of your children as your after-death agents, I respond with this rhetorical question: Is the efficiency you achieve worth more than the potential destruction in your children's sibling relationships?

Besides, many of the assumptions raised by these points can be countered with real fact.

- Distance can be overcome by fax, e-mail, and overnight mail.
- Having more cooks does not automatically mean that it will be more difficult to reach consensus. Also, you can always include a "majority rule" provision to ensure that no decision or action is bogged down by failure to reach unanimous agreement.
- Your nonbusiness child is just as qualified as your business child to perform the basic functions of the after-death agent.
- Your children will likely not disagree with each other, because even extremely recalcitrant and obstinate people realize that the more monkey wrenches they throw into the works, the longer the delay in getting their share of the inheritance.

Of course, there are reasons that are obvious for leaving a child on the outside of the Living Trust fence. For instance:

- You do not want to appoint a child whose reasoning has been adversely affected by substance abuse.
- You will not appoint a child who has been estranged from the family for many years.
- You will not appoint a child who has a physical or psychological problem that would definitely impact on the ability to make decisions that affect the inheritance distribution process.

Then there is the reason we encountered when my father and I were on the road promoting our previous book. We were being driven in a nice Lincoln Town Car to appear on *The Dr. Laura Show.* During the trip, the driver said that he had read our book and was left wondering about our advice to almost always name all the children as after-death agents. The driver said that he was the youngest of 12 siblings, and that it would be very tough to get everyone together for all the work that needed to be done. My father agreed, saying, "That's a lot of people to act together. Signing every document—the deed, the bank and brokerage assignments—would be a formidable task. Not everyone should serve as a successor trustee. Your parents should just select a few of the children who represent every near-generation."

My father added, "Buddy, thanks for your question. I've never really thought about the problem of 12 children serving as successor trustees. You've given me a brand-new exception. If I ever write another book, I'll be certain to mention this incident."

Well, my father might not be around to make good on his representation, but I still am. Here you go, Limo Guy! I apologize for not getting your name before we arrived at our destination.

Financial Advisor Alert

If there is one alert that I want you to take away from this book, it's this one! Ask your clients whether they have named all of their children as their after-death agents. If not, then you have to inquire further as to their reasoning.

Does this feel like prying? That such inquiry is beyond the scope of your duties as their money and investment strategist? Well . . . too bad! Get over it! In my mind, attempting to prevent family conflicts over money division and control *is part of your job description*! You are on the front lines of your clients' financial life, and if you don't raise this issue for the protection of their family connection, no one will.

So . . . pry away! Why did your clients name only one of two children as their after-death agent? Or two of three? Or one of three? If their answer has anything to do with efficiency or qualifications—and nothing to do with substance abuse, family estrangement, incapacity, or incompetency—then warn them of the potential family fallout from their decision and strongly urge them to change their Living Trust to name them all.

THE SECOND QUARTER

LIVING WITH YOUR LIVING TRUST DURING THE LIFETIMES OF YOU AND YOUR SPOUSE

Having read the previous chapters, you now know that the Living Trust is an after-death power of attorney that contains the inheritance instructions of your spouse and you. But, notice the word *living* in Living Trust? Even though the Living Trust is, at its core, an inheritance document, you still have to know how to use it during your joint lives. In other words, I have gotten you through the part about knowing what the football is; now I have to provide you with drills so that you learn how to throw it.

Fortunately, the care and feeding of your Living Trust during the joint lifetimes of you and your spouse is not a high-maintenance endeavor. Remember, you are the Living Trust . . . the Living Trust is you. You continue to manage your daily financial affairs as if you did not have one.

Still, there are several matters that pop up that directly involve your Living Trust, such as what to do when you sell real estate or what you should tell your children about the establishment of your Living Trust. The purpose of this Second Quarter is to train you so you can better recognize those matters and respond accordingly.

Functions of Your Living Trust While Both You and Your Spouse Are Alive

OR,

DON'T QUITE FORGET ABOUT YOUR LIVING TRUST AFTER YOU HAVE THROWN IT INTO YOUR SAFE-DEPOSIT BOX

If you are like most people, you do not want to become vested in any high-maintenance endeavor that takes you away from the true passions of your life (e.g., family, athletics, etc.). So it probably comes as welcome news when I tell you that after you establish and fund your Living Trust, there is nothing more you have to do with it. Put it in your bookcase, desk, or safe-deposit box, and allow it to collect dust.

This is a bit of a lie . . . but not much of one. I stretched the truth (insert your own lawyer joke here) to make the point that there is almost nothing more you need to do with your Living Trust after you have signed it and transferred assets to it.

As I have said previously throughout this book, you are the Living Trust . . . the Living Trust is you. You get all income and principal of the Living Trust assets, you are the manager of the Living Trust assets, and you are the owner of the Living Trust assets. You have the power to wheel and deal with the Living Trust assets in any way you see fit. You don't need to whip out your Living Trust to look up any instructions on how to conduct your normal everyday financial activities. You just do them.

However, please note the word *almost*, which immediately precedes the word *nothing* in the second paragraph of this chapter. Certainly, you do not need to refer to, or whip out, your Living Trust when you are handling your day-to-day financial affairs. However, there are a few situations in your life that will require you and your spouse to carefully review the Living Trust's instructions as they relate to handling some day-to-day financial affairs. As your Living Trust advisor, it is my job to make sure you are aware of those situations so that you can be prepared.

Financial Advisor Alert

While your clients don't need to have physical proximity to their Living Trust on any kind of regular basis, *you should* get your hands on it in order to answer the important inquiries that I've laid out for you throughout these Alerts. Does it name all the children as after-death agents? Does it have the required basic provisions that are essential to its validity? Does it appoint a third-party lifetime agent to help the surviving spouse manage and control the Living Trust assets if the "financial spouse" dies first? And so on. Most likely, your clients will not recall how these matters were handled. You bring value to your relationship by reintroducing them to their Living Trust for such a discussion.

Situation 1: Revoking Your Living Trust

Your Living Trust provides that you or your spouse may revoke the Living Trust in its entirety, and without the consent of the other. No, I haven't snuck into your house and looked at your Living Trust and seen that provision. But for the reasons I discuss in the next few paragraphs, all Living Trusts established by married couples have a provision that gives one spouse the power to revoke the Living Trust—unilaterally!

Isn't that something? After all the money, time, and effort you spent establishing your Living Trust, either spouse can cancel it. Once revoked, the inheritance instructions stated in the document are canceled, and the Living Trust assets must be returned to the persons who owned those assets prior to their transfer to your Living Trust, which means you and your spouse! For example, if you and your spouse owned your house as community property before you transferred title to your Living Trust, the house comes back to you and your spouse as community property.

The most common reason why persons may revoke their Living Trust is separation or divorce. If you are no longer with your spouse, the last thing you want is to maintain a Living Trust that gives your ex-spouse the use of your half of the Living Trust assets if you die first.

It should be no problem to revoke your Living Trust. You and your spouse know the score. Both of you realize there are innumerable financial concerns between you that must be untangled, and your Living Trust is one of them. This makes complete sense. If your marriage is no longer, it follows that your Living Trust should also be no longer. So, you go to the lawyer who drafted your Living Trust, you tell him or her to prepare the document that nullifies your Living Trust, and both you and your spouse sign it. Sounds simple, right?

Wrong! After all, there is probably a reason you are getting divorced—maybe you and your spouse cannot agree on anything, or maybe you frequently fight over finances. With this thought in mind, imagine that you approach your separated spouse saying, "My lawyer says we need to revoke our Living Trust. Sign here, please." Do you think your separated spouse will sign? As we lawyers say, no way! With your Living Trust leaving half of your assets to your separated spouse, or the right to use your half for life support, medical costs, and general maintenance, your separated spouse may hope that you die first before the divorce process has been completed, with the Living Trust in full force and effect.

In order to protect your assets and prevent this from happening, we Living Trust lawyers always take into account the worst-case scenario of a separated spouse refusing to sign a revocation. As a result, your Living Trust will have a provision that allows one spouse to unilaterally cancel it. Be sure that this "revocation instruction" clause in the Living Trust describes the exact manner in which the revocation takes place, which, typically, requires that it be in writing with a copy of that writing sent to your ex-spouse.

Financial Advisor Alert

Other than grief from the death of family or a close friend, nothing more adversely affects the rational thinking process than divorce. It is all-consuming to the point where little thought is expended for anything else. So…you have to do the thinking for your divorcing client who established a Living Trust with his or her soon-to-be ex-spouse. Meaning, you have to instruct your client to revisit an estate planning attorney to revoke that Living Trust. Otherwise, if your client dies before the divorce becomes final, the surviving spouse may get ownership of all the Living Trust assets.

If you choose to sign this revocation, I caution you to follow strictly the instructions stipulated in the Living Trust. Exact compliance with those instructions is mandatory. One deviation from those instructions can result in your ex-spouse claiming that the Living Trust was never validly revoked, which, as a result, gives your ex-spouse your half if you die first.

Remember, if your separated spouse does not sign the revocation, too bad for your separated spouse. You have the power to unilaterally sign the revocation, and it's a done deal. Your Living Trust can be revoked with just one signature.

After your Living Trust is revoked, there are two more matters you must address in order for all remnants of that inheritance plan to disappear: reclaiming your half of the Living Trust assets and destroying your "I forgot will."

Reclaiming Your Share of the Living Trust Assets

Once your Living Trust is revoked, you must reacquire your share of the assets you previously transferred to your Living Trust.

How do you reclaim your half of the Living Trust assets? You ask your spouse to cooperate in signing deeds, bank forms, brokerage forms, and all other documents to transfer title of the assets out of the Living Trust and back to you in your individual names. If your spouse will not cooperate, you call the attorney who drafted your Living Trust to get him or her involved in securing your spouse's signatures on those documents. If that doesn't work, then your divorce lawyer gets to make more money by filing a petition with the court that requests an order transferring the Living Trust assets back to you and your spouse.

Destroying Your "I Forgot Will"

After you revoke the Living Trust, you must now destroy the "I forgot will" that you may have completely forgotten you signed when you established your Living Trust.

As I previously pointed out to you, when you established your Living Trust, you also signed an "I forgot will" that left all of your non–Living Trust assets to your Living Trust upon your death. If you do not destroy your "I forgot will" after you cancel your Living Trust, all of your assets—which are now non–Living Trust assets— are left to a canceled Living Trust. A canceled Living Trust cannot receive those assets. It is as if your will left all of your assets to nobody. If that occurs, then the probate code of your state imposes its default inheritance instructions on your assets—and the law does not really know what your true intentions were.

Therefore, if you and your spouse separate or divorce, you must run to your attorney's office to sign two documents. One is the revocation of your Living Trust. The other is a quickie will that leaves all of your non–Living Trust assets (which is now *all* of your assets) to beneficiaries other than your ex-spouse.

Financial Advisor Alert

Revoking a divorcing client's Living Trust is just *one step* to ensure that the soon-to-be ex-spouse does not end up with all the Living Trust assets. The *second step* of preparing a new testamentary document is just as important. In this new document, whether it is a new will or new Living Trust, your client will leave his or her share of the former Living Trust assets to persons other than the soon-to-be-ex-spouse. Without this new inheritance document, and because your client revoked the Living Trust, your client will not have any inheritance instructions. And if your client dies "naked," then the laws of intestacy of your client's state will dictate who gets his or her assets.

Situation 2: Amending Your Living Trust

Your Living Trust provides that you and your spouse have the power to amend it at any time. That makes sense. If you had a will, you could change it by signing a codicil. With a Living Trust, which is like a will in that it contains your inheritance instructions, you can change, delete, or restate any of its provisions by signing an amendment.

Why would you amend your Living Trust? Actually, the question should be, why *wouldn't* you amend your Living Trust?

If you establish your Living Trust in your 40s or 50s, you are still in the productive prime of your life, your children are young, and your financial picture occasionally becomes redrawn. Your Living Trust will speak to your life at that time, with provisions that deal with the management of your children's inheritance if you die prematurely while they are minors.

Then, when you are in your 60s or 70s, your children are grown and your financial picture becomes a bit more permanent. Along with these life changes come new provisions in your Living Trust that deal with minimizing the estate tax and protecting your children's inheritance from any risks of loss in their lives that you perceive (e.g., divorces, addictions, financial immaturity).

Finally, when you are in your 80s and 90s and your life expectancy can be measured in single digits, now it's for real. Your financial picture is set, and you know how much estate tax planning must be done. You know who your children have become, and you have the information you need to make informed decisions on how and when they should receive their inheritances. You have grandchildren who are precious to you whom you want to include as beneficiaries to help them get a leg up in life to buy that home, begin that business, and start that family. Once more, you amend your Living Trust to accommodate those changes.

Of course, there are amendments to Living Trusts that are not so sweeping. Whereas many of your changes will involve a complete rewrite of the document, such as those that address the changes in your family and finances as just described, many more will address only one or two issues. The amendments to a Living Trust that are, in my experience, most common are:

- An amendment to change the person who serves as your lifetime agent in the event of your incapacity.
- An amendment to change the persons who serve as your after-death agent.
- An amendment to add or delete specific bequests of cash or other assets.
- An amendment to delete a specific gift of an item after you no longer own that item.
- An amendment to disinherit a child or a grandchild.
- An amendment to include provisions to minimize or eliminate the estate tax upon the deaths of both you and your spouse.
- An amendment to leave a beneficiary's inheritance in a protection trust (discussed in Chapter 18), as opposed to leaving it to that beneficiary outright.
- An amendment to change the inheritance instructions so that they no longer promote conflict between your children in the inheritance arena.

Financial Advisor Alert

When you review your clients' Living Trust with them, it may be their first look at the "who gets what" part in quite a long time. And chances are those inheritance instructions will speak to circumstances that no longer exist. The share going outright to their "perfect son" may now need to be controlled by a third party to protect it from that "perfect kid's" penchant for, say, crazy spending. Or conversely, the Protection Trust they inserted for third-party control of their "less-than-perfect" child is now overkill because the vice that created the need for that control has faded into distant memory.

Whatever changes have taken place in your clients' world, you must lead them into a review (even a cursory one) to ensure that their Living Trust's inheritance instructions comport with facts as they presently are—and not what they were.

Financial Advisor Alert

Whether your clients amend one sentence or make a complete overhaul, a Living Trust amendment does *not* change the name or date of the Living Trust. It still retains the original name and original date. For example, if Speed and Trixie Racer established the "Racer Family Trust" on January 1, 2015, then unless it's revoked, their Living Trust will *always* be titled the "Racer Family Trust Dated January 1, 2015." This is true even if Speed and Trixie execute an amendment every day for the rest of their lives. This means that the accounts that are vested in "Racer Family Trust Dated January 1, 2015" retain that name and date.

So when your clients ask you whether you have to retitle their Living Trust assets after they have executed an amendment, you can confidently tell them it's not necessary.

After 30 years in this business, I would say the most common amendment is one that changes the disposition of personal property such as clothes, furniture, jewelry, antiques, automobiles, and collections to another person. I have many clients who relish coming to my office so they can replace the people in the "who gets what" provisions as they relate to their rings and things—sometimes five times a year. From my observation, I would say most of these are "I'll show you" changes, as in, "You disagree with me? I'll show you not to disagree with me!"

However, such changes are a waste of money for my clients, and, quite frankly, a waste of my time. For all the amendments that deal with personal property, I could spend the same time focusing on more intellectually challenging amendments that completely restate an entire Living Trust.

In order to save my clients money—and my sanity—I came up with the Personal Property Memorandum Provision, which I now incorporate into all my Living Trusts. As your Living Trust advisor, I recommend that you incorporate a provision of this nature into your Living Trust. It states that . . . well, just read it yourself. It's self-explanatory:

Following the death of the Surviving Spouse, the After-Death Agent shall distribute all personal property in accordance with any written, signed, and dated Memorandum left by the Surviving Spouse that directs the distribution of such Property. Should the Surviving Spouse leave multiple memoranda that conflict as to the disposition of any item of personal property, that memorandum which is the last memorandum signed by the Surviving Spouse shall control as to those items which are in conflict.

Get it? Once this provision is inserted into your Living Trust, you will have the power to write on any piece of paper—a legal pad, a cocktail napkin, an index card—your instructions on who gets your piano, your necklace, your soda-pop can collection, your first edition of *Detective Comics* No. 27 (which depicts the first-ever appearance of Batman). If you want to change your mind as to who gets an item, you simply make the change yourself on that document by crossing out the old and filling in the new, or destroying the old document and creating a new one, and placing that changed or new document in the same location where you keep your Living Trust.

If you die without creating a Personal Property Memorandum Provision, or if you have a memorandum that does not cover the disposition of all of your personal property, your Living Trust should provide that such nonmemorandum items will be distributed to your children "as they so shall agree." If you do not have a Personal Property Memorandum Provision in your Living Trust, I advise that you have your lawyer prepare an amendment to your Living Trust to put one in there.

But regardless of the size and extent of the amendment to your Living Trust—from a one-pager to a complete restatement—amending it during the joint lifetimes of you and your spouse requires the mutual consent and approval of both of you. That's right. You read correctly. Although revoking your Living Trust requires only one signature, an amendment requires both signatures.

You Read Right! It Takes One Signature to Revoke, but Two Signatures to Amend

What's the deal? Since revoking seems more severe than amending, why should only one signature be required to destroy a Living Trust when two signatures are required for a mere amendment? Quite simply, because one spouse cannot have the unilateral power to change the terms of the Living Trust. If such singular power were allowed, the Living Trust could potentially never be settled.

To illustrate this point, imagine the following scenario. You and your spouse have an argument. You think Jean-Luc Picard is the best *Star Trek* captain ever, while your spouse believes the same about James T. Kirk. Of course, your spouse's Kirk-centric position is preposterous and demonstrates your spouse's dire need for therapy. But for now, both of you are really steamed at each other. Caught up in the heat and passion of this issue, you run down to your lawyer's office, pound your fist on the desk, and say, "I want that horrible Kirk-loving spouse of mine out of the Living Trust, and cut out the children from my spouse's first marriage while you're at it!"

Financial Advisor Alert

Yes, I think Captain Picard totally rules over Captain Kirk. Strict adherence to the prime directive is always preferable to cowboy diplomacy.

The lawyer prepares the amendment and you sign it. Somehow, your spouse discovers the amendment and says, "Oh yeah? Two can play at that game!" Your spouse runs down to the lawyer for an amendment replacing the old provisions, and adding new ones that cut *you* out.

As you can see from this outlandish example, single-handedly amending the Living Trust can become a cyclical game of establishing financial superiority over the other person. Since both of you brought your Living Trust to life, both of you must consent to all changes that are written during your joint lifetimes, or chaos and anarchy could ensue.

Like your Living Trust, an amendment is a legal document. It has to have the proper legal stuff in it for it to be valid and effective, and this legal stuff is mentioned in your Living Trust. It will say that the amendment must be contained in a notarized or witnessed document that is signed by the settlors—you and your spouse—and delivered to the trustees—who are also you and your spouse.

How do you deliver a document to yourselves? You just simply sign a statement in the amendment that says that the "Trustees hereby acknowledge delivery of the herein amendment from the Settlors." I know that sounds kind of crazy, but that is the way it's done.

Financial Advisor Alert

Your clients may still have uncertainty about the two hats they wear in the Living Trust context. You may have to remind them that they are trustees (whom I refer to as "lifetime agents" in this book for simplicity) who have the duty to hold, manage, and control the Living Trust assets for the benefit of themselves as the settlors ("owners") who own the Living Trust assets. Refresh them about there being no difference in owning their assets outright and owing them in this dual settlor-trustee manner. To those who ask, "So why then the Living Trust?" you respond that the Living Trust's main goal of probate avoidance can only be accomplished if the Living Trust looks, smells, and feels like a true trust. And the Living Trust requires the creation of the offices of settlor and trustee to be "alive" and valid.

A Word of Warning

If you require an amendment to your Living Trust, **don't attempt to prepare it yourself!** I have seen dozens of self-prepared amendments that are laugh-out-loud incorrect. But what is less humorous is that I will not make these discoveries until *after* the self-preparers are dead, and little can be done to prevent that amendment from failing.

As your Living Trust advisor, I warn you that this is a scene you do not want to create. Let me tell you about that scene, which I have seen repeated in my office more times than I want to recount.

You die and the persons who believe themselves to be the beneficiaries of your Living Trust come to my office for advice on receiving their shares of your Living Trust assets. I say, "Show me the document that names you as the beneficiaries." They whip out a document that you prepared on your own, titled "Amendment to Living Trust." I review the document and, yes, it states that the persons in my office shall receive your Living Trust assets. For those persons, so far, so good.

Before I pronounce that the persons in my office are, in fact, the beneficiaries of your Living Trust, I want to see the original Living Trust—the one that was amended by your self-prepared amendment. Why? Because I want to see if the amendment was prepared in accordance with the instructions contained in your original Living Trust.

So, your beneficiaries give me your original Living Trust. I turn right to the section dealing with revocation and amendment. I read that section. It requires that the amendment be notarized. I look at your amendment. It's not notarized.

I look up from the pages of your original Living Trust at the persons in my office who had natural expectations that they would receive your Living Trust assets. I am about to devastate them with the news that the amendment you prepared is not valid and, as a result, they will receive none of your Living Trust assets. How do I break this news to them? I learned a long time ago not to beat around the bush. Just do it.

With a tone of sadness as sincere as I can summon, I quietly make the announcement: "I'm sorry to say that you take nothing under the amendment. It is invalid due to the failure to comply with the original Living Trust's established amendment procedure. All the Living Trust assets will be distributed to the beneficiaries described in the original Living Trust." At first, the news does not register. It does not enter or compute. But ultimately, after the shock, denial, and explanations, those persons come to realize to their personal horror that due to your error, they will not receive any of your Living Trust assets.

Nothing is more likely to cause a small riot in my office than the beneficiary who, in a few seconds, goes from a financial windfall to potentially zilch.

Perhaps the mistake can be fixed by petitioning the court to rescue the intentions stated in amendment. But if not, and no other fix is available, it becomes a failed amendment and will have no effect whatsoever, leaving the beneficiaries without the inheritance described in that document.

Do not let this happen to you. If you want to change your inheritance instructions, have an experienced attorney do the changing. It may seem simple enough to prepare the amendment yourself, but you might miss something that can cause the inheritance instructions on that document to not be carried out.

Financial Advisor Alert

Living Trust amendments constitute most of my estate planning business. As our clients advance in age, so too do their inheritance wishes. Thus, it is quite likely that your clients have amended their Living Trust's inheritance instructions. Your function is to ascertain whether that amendment was attorney-drafted or client-drafted. If a do-it-yourself job, then strongly urge them to run it by an attorney to see if it comports with their Living Trust's requirements for a valid amendment.

Situation 3: Either You or Your Spouse No Longer Acts as a Co-Trustee

In the section of your Living Trust that appoints specific persons or entities to act as the trustee, there is a provision that states, in essence, that both you and your spouse serve as co-trustees at present. It further states that if one spouse is not able or is not willing to act as a co-trustee, the other spouse continues on as the sole trustee.

These provisions come into play when either you or your spouse dies, becomes incompetent, or resigns.

You or Your Spouse Dies

This is a no-brainer. You are not able to act as a co-trustee if you are deceased. Certainly, you may still be willing to act, but your phantom is not a legally viable or recognized entity. That's just life in the Big City.

You or Your Spouse Becomes Incompetent

There is a significant likelihood that you or your spouse will become legally incompetent at some point during your joint lifetimes. Your Living Trust considers this possibility and allows the competent spouse to carry on as the sole trustee of your Living Trust without the need for court involvement.

The big question in this situation, however, is how incompetence is determined. This is not a casual matter. You cannot just run to your attorney's office and pronounce that you are now the sole person in charge of your Living Trust assets because, in your opinion, your spouse is mentally addled. The attorney will think *you* have gone daft, or that you are making a power play for complete control of the Living Trust assets.

To prevent such attempts at complete control, your Living Trust provides standards by which incompetence is measured. These standards are not uniform, and we lawyers often differ on what they should be. But no matter the differences, they need to provide assurance that a proper determination of incompetence is made to prevent one spouse from illegitimately taking over the family money.

As your Living Trust advisor, I suggest to you and to my clients that you stipulate in the Living Trust that one spouse can be determined incompetent to be a co-trustee if the other spouse obtains two letters written by licensed physicians on their stationery. Both letters must state that you have become mentally or physically incapacitated to the extent that you can no longer manage your financial affairs. Furthermore, to avoid collusion between your spouse and the physicians, the letter-writing doctors cannot be related to you or your spouse, and they cannot be related to each other.

Once those letters are obtained, your spouse automatically becomes the sole trustee of your Living Trust. He or she now has the singular power to execute all documents binding the Living

Trust, including checks, deposit statements, withdrawal statements, deeds, escrow documents, contracts, and the like. As this is a lot of financial power, I again suggest that you be sure to include a very clear statement in your Living Trust that defines how incompetence is measured and determined.

You or Your Spouse Resigns

There is no law or trust provision that forces you to stay on as a co-trustee. If you no longer want to serve, you can sign resignation papers.

Why would you want to resign? Why would anyone voluntarily give up control of the Living Trust assets? Using my clients' experiences as a guide, resignation occurs when you have become ill to the point where managing the checkbook has become a slow and difficult process. Ultimately, you realize that the family finances would be handled more expeditiously and efficiently if you are no longer in the process.

Resigning is not just for the addled. Perhaps you are the type of person who wants to die first so you won't be left with the bookkeeping. If so, you may want your money-managing spouse to handle everything. Or, maybe you believe that too many cooks spoil the broth and that your Living Trust assets would best be handled by one of you.

Whatever the reason, you cannot just remove yourself as a co-trustee by simply throwing up your hands and shouting "That's it!" Your Living Trust provides that your resignation must be stated in writing, signed by you, and delivered to the remaining co-trustee. The signing is not as dramatic as you might think. It's not like the cinematic depiction of resignations where you (1) storm into the high-rise building conference room, (2) stride over to the long conference table surrounded by executive types who all resemble the Monopoly guy, (3) slam down your resignation papers on the table, (4) sign them, (5) throw them in the direction of the evil executive guy heading the table, and (6) storm out the door. No, it merely involves a call to your attorney to tell him you do not want to be a co-trustee. Your attorney will then prepare the appropriate legal documents and set up an appointment.

During that appointment, your attorney will make sure you read and understand the effect of the resignation, which is that the sole management and control of the Living Trust assets will be in the hands of your spouse. If you can handle the prospect of your spouse having the sole power to bind you to all transactions relating to your Living Trust assets, and if you truly want to resign, go ahead and affix your signature. But, as your Living Trust advisor, I suggest you really ponder this resignation before you sign that paper.

Financial Advisor Alert

Whether your married client is removed as a co-trustee by death, incapacity, or resignation, your client has to prove that he or she is now the sole trustee of the Living Trust. Prove to who? The bank managers. The brokerage account representatives. The customer service center at the life insurance and annuity companies. Really, all of the "live people" at the financial institutions at which your clients have their assets—because the ownership of those accounts must reflect that only one trustee is in charge and only one trustee's signature is required to wheel-and-deal with the Living Trust assets. (And if your client sells the house, apartment building, or other Living Trust real estate, such proof must also be presented to escrow and the title insurance company.)

You can *really* show your value to your sole trustee client by assisting with this process. Make a conference call with your client and that live account representative and ask what your client needs to present in order to establish that there is now only one Living Trust sheriff in town. (Most likely, it will be a copy of the Living Trust and the document showing the death, incapacity, or resignation of the former co-trustee; but don't be surprised if more is required, such as a letter from the attorney who drafted the Living Trust stating, in essence, that it is still in full force and effect.) Then make an appointment for your client to visit that representative. Not only will the representative have the relevant documents for your client's signature at the ready but will also ascertain beforehand what other documents and processes are needed for the account trustee "changeover" and advise your client accordingly at that meeting.

The Low-Maintenance Living Trust

Living with your Living Trust is a low-maintenance proposition. While both you and your spouse are alive, living with your Living Trust essentially means keeping it handy in the event either you or your spouse wants to revoke it, or if both you and your spouse desire to amend it. It's that simple. In this chapter, you have received the proper training on how to approach and implement those courses of action.

But we are not done yet. Living with your Living Trust also requires attention to various matters relating to the real estate you transferred to your Living Trust, and involves consideration of discussing your Living Trust with your children or other beneficiaries. Those subjects are discussed in the following two chapters in this Second Quarter.

The Five Concerns about the Real Estate You Transferred to Your Living Trust

OR,

YOU STILL OWN YOUR HOUSE!

There is no special trick to ensure that you continue to own the real estate you transferred to your Living Trust. You own it. There is nothing to do other than continue to do nothing—as you were doing before you established your Living Trust.

However, as I train you on how to live with your Living Trust while both you and your spouse are alive, I must engage in a training session on five concerns that you must consider when dealing with real estate that has been transferred to your Living Trust.

Financial Advisor Alert

Even though you are your clients' advisor on all things financial, you should still take note of the real estate–related Living Trust matters that I discuss in this chapter. Your clients' house, apartment building, commercial property, and other real estate concerns are likely their most valuable assets, and you do your clients a service by having the ability to point out, at least, the basics of real property matters in the Living Trust context.

First Concern: Owning Your Living Trust Real Estate

When I explain to my clients that they need to transfer their real estate to their Living Trust, I often see them wince in discomfort, as if they had been hit in the chest with a tennis ball. As one client said, "Mr. Condon, I feel very uncomfortable transferring my house to my Living Trust. This is my house. I want to make sure it stays in my name."

As an experienced attorney and property holder, I do not dismiss this concern lightly. Real estate is almost always the most valuable asset a person owns, and people are uncomfortable signing anything that potentially affects their ownership of it. However, the Living Trust is effective only to the extent that there are valuable assets in it; therefore, the real estate must be transferred to it. If not, your Living Trust will sit as an empty bucket and, as a result, a probate procedure will be required after death to transfer the real estate to the Living Trust. The money used to pay me for setting up the Living Trust might just as well have been thrown into the street.

Recall the most important words of advice that I have offered about the ownership of the assets in your Living Trust: You are the Living Trust . . . the Living Trust is you. In other words, you are the owner, manager, and beneficiary of the Living Trust assets. Therefore, when you sign a deed transferring title from you as an individual to you as trustee of your Living Trust, you do not take away any rights related to the title and interest of your house.

Financial Advisor Alert

More than a few clients have been riddled with anxiety over the concern that they no longer own their house after transferring it to their Living Trust. But they find great relief when offered a second opinion from a trusted professional that no ownership rights are lost after that transfer. You need to take on the role of that trusted professional and give those folks that reassurance.

Second Concern: Transferring Real Estate to Your Living Trust without Risk of Property Tax Reassessment

One of the most common questions I get from clients when I establish their Living Trust is this: "Mr. Condon, when you record the deed that transfers my house to my Living Trust, will the property taxes go up?"

Here is my answer: No. Here is my answer again: No. And let me give you my answer for a third time: No.

Why am I being so relentless in telling clients that the property taxes on their house will stay the same after the house is transferred to their Living Trust? Because they are so fearful that such a transfer could trigger a reassessment. My clients bought their homes decades ago when property values were very low; and with lower values come lower property tax bases. But, if those bases somehow become increased to current fair market values, the bases will increase substantially, which will cause the property taxes to skyrocket to the point where my clients will be taxed right out of their homes. That is not a pleasant prospect for my clients, who are often property rich and cash poor.

But again, transferring real estate to a Living Trust will not cause a property tax reassessment. Let me give you the ultimate proof. I practice in Los Angeles County, where sits the Los Angeles County assessor's office. The assessor's only function is to raise money for the county by increasing property taxes. The assessor can raise property taxes in only two limited situations: when real estate is built or improved (not our focus here), and when there is a transfer of ownership of real estate. The assessor is very aggressive on increasing property taxes on transfers, but cannot increase taxes on transfers of real estate to a Living Trust, because a transfer to a Living Trust is not a transfer! Even the money-hungry assessor realizes that a transfer to a trust is not a real transfer of ownership, because the settlor (owner), trustee (manager), and beneficiary are the same person as the transferor.

Many of my clients own real estate in other states. During my 30-year practice, I have dealt with the assessor in counties in almost every one of our United States. From these experiences, I have come to two conclusions. One, if you ever attempt to navigate the deed-recording systems in Hawaii or Louisiana, with their byzantine and absolutely confusing procedures and requirements, you will go slightly mad. Second, no transfer of real estate in any state to a Living Trust will result in an increase in any real estate tax.

So, have no fear or trepidation when your lawyer asks you to sign that deed. If your transfer results in an increase in property taxes, then someone screwed up. I cannot state it more plainly than that.

Financial Advisor Alert

Some Living Trust clients assume their real estate's property tax basis naturally increases when the trust transfer deed is recorded—and pay that increase without a fight. To combat that surprisingly common assumption, ask your clients whether their property taxes increased following the recording of the deed that transfers title to their Living Trust. Their answer will likely be no. But if yes, express shock and indignation and get them running to the attorney who performed that transfer to look into it immediately. Either the lawyer screwed up, or the county assessor somehow missed the "reassessment exclusion forms" the lawyer submitted with the trust transfer deed.

The next time you have to concern yourself with your Living Trust real estate is if you sell or refinance it.

Third Concern: Selling Living Trust Real Estate

Selling the house or other real estate that you transferred to your Living Trust is just like a sale without the Living Trust component. You decide to sell, you find a real estate broker, your house gets listed for sale, you accept an offer, escrow closes, and you walk away with the sale proceeds.

However, because your property is titled in the name of your Living Trust, you may find yourself getting this type of phone call from the escrow officer after you have accepted the offer, but before escrow closes:

> **Escrow:** Mr. Bookreader?
>
> **You:** Yes?
>
> **Escrow:** This is escrow calling. I just got a call from the title insurance company. They just noticed that the house you are selling is in your Living Trust. They require more information.
>
> **You:** What kind of information?
>
> **Escrow:** Well, they said they need to see your Living Trust.
>
> **You:** Why? That's a private document.
>
> **Escrow:** If you don't let them see your Living Trust, they will decline coverage, and that will kill the sale.
>
> **You:** My lawyer never warned me about this!

What is going on in this situation? Well, before you can sell your real estate, the purchaser will want a title insurance policy, which assures that he or she has clear title to the property being purchased. So, the purchaser approaches a title insurance company to buy that policy. The insurance company then performs a search of the title to your property and shows the latest vesting to be in the names of you and your spouse as trustees of your Living Trust.

Certainly, you know that you established your Living Trust, and that you and your spouse are the trustees with the power to wheel and deal with assets in the Living Trust in any way that you desire. But the title insurance company does not. It wants to be 101 percent certain that you are the Living Trust and the Living Trust is you, and it wants proof that you and your spouse, as trustees, have the power to sell real estate contained in your Living Trust. To achieve that certainty, the insurance company wants to see particular portions of your Living Trust, which are:

- **The declaration of trust**—the part that declares your intention to establish a Living Trust.
- **The trustee section**—where you identify yourself as the manager of your Living Trust.

- **The trustee's powers section**—to prove that you have the power to sell trust assets.
- **The signature page.**

So what do you do? You whip out your Living Trust, find those portions, make copies, and send them to escrow. If you do not have your Living Trust handy, call the lawyer who drafted it for you and tell him or her (nicely) to send escrow those portions from the copies in the office files. I get those kinds of calls every day. And although it is a bit of a nuisance to schlep to the file room, get the file, make the copies, and provide them to escrow, it is a process that every Living Trust attorney knows is part of the job—and should be included in the fee you paid the attorney to draft the documents. So, do not feel guilty when you issue that instruction. Your lawyer will grumble, but expects to receive that call and will get those copies to escrow.

In any event, with these four portions, you are able to prove to the title company that you own the property in a validly established Living Trust. Therefore, you are empowered to sell it if you wish.

Fourth Concern: Refinancing Living Trust Real Estate

As an attorney, I would like to tell you that refinancing Living Trust real estate is easy. Much of the time, it is. But as your Living Trust advisor, I must caution you that sometimes it is very difficult, because many lenders and title insurance companies are unwilling to participate in the transaction unless the real estate is in your individual name. As unfair as it sounds, this unwillingness may require you to sign a deed that transfers your real estate from your Living Trust back to your individual name before you can refinance.

If you are so forced to retransfer your real estate to your individual name as a condition to refinance, the escrow company will prepare the deed, which you must sign. **But escrow will not put your real estate back into your Living Trust when the refinance has been concluded!** In other words, you will be responsible for then preparing a deed that again transfers your real estate back in the Living Trust. If you do not do so—either because you do not know how to or because you may not remember that the real estate is no longer in your Living Trust—then the real estate will remain in your name.

This situation can be extremely problematic and can ultimately cost your Living Trust beneficiaries a lot of time and money. For instance, if you die before you retransfer the real estate back to your Living Trust, your beneficiaries will have to establish a probate procedure where they must submit your "I forgot will" for approval. In doing so, they will have to obtain an order from the court that authorizes the transfer of your real estate to your Living Trust. Thus, this process essentially nullifies the reason you established a Living Trust in the first place.

I have participated in three probates where the only asset going through the process was forgotten real estate. The waste of time and funds was not lost on the beneficiaries, who attempted to blame me for the screwup and hold me liable for the costs, as typified by the following conversation I had with a representative of one set of beneficiaries:

Attorney for Beneficiaries: Mr. Condon, my clients have to probate their father's will because his home was not in the Living Trust at his death. You need to pay for that.

Me: Why?

Attorney: Because the property was not in his Living Trust.

Me: I know that. That's the second time you have told me that. But why do I need to do free probate work?

Attorney: Because you should have known that he was going to take his house out of his Living Trust to do a refinance.

Me: He refinanced?

Attorney: Yes. And you should have known that.

Me: How should I have known? I have not seen or spoken to him in nine years.

Attorney: Oh! Never mind.

Of course, had I known about the refinance, I would have been in the position to advise the client accordingly. But in any event, I do not want you to suffer such a similar stress-filled conversation with people attempting to find someone to pay for the inadvertent mistake of another. So for my sake, if not for your beneficiaries' sakes, make sure you remember to call your lawyer to put your real estate back into your Living Trust after your refinance is concluded.

> ### Financial Advisor Alert
>
> Ask your clients whether they have refinanced their house or other real property since they established their Living Trust. If yes, then take it upon yourself to look up the title to see how the title is vested. Ask any real estate agent or broker to search for the latest title vesting of the property that your clients refinanced. The broker or agent will be happy to accommodate you. Or if you have had prior dealings with a title insurance company's customer service department, call up a representative and directly make that request. Don't be surprised if you discover that your clients' refinanced property was not transferred back to their Living Trust after the conclusion of the transaction. That happens a lot.

Fifth Concern: Requiring the Signatures of Both You and Your Spouse to Sell Living Trust Real Estate

Before establishing your Living Trust, you and your spouse owned your checking account in some form of joint ownership. When you opened that account, you told the new account representative that only one signature was required to negotiate checks. Of course, this is a very common arrangement, as you do not want the hassle of running to your spouse every time you write a check.

When we lawyers establish your Living Trust, we do not want to interfere with that arrangement. If one signature was good enough to negotiate checks written from a joint account, then one signature is good enough to negotiate checks written from a Living Trust account where both you and your spouse are the trustees. So, in the section of your Living Trust that sets forth the powers of the trustee, there is a standard (read: boilerplate) provision that says that only one signature of either trustee is required to transact with Living Trust assets.

As your Living Trust advisor, I must warn you that this singular power of one trustee to enter into transactions with your Living Trust assets also covers real estate assets! If you are like most of my clients, you do not want your spouse to have the ability to sell or refinance your Living Trust real estate without your participation. Rather, you expect the continuation of the pre–Living Trust requirement of mutual consent and signatures of both you and your spouse regarding any matter relating to the real estate.

If this comes as a shock to you, you can imagine how one of my clients felt when he discovered the effect of this provision the hard way. Mr. and Mrs. Southerland signed a Living Trust that contained such a "power of one" provision. She wanted to sell their four-unit apartment building because she was tired of dealing with "crazy tenants." He, however, believed in the magic of appreciating real estate. This conflict exploded when he discovered that she had sold the building! He did not notice that the sale had taken place until after he contacted a tenant to ask about the status of a late rent payment. It was not late; it had just been sent to the new owner.

There is nothing inherently wrong with allowing one spouse to bind the trust or singularly function on behalf of the Living Trust. Indeed, some folks like the convenience of one signature binding real estate transactions. If you dread selling or refinancing your house because of seemingly endless document requirements, you may find yourself in that category. However, this "power of one" provision is often part of the small print of the Living Trust that is at risk of being overlooked by the attorney, so much so that I have brought it to your attention in this chapter.

Thus, if you do not want your real estate to be swept up in this one-signature-for-all-assets provision, you have to tell your lawyer to incorporate the real estate exception, specifying that only one signature shall be required to transact all Living Trust assets *with the exception of real estate.* Real estate shall require both your signatures during the joint lifetimes of you and your spouse.

Financial Advisor Alert

One of the Living Trust's basic selling points is that the settlors' financial lives do not change. Your clients' post–Living Trust check writing, investing, spending, and wheeling-and-dealing carries on in the same manner as their pre–Living Trust existence. All without having to schlep their Living Trust everywhere to check whether they have the power to engage in the transactions at hand ... because the "Trustee Powers" section gives them the authority to engage in any transaction with Living Trust assets. Buy. Sell. Invest. Refinance. Borrow. Lend. Repair. Insure. Maintain. Exchange. Gift. Everything except burn for the insurance money.

As a result, your married clients will likely not have reviewed their Living Trust to ascertain whether it empowers one spouse to bind both to transactions involving Living Trust assets. So ... do this for them. Look under the section titled "Trustee Powers" (or words to that effect) and peruse the paragraphs to see if it gives such unilateral power. If so, then discuss with your clients whether they wish to amend the document to include the real estate exception.

Concerning Yourself with the Five Concerns

Do not fret that transferring your real estate to your Living Trust diminishes your bundle of rights to your real estate. You still own your real estate as it sits in the Living Trust just as you owned it before you owned it as trustee. However, as I pointed out in this chapter, selling and refinancing your Living Trust will require you to engage in additional steps to satisfy the needs of outside agencies involved in those transactions. Your Living Trust advisor (me) is advising you that the additional work is a meager price to pay for the benefit of probate avoidance that your Living Trust gives to your beneficiaries.

CHAPTER

Should You Tell Your Children about Your Living Trust?

OR,

DON'T DISMISS THE CHANCE TO HAVE A FAMILY INHERITANCE MEETING—ESPECIALLY IF THE LAWYER WON'T CHARGE YOU

Your Living Trust is a private document. There is no legal obligation thrust upon you to share its contents with anyone. After you bring it home, you can store it under lock and key and hide it from the world. And if you are like most of my clients, your first instinct will be to do just that. As you place it in your safe-deposit box, you mutter aloud (perhaps with glee) that your children will never see this document as long as you are alive.

But as your Living Trust advisor, I advise you to run against that instinct. In fact, I want you to do a 180-degree turn. I not only want you to inform your children about your Living Trust, I want you to tell your children the size of their expected inheritance!

Are you appalled and shocked at this advice? You may very well be. Of course, you may be the rare breed that considers yourself an open book when it comes to family money matters. Most likely, however, either the thought of disclosing inheritance information to your children has never entered your mind, or you have dismissed it out of hand at its mere suggestion.

Financial Advisor Alert

Your clients have the natural and instinctive desire to enhance their assets during their lifetime. With your advice and assistance, they make investment decisions appropriate for their circumstances, and create a financial plan designed to meet their lifestyle standards with an eye toward asset protection and productivity. It's the American way! So—doesn't it follow that your clients should also take necessary steps for a smooth and trouble-free transfer of those hard-earned assets to the next generation? In my mind, it makes no sense for you and your clients to knock yourselves out creating wealth just to see it dissipate from chaos, conflict, estrangement, litigation, addiction, financial immaturity, and other risks of loss. For the reasons I set forth in this chapter, the family inheritance meeting is the most helpful "tool" to prevent such problems and the losses that stem from them.

And we estate planning attorneys need *you*—the financial advisor—to get the families to that table by touting to your clients the meeting's positive purposes of post-death wealth *and* family preservation.

In this chapter, my goal is to change your mind. I will motivate and encourage you to conduct a family inheritance meeting by giving you plenty of reasons why it should take place. And once you are so motivated, you will know how, when, and where that meeting should occur.

Why You Don't Want to Conduct a Family Inheritance Meeting . . .

As an experienced attorney, I have heard my fair share of reasons for clients' nondisclosure of their Living Trusts to their children, and I am sure many of you share these same reasons. Please find yourself in one of the following excuses that I have heard during my 20 years of practice:

- "I like my privacy. End of story."
- "If my kids know what they're going to inherit, they will do nothing with their lives."

- "My money is none of my kids' business."
- "My children will be very upset with my inheritance plan. I just don't want to hear it. Let them go crazy after I die when I won't be around."
- "I am Swedish. And one thing Swedes don't do is talk about such personal matters with their children."
- "I would love to tell my children about their inheritance. But we've never really talked about money before. It would be too awkward."
- "My children live all over the place. No way would you ever get them into one room for a meeting."

And Why I Don't Respect Your Reasons as to Why You Don't Want to Conduct a Family Inheritance Meeting

I have heard variations of those excuses from almost all of my Living Trust clients (except the one involving the Swedish couple, which is the only time those words have been spoken to me). With every Living Trust I prepare, I offer the clients—for no extra fee— the opportunity to invite their children into my office to discuss the Living Trust and its inheritance instructions. For every 100 such invitations, perhaps two are accepted. I am not a psychologist, but these numbers strongly suggest to me that talking about inheritances with our children is not part of our DNA.

Nonetheless, I keep plugging away with these invitations, because I believe that the family inheritance meeting should be an integral part of the Living Trust process, for several reasons:

- The meeting is an opportunity to educate your children on the form and function of the Living Trust. Let them hear about what it does and how it avoids probate. Let them look at its pages and see their names in the inheritance instructions. If you fear that the voluminous documents will overwhelm them, they can take small bites.
- Your children are already thinking about their inheritance. Of course, they are not telling you this, because they do not want to give you the false impression that they want you to

die. They are just being normal children who wonder about their financial status, money, and their inheritance. Take away this grand mystery by letting them get a hands-on feel for your inheritance plan.

- Your children might have a distorted view of your financial situation and may have made their plans based on that distortion. Perhaps they have failed to take into account how the estate tax will diminish their inheritance. Maybe they believe you are worth a lot more than you truly are. Perhaps one child does not know he or she is receiving less than your other children . . . or nothing at all. You are doing your children a kindness by giving them a roughly accurate view of your financial picture so they can adjust their expectations—and their plans—accordingly.

- Your children need to know that they are named as your lifetime agents who take over your Living Trust assets during your lifetime in the event of your incapacity. Speaking rhetorically, how will your children know they are your lifetime agents unless you tell them? And how will they know what the role of lifetime agent requires unless they first have that information? It simply does not make sense to keep your children in the dark about your Living Trust when, in fact, they may become your lifetime agents.

- Your children need to familiarize themselves with the Living Trust documents during your lifetime so that they do not seem so daunting after your death. There are few events more stressful in your children's lives than the deaths of both parents. Imagine how that stress is exacerbated when shortly after the funeral they are first presented with several thick and lengthy documents written almost entirely in legalese, which they have to read, navigate, and understand while the beneficiaries are breathing down their necks saying, "Where's mine?" You do not want that for your children. Take away that bewilderment and floundering by going over the Living Trust with them during a family inheritance meeting.

- Your children need to know about the process of administering a Living Trust. Although the concept of the Living Trust is simple—your after-death agent signs the documents transferring title of your assets from your Living Trust to your beneficiaries—they must still engage in a process that involves preparation of estate tax returns, drafting of deeds, dealing with the IRS, communicating with bank and brokerage representatives and completing many of their required forms, and on and on. They should have some semblance of understanding this process while you are alive so they are mentally prepared to handle it after your death.

- The family inheritance meeting can smooth over the potential conflicts about your inheritance instructions that could arise after your death. For example, perhaps you decide to leave more of your assets to your struggling schoolteacher daughter and less to your successful doctor son because, you think, your daughter needs it more. While you believe you are achieving economic justice, your doctor son sees it slightly differently: "My parents have punished my success and rewarded my sister who works fewer hours than I do! How dare they?" Your son cannot be angry at you because, well, you are dead. So, he transfers that anger to his sister, and he never talks to her again.

  This type of situation can be avoided if your asset allocation plan is discussed at a family inheritance meeting. During that time, your son would be able to openly disagree with your plan and hear your rationale for the allocation. In other words, the family inheritance meeting allows you to raise the conflicts now so they can be handled, discussed, and, perhaps, smoothed over while you are alive. If you do not want to face what you believe will be a contentious atmosphere, as your Living Trust advisor I must caution you into it with this statement: By not addressing the conflict now, you allow it to fester after your death to the extent that it will undermine your children's sibling relationships.

- You have spent considerable time, money, and effort in putting your Living Trust together. You did this because you desire that your children receive their inheritance in the most cost-free and hassle-free manner possible. If your Living Trust is primarily for them, does it not follow to clue them in to it?

- You may have assets that are literally all over the place, and you need to tell your children what you have and where it can be found. A limited liability membership interest in a property in Texas. A limited partnership share in a gas lease. A bank account in Nevada. Some cash offshore in the Cook Islands. An IRA in a brokerage account in Delaware. Without the meeting, your children may not be able to track everything down, or realize that your engagement ring is hidden in the hem of your favorite red skirt!

If you do not believe that people are capable of hiding their assets in obscure places, let me tell you that on a few occasions I have had to hire a private eye to trace and locate missing assets. In particular, when one of my clients passed away, his children suspected that he had bank accounts and real estate investments outside California. Although he was originally from New York, he often relocated to such places as Miami, Baltimore, Israel, and Los Angeles. Therefore, they believed he had assets in those various locations. They were right, and eventually we located their father's assets, but not without spending a lot of time, effort, and money. This was not a situation where he was hiding assets or financial information on purpose. Rather, with advancing age, he just did not remember the nature and extent of his holdings. Regardless of the reasoning, if my client had allowed me to arrange a family inheritance meeting, he could have saved his children the aggravation and expense that came from having to trace his assets following his death.

How to Conduct a Family Inheritance Meeting

I have previously told you that I make sweeping generalizations in order to help get a point across. However, my statement that you need to have a family inheritance meeting is not one of them. For the reasons I discussed, this meeting is an important part of the process of establishing your Living Trust, even if your Living Trust is the most conventional, garden-variety Living Trust in the world.

Now that I have converted you to my will, your next inquiry becomes how to convene a family inheritance meeting. Ideally, it should take place in a somewhat formal setting that impresses on your children that this is Serious Time. This is not at your family Labor Day backyard barbecue with your grandchildren running around underfoot. It is not in your living room after the belt-busting Thanksgiving dinner with the Dallas Cowboys on television in the background.

There are four essential steps to having an effective family inheritance meeting.

1. The meeting should be at your Living Trust attorney's office—with your lawyer heading the table in the law library or conference room. This is a very official setting and does more than anything else to send your children the message that this is a serious conversation.

2. Your children must attend the meeting. If this demand comes from you, your children may not take the matter seriously. Therefore, I suggest that you have your Living Trust attorney set up the meeting and invite your children. Nothing will make your children jump into action more than getting a call from their parents' attorney.

3. Do not accept excuses from your children who claim that they cannot attend. It is likely that your attorney's invitation will be met with false bravado ("Whatever my parents do is okay"), insincerity ("Tell them to just go ahead and spend it all"), or lack of caring ("I'm too busy"). To those comments I generally respond with this: "Okay, then I guess you won't mind if your parents leave you out of the Living Trust." You want to see quick? They come a-runnin' after this comment! A child who truly cannot make it can be present through speakerphone.

4. Prepare an agenda for the meeting with your attorney. As your children are all gathered around in the official setting or present through speakerphone, ask your attorney to give the opening statement. Perhaps he or she can begin by saying, "Your parents have done a marvelous thing. They have undertaken significant effort to make sure that your

inheritance comes to you in the most time-efficient and cost-effective manner possible, and they have accomplished this with the Living Trust." At that point, the attorney can summarize your Living Trust and give your children the highlights. I recommend that you meet with your Living Trust attorney before this meeting to discuss the information of the Living Trust that you will disclose and to determine these "greatest hits."

Financial Advisor Alert

Ask your clients to allow you to attend the family inheritance meeting. With two professionals present (you and the attorney), your mutual clients will perceive that a "team" has been formed for their family unity and financial benefit. Believe me, that perception alone will leave your clients feeling very safe and protected. Also, the attorney will bring you into the conversation for your input on certain aspects of the clients' financial and investment plan, such as how the assets are currently vested and how the post-death transfer of those assets takes place.

With your presence and participation, you are not just a name on your clients' financial records and statements they feel uncomfortable about contacting and trusting; instead, you are their parents' "financial guy" who took the time and trouble to meet with them at the attorney's office to help the family "cause."

Your Lawyer Should Not Charge for the Family Inheritance Meeting

What will your attorney charge for these efforts? It should be . . . nothing! You should not have to pay extra for your lawyer's participation in the family inheritance meeting, because it is too important to be considered anything other than an integral part of the Living Trust process. Therefore, before you hire the lawyer, I suggest that you respectfully mandate that his or her presence at a family inheritance meeting be part of the Living Trust package. If the lawyer balks at this instruction, move on to another attorney until you find one who will agree.

Of course, you can always convene the meeting on your own. Just make sure that it takes place in a manner that lets your children know that it is serious business. In other words, turn the television off and gather around the dining room table. Hand them each a copy of your Living Trust, give them the cook's tour of your inheritance instructions, and ask for questions and comments. Then you are off to the races.

THE THIRD QUARTER

LIVING WITH YOUR LIVING TRUST AFTER THE DEATH OF YOUR SPOUSE

As a Living Trust attorney, one of my main functions is to assist the surviving spouse in administering the Living Trust following the death of the "first spouse to die," whom I shall refer to as the deceased spouse.

Dealing with surviving spouses is the second most gut-wrenching part of my job. (The first is working with clients whose children have died before them.) I remember Mrs. Abernathy, who said to me after her husband died, "Mr. Condon, I didn't want to even think about my husband dying before me. I couldn't imagine how my life would be without him. I really hoped I'd go first so I wouldn't have to find out. But he's gone, and I don't want to do anything. I don't care about my Living Trust. I just want to disappear."

Mrs. Abernathy is not alone in her thinking. I have heard this refrain from many of my clients who similarly cannot bear even the mere thought of life without their spouse.

Like my mother. Esther was born and raised in Knoxville, Tennessee. She met my father in the resort town of Highland Springs, California, about 30 miles shy of Palm Springs. They met while playing Ping-Pong. After marrying my father a mere six months later, she quit her job as a filing clerk for the FBI. Supporting her husband became her main function. She lived that existence for 50 years, until in August 2006 my father died of lymphoma, a condition that he handled one way or another for almost 20 years before his death. My father, who was a longtime athlete whose credo was, "Surfing is life—all else is mere detail," most lamented how his illness impacted his ability to surf, ski, play tennis, and ride dirt bikes. But when his illness prevented him from doing what he wanted, he did what he could—with such "fallback" activities as walking and weight-lifting. My mother was inconsolable when he died, and still is. Not a week goes by when I do not hear her express the same sentiment as Mrs. Abernathy and dozens of other surviving spouses whom I have encountered during my practice: "I wanted to die first."

I intellectually understand that I must communicate to the surviving spouse the laundry list of goals that must be achieved to assure the success of the Living Trust established by both spouses. But it is often difficult to make effective contact with a surviving spouse who has chosen the path of least resistance—that is, withdrawing from all matters relating to Living Trust business.

As crass as it must seem, I must convince a surviving spouse that she must come to grips with her husband's death to the extent that she can deal with the numerous Living Trust issues that must be addressed. If not tended to, the thousands of dollars that the couple spent on their Living Trust may be wasted because no efforts were made to effect the provisions in the Living Trust that would, on the surviving spouse's death, save the beneficiaries tens of thousands of dollars in probate expenses and estate taxes.

I know these words are harsh, but they are designed to motivate you to take action. I have dealt with many surviving spouses in this manner. Most times, I get thanks for giving them a kick in the pants. However, a few times I have been fired for coming across as too insensitive. But ultimately, I have no regrets, because I am doing my job of helping clients deal with the business of achieving the goals of a Living Trust, which are the subject of the following chapters in the Third Quarter.

10

Will You Divert Your Deceased Spouse's Half of the Living Trust Assets from Your Offspring?

OR,

HOW TO MAKE YOUR CHILDREN FRET AND HOPE THAT YOU WILL DO THE RIGHT THING

During the joint lifetimes of you and your spouse, you both owned your Living Trust assets together. You owned half. Your spouse owned half. When your spouse died, you became the owner of both halves as one whole.

But, for purposes of explaining the main issue of this chapter, I need to characterize the Living Trust assets as "your half" and "your deceased spouse's half."

Before I get into the main issue of this chapter—possibly diverting your assets from your offspring—let's begin by discussing the goals of the Living Trust after the death of your spouse.

> **Financial Advisor Alert**
>
> The concerns discussed in this chapter arise in second marriages when there are children of the first marriage. If one or both of your husband-and-wife clients are on their second time around, you must raise the idea of inserting a plan in their Living Trust that prevents the surviving spouse from completely diverting the Living Trust assets from the family bloodline.

The Three Goals of Living Trust Management after the Death of Your Spouse

After the death of one's spouse, there are three goals that must be achieved in order to have a successful Living Trust.

Goal 1: The first goal is to protect your ownership and control of your Living Trust assets for the remainder of your life. In other words, if you become incapacitated to the point that you cannot manage the Living Trust assets, you want to be sure that some good person will step in as your lifetime agent to use the funds for your benefit, and not run off with them to Brazil during Carnival.

Goal 2: The second goal is to make sure that your deceased spouse's share of the Living Trust assets will *not* be diverted by you, the surviving spouse, to your new boyfriend, your new girl-friend, your new spouse, or your new spouse's children from his or her first marriage. In other words, while you may want to divert the Living Trust assets from your bloodline, I can tell you with all certainty that your deceased spouse does not want to see that happen.

Goal 3: The third goal only applies if you are really rich. That is, if you and your deceased spouse's wealth exceeds your com-bined exemption amounts (which I discuss in Chapter 13), then the third goal is to capitalize on the opportunity your Living Trust gives you to save estate taxes for your children after your death. In other words, you would implement provisions in your Living Trust now—during your life—to make sure your children pay less estate tax years later when you die.

In order to help your Living Trust achieve these goals, I need to meet and confer with the surviving spouse on at least an infrequent basis. But as you can well imagine, many surviving spouses are consumed by grief and unable to deal with any type of business matter. As such, the most important issue initially becomes Goal 2, which is the focus of this chapter. After all, we do not want a grieving widow or widower to suddenly be taken advantage of, especially when it comes to diverting assets away from your children and your first spouse's intentions.

Does Your Deceased Spouse Approve of Using Half of the Living Trust Assets to Support Your Second Spouse?

When your spouse died, you came into full control of both halves. You get the income from both halves. You get to dip into the principal of both halves. You get to wheel and deal with both halves. You have the power to use your deceased spouse's half any way you want. This is consistent with all normal expectations of husband-and-wife assets.

This sounds like a pretty good arrangement for you, the surviving spouse, but not so much for your deceased spouse. Why? Because having the power to do anything you want with your deceased spouse's half includes the power to leave that half to your new spouse, girlfriend, boyfriend, caretaker, or significant other. That ghostly whisper you hear over your shoulder is your deceased spouse saying, "Honey, you can do whatever you want with your half. But I don't want my half to end up with some opportunistic trollop. Make sure you leave it to our children."

Remarriage among widows and widowers is commonplace. After spending a lifetime with your spouse, you don't want to be alone, unless you crave your new solitary life where you can focus totally on your own needs and desires. Thus, even if you do not realize it now, you may remarry, and your new second spouse will probably become the primary focus of your existence.

It is hoped that your children (whom I refer to in this chapter as your "first children" because they are the product of your first marriage) will be happy for you when you marry this second spouse. They will revel in the knowledge that you will not be alone for the remainder of your days. But let me give you a taste of reality from the trenches. In the many situations I have encountered when my surviving spouse clients have remarried, I run into many first children who are happier for themselves than for their parents. Why? As one first child put it so succinctly: "Mr. Condon, I can't tell you what a relief it is for me that Dad hooked up with a new wife. Now he has an automatic caretaker! If he becomes incompetent, she can schlep him to the doctors. She can change his diapers. Then I can be free to do my thing, which is skiing, surfing, and tennis."

Such a lovely sentiment. When I hear such words from my clients' first children, I always wonder what family baggage came to bear that caused them to effectively divorce their parents at the time when their parents needed them the most. But what goes around often comes around. There is no such thing as a free lunch. The first children's relief that your second spouse will provide the lion's share of your care will rapidly dissipate when they realize they now "compete" with your second spouse for the Living Trust assets after your death.

Is this a valid concern? You betcha! Your Living Trust has a provision that states, in essence, that you have the power to change the inheritance instructions. If you love your second spouse, and if your relationship with your first children has flattened over time, it is only natural that you would want to change those instructions to name your second spouse as a beneficiary.

Every week, I get a call from first children who are scared to death that their surviving parent will leave all the Living Trust assets to their stepparent. Sadly, there is nothing the first children can do to prevent this occurrence. If the surviving parent wants to cut them out of the Living Trust, it can be done because of the surviving spouse's complete power and control of the Living Trust assets.

However, your first children will be relieved to know it's not a done deal. There are certain protective plans that can be built into your Living Trust that take away the surviving spouse's power to amend the deceased spouse's half of the Living Trust in any way that affects the first children's inheritances. But these protective plans have to be put into the Living Trust when you and your spouse first established it together.

Are there any protective plans in your Living Trust? Did you even discuss this issue with your attorney before you and your spouse signed it? Perhaps your attorney was not experienced enough—or too busy—to suggest the possibility of the Living Trust assets being diverted from the bloodline by the surviving spouse.

Or perhaps your attorney did raise this issue with you and your spouse, but you dismissed it. Like many of my clients, you may rely on faith that the surviving spouse will "do the right thing" and make sure all of the Living Trust assets ultimately go to the first children. Regardless of the reasons, you must remember this important message: The possibility that your children may suffer some inheritance loss because of the remarriage of a surviving parent is something that must be discussed and considered between you and your spouse at your first Living Trust meeting.

Financial Advisor Alert

This is one of those "how dare you" matters that may make you reticent about raising this issue. Because that's the response you fear may be forthcoming for being perceived as having cast aspersions on your clients' character or overstepping your "money boundary." Get over it! It's part of your job to prevent abuse of your clients' financial assets. Does diversion of the Living Trust assets to the surviving spouse's next spouse or significant other constitute financial abuse? Absolutely! Even your clients would say so.

Still, you will find that your second-time-around clients have never raised this issue among themselves out of concern for conveying the wrong impression. ("What?! You think I would cut out our kids if you die first?! See you in divorce court!") So, it's up to you. When your clients are in a second marriage–first children situation, you *must* make them aware that the survivor among them may have the power to leave all the Living Trust assets to someone other than their children and to discuss this further with their attorney.

Fretting and Hoping—by Your First Children

Now that your spouse is dead, what can your first children do to prevent you from diverting your deceased spouse's half to your second spouse if you have a Living Trust without any protective plan? Really, all they can do is hope that you and your spouse recognized this issue and put in the appropriate provision in your Living Trust to limit the surviving spouse's ability to change the inheritance instructions of the deceased spouse's half.

If your Living Trust does not have any protective plan, then you are the owner of both halves, and your first children must lie awake at night fretting about the possibility that you will divert their inheritance to your second spouse, and hoping you will do the right thing. As my father used to say, sometimes you run into problems that have no solution. In this case, I suppose fretting and hoping is the only remedial measure your first children can implement.

Preventing Your First Children from Fretting and Hoping So They Can Get Some Sleep

For purposes of carrying this admonition all the way through, let's assume that your Living Trust does contain a protective plan that prevents you from messing with your deceased spouse's half. What, then, are those plans and what are their effects?

One protective plan simply requires that on your deceased spouse's death, the deceased spouse's half will go out of the Living Trust and directly to your first children. The outright distribution of your deceased spouse's half to your first children absolutely guarantees you will never get your grubby mitts on it. Of course, you, the surviving spouse, would be deprived of the use of that half, and you would never sign a Living Trust that does that. After all, the goal is ensuring that the deceased spouse's half ends up with the first children, not impoverishing the surviving spouse.

Instead, the more acceptable protective plan (at least, to you) is the transfer of the deceased spouse's half to a *marital trust*. The marital trust is not contained in a separate document. It's part of the inheritance instructions of your Living Trust. In the marital trust, it is stated that you, the surviving spouse, receive all the income from your deceased spouse's half, and you have the right to dip into the principal for your health and support. Later, when you die, your deceased spouse's half goes out of the marital trust and to your beneficiaries.

Financial Advisor Alert

Take a look at the section in your husband-and-wife clients' Living Trust that deals with distribution of the trust estate following the first spouse death. Even if drowning in legalese, the words *marital trust* (or another name like *Q-tip trust*) will be fairly evident. If not present, then paint for them the prospect of SSAD (surviving spouse asset diversion) and get them to call their attorney for further discussion.

Financial Advisor Alert

If the marital trust provisions are present in your clients' Living Trust, there may be a sentence that says, in effect, that the surviving spouse must first spend down his or her entire half of the Living Trust assets (the survivor's trust portion) before using the deceased spouse's marital trust portion. Or conversely, it may say that the surviving spouse can resort to marital trust assets *without first having to run through the survivor's trust assets*.

Such a huge impact! Whether the surviving spouse can avail himself or herself of the entire trust estate at will—or just one-half until that half is gone—is a game-changer for the surviving spouse's quality of life.

But as significant as this sentence is, your clients will not know which one their Living Trust contains. So do them a big favor; find this language in their Living Trust, point out which version they have, and ask whether it matches their true intention. If not, then that language must be changed.

What about the half of the Living Trust assets belonging to you, the surviving spouse? Can that be controlled in the marital trust as well? No. Your half belongs to you, and you are free to do anything with it. Leave it to a new spouse. Leave it to a significant other. Leave it to your first children. Spend it. Throw it in the street. The fact is, no one and no trust can control what the surviving spouse does with the surviving spouse's half, except the surviving spouse.

Therefore, if you, following your spouse's death, need to marry someone so you won't be alone or to provide you with a caretaker you can call upon at all hours, or because you cannot find your way to the kitchen, you can reward your second spouse with your half on your death, and there is nothing to prevent you from doing so. But with a marital trust, you will not have the power to leave your deceased spouse's half to your second spouse, much to the relief of your deceased spouse and your first children. With the marital trust, your deceased spouse's half of the Living Trust assets is protected from you, while still providing economic value to you.

11

The Power to Change Your Deceased Spouse's Inheritance Instructions ... or Not!

OR,

IF YOUR CHILD'S VICE DISSIPATES AFTER YOUR SPOUSE DIES, ARE YOU ALLOWED TO CHANGE YOUR SPOUSE'S INHERITANCE INSTRUCTIONS TO MEET THAT CHANGE?

At the time you and your spouse established your Living Trust, the inheritance instructions were designed to speak to your children's circumstances as they existed back when you created the Living Trust.

For example, say you have two children—a son and a daughter.

Your son is a normal person. In my world, "normal" means he does not have any problems that pose a risk of loss to his inheritance. He is not an alcoholic, a drug addict, or a spendthrift. He does not belong to a crazy cult to which he will hand over his inheritance. He does not suffer from any mental or emotional infirmity that he must take medication to control. And there is no drama in your son's life, such as a wife with cash-register eyes, an income tax problem, or an actual or pending divorce, which will cause your son's inheritance to quickly dissipate.

For your normal son, you and your spouse believed his inheritance will not be caught up in any problems. So, your Living Trust leaves him in complete control of his share of the inheritance.

The Tyranny of Unjustified Lifetime Control

Your daughter, however, is another story. She has never managed her money properly, and you doubt she will attain financial maturity after your death. She spends like a socialite, throwing money away on clothes, the latest handbags, designer shoes, and expensive dinners and nightclubs where patrons think nothing of spending $400 on a bottle of champagne. You knew at the time you and your spouse established your Living Trust, and you know now, that any inheritance your daughter received would end up at nightclubs where the patrons think nothing of spending $1,000 on a bottle of champagne. It is quite obvious that her share of the inheritance must be controlled. It must be protected from her vice, and must be protected for her so it will be around to be used for her necessities of life.

Your spendthrift daughter cannot receive her inheritance outright. Your daughter's inheritance must be held by a third-party manager for the rest of her life so it will not be spent on the high life.

As a result of your daughter's behavior, you have taken the advice of your Living Trust advisor and established a protection trust. In other words, you and your spouse provide in your Living Trust that your daughter's share will be held in a protection trust for the rest of her life to ensure that a third-party institution controls and manages her inheritance to provide for her necessities of life. With this method, your daughter will never, ever, get to handle or spend her own money. (I discuss the protection trust in almost debilitating detail later in the book, in Chapter 18.)

Financial Advisor Alert

As you peruse your clients' Living Trust, it will be evident whether a protection trust has been created for their child's inheritance. You will see the name of the child incorporated into that subtrust's name (e.g., the "Randy Savage Trust" or "Randy Savage Irrevocable Trust") or such language as this: "The share to Randy Savage shall be held in a separate trust which shall be held, administered and distributed in accordance with the terms and provisions of the trust established for Randy Savage as stated below."

If the protection trust exists, you should ask your clients for the reasoning behind the establishment of that subtrust. Is their child an addict of some kind? Is he financially immature? Does she have creditor problems? Is he going through a divorce? If so, you must continue your perusal to determine whether the Living Trust gives the surviving spouse the power to change the protection trust, as I discuss below. In my view, the surviving spouse should always have the power to untie a child's "inheritance hands" if the vice underlying that tie-up somehow dissipates after the first spouse's death.

But guess what? A miracle happens. After your spouse's death, your daughter attends Shopaholics Anonymous, begins shopping at Walmart, and starts volunteering at a local soup kitchen.

To that I say, wonderful! Your daughter has become an exception to the rule that shopaholics wind up broke or filing for bankruptcy. But there is a problem. You have inheritance instructions that still speak to your daughter's addiction. Even though she has become a productive member of society, your Living Trust states that her inheritance will be withheld from her by a third-party manager for the rest of her life.

This is what I call the Tyranny of Unjustified Lifetime Control. The reason for the control no longer exists, but the control exists anyway. The question then becomes: Does your Living Trust give you the power to change the inheritance instructions after your spouse's death to meet your daughter's changed condition?

Even though I have never read your Living Trust, I can tell you with all certainty that it gives you the power to change the inheritance instructions on your half of the Living Trust assets. But in certain circumstances, your Living Trust *may* not give you the authority to change the instructions on your deceased spouse's half.

What is this stuff I have just seemingly thrown in from left field about your half and your deceased spouse's half of the Living Trust assets? Well . . . maybe not so deep in left field. If you read Chapter 10 prior to this Chapter 11, you may recall the words *marital trust*. If you see those words in your Living Trust, you are making a foray into the world we estate planning lawyers call *trust splitting*. As in—when your spouse dies, your deceased spouse's half of the Living Trust assets shall be allocated (by you, the surviving trustee/lifetime agent) to a *subtrust* called the marital trust.

The marital trust protects your deceased spouse's inheritance instructions. That is, while you get the income and/or principal of the marital trust for the rest of your life, you cannot change the marital trust's "who gets what" provisions. They are irrevocable.

While you have allocated your deceased spouse's half to the marital trust, your half is considered to be in your *survivor's trust*. The assets in the survivor's trust are considered your assets. Because they are your assets, you have all the freedom in the world to amend your survivor's trust to make sure your reformed daughter has direct access to her inheritance that comes from your half of the Living Trust assets in your survivor's trust.

So even though you can amend the inheritance instructions of your half (the survivor's trust) all day long, you cannot do so with your deceased spouse's half in the marital trust. When you die, the assets of the marital trust must be distributed in accordance with the inheritance instructions that exist in your Living Trust at the time of your spouse's death. And if those instructions state that your daughter's inheritance from the marital trust is "stuck" in an anti-spendthrift protection trust for the rest of her life, then that will be the case.

I also discuss the concept of a *trust split* after the death of your spouse in Chapter 13 in the context of estate tax planning and the allocation of your deceased spouse's half to a subtrust called the *exemption trust*. But for purposes of this discussion, your Living Trust may provide for a split of the Living Trust assets into exemption trust and survivor's trust subtrusts following the first spouse's death. By allocating your deceased spouse's half to the exemption trust, you determine that those assets will not be considered to be owned by you on your death. And if you don't own those assets, the IRS cannot impose an estate tax on them. In legal parlance, this is called "preserving your deceased spouse's exemption amount," and I discuss this in more detail a bit later in the book.

As with the marital trust, the exemption trust that contains your deceased spouse's half is irrevocable. You do not have the power to change its inheritance instructions. If you did, the IRS would consider you to be the owner of the assets in the exemption trust. Since you don't have the power to change the instructions of the exemption trust, your recovered daughter will never have full control over the portion of her inheritance that is "stuck" in the exemption trust.

This double life may prove quite maddening for your reformed shopaholic daughter. After your death, your daughter will receive your survivor's trust portion without any conditions or controls,, but she cannot touch the assets coming from your deceased spouse's subtrust—whether the marital trust or the exemption trust—because of the irrevocability of that subtrust's inheritance instructions.

Periscope from the Grave

However, there is a provision that I suggest you put in your Living Trust to rectify this problem. This remedy gives you, the surviving spouse, the power to change your deceased spouse's subtrust (whether the marital trust or exemption trust) to meet this changed condition. This provision is called the *limited power of appointment*, which means the power to change the inheritance instructions of the otherwise irrevocable marital trust or exemption trust.

This power is like your deceased spouse's "periscope from the grave." It allows you to imagine your deceased spouse seeing the changes in your daughter's life and expressing the desire that you, the surviving spouse, can change the inheritance instructions on your deceased spouse's share to meet your daughter's changed conditions.

This limited power of appointment is not self-executing. The changes to the instructions in the marital trust or exemption trust don't just magically occur simply because you want them to. The changes must be made in a fairly complex legal writing called the "Exercise of Limited Power of Appointment."

Don't try to prepare this document yourself. If your Living Trust creates this limited power of appointment, it will also require slavish conformance to all procedures stated in your Living Trust that are required for a limited power of appointment to make a valid and effective change of the exemption trust. I assure you that you would miss at least one of those requirements.

Financial Advisor Alert

There are several types of powers of appointment. The most common are the *general power of appointment* and the *limited power of appointment.*

The *limited* allows the surviving spouse to change the inheritance instructions *only among* your clients' children. Meaning, the surviving spouse cannot change those instructions to leave the marital trust or exemption trust assets to her newfound friend or that crazy charity that made a fuss over her. Rather, any change *can only be* children-related, such as removing a child's protection trust, leaving a child her inheritance outright, instructing that a child's share shall include certain assets, cutting out one child, increasing another child's shares—all of that.

Then there is the *general,* which allows the surviving spouse to make *any* changes to the marital trust or exemption trust's inheritance instructions. If the surviving spouse remarries and wants to leave her deceased first husband's share in the marital trust or exemption trust to her new husband, she can use the "general" to make that happen.

Obviously, it behooves both spouses for the surviving spouse to have the limited . . . because neither spouse wants the other to have that power. Check your clients' Living Trust to ensure that the surviving spouse only has the "limited" power over the marital trust or exemption trust, which will be largely like this: "The Surviving Spouse shall have the testamentary power to appoint all or any part of the principal of the [marital trust or exemption trust], outright or in trust, in favor of the Settlor's issue, or any one or more of them, in such proportion as the Surviving Spouse designates."

Financial Advisor Alert

You *must* be able to recognize a *general*. Why? Because a "general" in the context of an exemption trust will blow the whole purpose of the exemption trust! The exemption trust's chief purpose is to prevent the IRS from counting the deceased spouse's assets in the exemption trust as part of the surviving spouse's taxable estate when the surviving spouse dies. This can save a boatload of estate taxes. But if the exemption trust is subject to a "general," the IRS will count the exemption trust assets as part of the surviving spouse's taxable estate. Just as if there was no exemption trust.

So . . . here is the language of the "general." If you see this as part of the provisions that create the exemption trust, realize that the drafting lawyer screwed up and get your clients running to another attorney for an amendment: "The Surviving Spouse shall have the testamentary power to appoint all or any part of the principal and undistributed income of the Exemption Trust, outright or in trust, in favor of his or her estate or any one or more persons or other entities."

What If You Don't Want to Change the Inheritance Instruction?

There is, however, a downside of this limited power of appointment. There is nothing that *requires* you to exercise your right to change the marital trust or exemption trust.

Remember, the limited power of appointment gives you, the surviving spouse, the power to change the inheritance instructions of your deceased spouse's subtrust (marital trust or exemption trust), which contains your deceased spouse's half of the Living Trust assets to meet your daughter's changed condition. This power is vested in you, the surviving spouse

But what if you don't want to make that change? Sure, you can feel your deceased spouse's ghostly presence rooting for you to call the lawyer to get started on preparing the limited power of appointment to allow your reformed daughter full control over the exemption trust assets. But perhaps you don't want to spend the money on the lawyer for the "Exercise of Limited Power of Appointment." Or perhaps you fear that your daughter will relapse if she gets control of her inheritance. Or, maybe, you are a vengeful bastard who is bent on making your daughter pay for the hell she put you and your spouse through during the worst of times, and denying her control of any portion of her inheritance is, to you, the ultimate payback.

If, for whatever reason, you elect not to change the exemption trust, then that's it. Your daughter cannot go to court to have a judge force you to sign the "Exercise of Limited Power of Appointment," and your deceased spouse can haunt you for only so long before giving up. Your daughter will just have to be a victim of the tyranny of unjustified lifetime control.

Financial Advisor Alert

As the financial advisor, you will likely be privy to family circumstances that affect your clients' money. For example, if your clients' trust their child with financial decisions only as far as they can throw him, they will make it their business to tell you that. Why? Because they consider you their financial leader and instinctively feel it is something you need to know. So . . . you advise your clients to take steps to protect their child's inheritance from himself, which includes getting them to establish a Living Trust that leaves their child's inheritance in a protection trust. Lovely!

Your clients will also not hesitate in telling you when their child eventually attains financial maturity. That's happy news. But, what if that news comes after the first spouse's death . . . and after the funding of that spouse's exemption trust and/or marital trust?

A good Living Trust is a flexible Living Trust. It should allow your surviving spouse clients to change the inheritance instructions of the deceased spouse's marital trust and exemption trust if circumstances dictate. If that Living Trust (hopefully) contains a "limited," your clients will have the ability to change the exemption trust and marital trust so that their child has control over his own inheritance (instead of a third party).

Should you suggest to your clients that their child's protection trust is now overkill and they should consider exercising that "limited" to eliminate the protection provisions—and make a similar change to the survivor's trust? I say yes. Otherwise, that child's "inheritance hands" will be tied without justification. If the reason for the rule no longer applies, then don't apply the rule.

There is also the risk that you, the surviving spouse, can use the limited power of appointment to reduce or eliminate your daughter's share of the marital trust or exemption trust. This is you saying, in effect, "It's my way or the highway. You'd better watch your step around me or I will not only cut you out of my half, I will cut you out of your mom's half as well."

Financial Advisor Alert

Not many people use "the inheritance" to change their children's behavior. That's typically the stuff of cinema. But you will have a few clients who match that type. The ones who "lord it over" their children with threats of changing their Living Trust to cut them out. ("I'll show those kids what they get by not calling me. Nothing!") Is there a role for you to play here by being the voice of reason? To somehow convince them to not use the Living Trust to assist their power trip? Probably not. Your client's troubled relationship with the children commenced well before you entered the picture. If your client must resort to inheritance-related threats to move the children to some action, then that effort will likely not bear fruit. People holding heavy family baggage cannot be easily moved.

Obviously, I do not counsel the use of the limited power of appointment in such an antagonistic fashion. The Living Trust is supposed to contain your legacy to your children, not be used as a weapon against them.

Not every problem has a solution, but if there were a solution in this case, it would be a sarcastic one: time travel.

Your daughter would have to travel back to the moment when you and your spouse were discussing your Living Trust with your attorney. Armed with the knowledge that the surviving spouse can, for any reason, decline to change the inheritance instructions of the deceased spouse's subtrust (marital trust or exemption trust) to meet her changed conditions, she could ask your lawyer to insert into your Living Trust a provision that gives someone other than you, the surviving spouse, the power to make that change: a trusted family member, a trusted friend, a professional trustee, or any other person or entity that could approach this situation and circumstances in a manner more objective than you.

And, to combat the random urge to change your daughter's share in a downward direction, your Living Trust can provide that there will be no change to the deceased spouse's subtrust (marital trust or exemption trust) that can deprive your daughter of the full amount of her share of her inheritance from that subtrust.

CHAPTER 12

Dealing with Your Living Trust If You Remarry

OR,

THE BATTLE ROYAL: YOUR SECOND SPOUSE VERSUS YOUR FIRST CHILDREN

Take a quick moment to reread the subtitle of this chapter. Do you feel that my word choice is a bit peculiar? For anyone who has remarried after the death of a spouse, who has become the new wife of a recent widower, or who has inherited a new stepparent, you will agree with my choice of words. Trust me; if you choose to remarry and you later die before your second spouse, your Living Trust will result in a clash of the beneficiaries—a battle of your first children versus your second spouse.

Financial Advisor Alert

This chapter mainly addresses the "waiting game" that arises in this inheritance scenario. If your client remarries after the death of her first spouse, your client will likely amend the Living Trust so that the second spouse is taken care of for the rest of his life. The second spouse is named as the successor trustee who shall have the power to wheel-and-deal with the Living Trust assets. The second spouse will get all income. The second spouse will get the right to reside in the residence. The second spouse may even get to dip into the principal for health, support, and education. When the second spouse dies, the first children receive distribution of the remaining Living Trust assets.

Of course, this creates a situation where the first children have to wait for the second spouse to die so they can inherit. The effects of this waiting game on the participants can be quite onerous . . . especially for the second spouse who may become emotionally wrought with the knowledge that some people "out there" are rooting for a quick and sudden death.

But another game is afoot in this context, which you may get pulled into: the hotly contested battle of *high income vs. high growth*. While the first children play the waiting game, they want to know that today's investments will not be reduced by inflation. For them, a thousand dollars today should be worth way more when the second spouse dies. That goal will be achieved if your second spouse client invests in capital growth assets. But what does the second spouse want? High-income yielding assets to maximize the income to which she is entitled—especially if she doesn't have the power to dip into the principal. The first children may threaten you with litigation if you don't advise your second spouse client to accomplish a more balanced investment mix.

Are you, the financial advisor, legally accountable for not advising your high-income-loving second spouse client to invest with a view toward both classes of beneficiaries? (Meaning, the second spouse income beneficiary and the first children remainder beneficiaries.) It's a stretch—but one that may be shortening. In several states, courts have held a third party liable to trust beneficiaries for "aiding and abetting" a trustee in committing breaches of duties that the trustee owes to those beneficiaries. One of those duties is impartiality, which means that the trustee's investment mix of the Living Trust assets *must* not benefit one class of beneficiaries over another. So if you advise the trustee—your second spouse client—to invest for maximum income, you could find yourself at the receiving end of a lawsuit brought by the first children in which they allege you have conspired with the trustee to violate the duty of impartiality and attempt to hit you for damages in the amount of lost profits and appreciation.

Don't think this can happen to you? Listen (or read, actually), there are a million litigation-centric lawyers out there who think nothing of taking on near-specious cases just to extort a settlement. That's what litigators do: File a lawsuit and ask questions later. Throw spaghetti at the wall to see what sticks. Do you want the prospect of such litigation looming overhead? Invading your thoughts at night and preventing you from enjoying *Breaking Bad* or *Better Call Saul?* Neither do I.

So what do you do to prevent this somewhat unlikely but still entirely possible scenario? Prevent this problem from coming up in the first place. While both parties are living, ask the spouse with the children from the first marriage whether she has amended her Living Trust to provide for her second spouse. If so, grab that Living Trust and read the part about what happens if she dies before her second spouse. You will likely see a subtrust established for the second spouse that provides him with a lifetime right to receive income and reside in the residence. Then look for a provision that says, in essence, that the trustee should manage and invest the trust estate in favor of the second spouse without regard to preserving the trust estate for the remainder beneficiaries (the first children). With that provision, you can put the second spouse entirely in high-income-yielding assets without having to look over your shoulder for low-flying litigation. Why? Because that provision allows the second spouse's interest in high interest to predominate over the first children's interest in high growth. While not every legally imposed trustee duty can be "written away" with contrary Living Trust provisions, the duty of impartiality can easily be superseded with such a provision that instructs who shall be "favorite."

If you don't see any such "favoritism" provision, then the duty of impartiality applies. Now you inform the parties that its absence will create a breeding ground for the "Big Battle" if the spouse with the first children dies before the second spouse. Then it's up to the spouse with the first children. If she wants the trustee (probably the second spouse) to treat all beneficiaries impartially, with an equal mix of high income and high growth, then she need not make any change. But if she wants to ensure that her second spouse gets the maximum income possible, then she needs to have her attorney prepare the appropriate amendment.

The Clash of the Inheritors

If you do not believe me, consider the following stories, which I witnessed firsthand throughout my 20 years as an attorney.

The Case of the Homicide Detective

I remember a time when I was questioned by a homicide detective looking into the death in an automobile accident of a second wife of one of my deceased clients. Apparently, there was a hint of foul play, or why else would the police have shown up at my office requesting a look at the client's file?

The reason for the scrutiny was that I prepared a Living Trust for the deceased client that gave economic support to his second wife from his Living Trust assets for the rest of her life. The Living Trust also provided that upon the second wife's death, the Living Trust assets would go to the deceased client's children from his first marriage (the first children). After the detective left my office, I heard that he gave the first children a long and hard look. While they certainly had the financial motive to end her life prematurely, nothing tied them to the accident. But in my heart of hearts, I felt that something sinister had been afoot.

The Case of Not Waiting

I remember meeting with another deceased client's first children after his death. Although they were stricken with emotions, I explained to them that their father's Living Trust supported his second wife for the rest of her life and that the first children would get the leftovers upon her death. One of the first children looked at me and said, "I ain't gonna wait." I deal with a lot of people, and I like to think I can tell when someone means what he says. With the chill in his voice and his icy stare, this guy seemed deadly serious.

Did he actually do something to lessen his long wait? Since that meeting, I never had any dealings with those first children or the second wife. But, although I have never seen their names in newspaper headlines ("Second Wife Dies, First Children Under Suspicion"), I have no doubt that those first children caused distress to the second wife with frequent reminders that she was living too long to suit their taste.

The Case of the "Are You Okay?" Phone Calls

I remember that after one client died, his second wife told me she was getting two or three phone calls a week from the first children to see if she was "okay." As she said to me, "I can hear the disappointment in their voices when I pick up the phone and say, 'Hello.'"

The Case of the Wasteful House Guest

I remember the second wife with the right to live in her deceased husband's home for the rest of her life. She told me the first children made her life a living hell with intermittent letters and calls, saying, in essence, "You're letting the house fall into disrepair. This is a waste of the first children's future inheritance. Do something!"

The Case of a Lawsuit

I remember the second husband who had been given the right to all income generated from his deceased wife's Living Trust assets. Naturally, he invested in securities that would yield the highest amount of income. But the first children, who would receive those assets after the second husband's death, wanted him to invest in growth investments. So, they sued him for maximizing income at the expense of growth.

The Case of the Disney Cruise

Just one more. Be a fly on the wall for this conversation that was related to me by one second wife after the death of her husband:

> **Stepgrandson:** Hey, Stepgrammy! Guess what? Daddy and Mommy and me—we're all going on a Disney cruise for two weeks!
>
> **Second Wife:** Oh, that's marvelous. When are you going?
>
> **Stepgrandson:** Mommy says we're all going to go as soon as you die!

Divide and Conquer

Early on in my estate planning career, it seemed wise and appropriate to create Living Trust instructions that provided lifetime support for the second spouse. Upon his or her death, the Living Trust assets would be dispersed to the first children. In my mind, this plan was fair because the first children would normally have to wait until the deaths of both parents before receiving their inheritances. Waiting until the death of the second spouse would be somewhat the same.

After years of practicing, in conjunction with the changing marital trends, I realized that it isn't the same. In the world of elderly men and women marrying people who are half their age, I began to wonder how old first children might be when the second spouse dies. In their 70s? In their 80s? Maybe not even alive at all.

Then, I began to put myself in the first children's shoes. How would I feel if I could not get my inheritance until my life expectancy could be measured in single digits? That's a long time to wait to enjoy your inheritance. Not only do first children have to wait to inherit, but the factor causing the wait is the far-off death of a person who may be nothing more to them than some random stranger.

I also began to put myself in the second spouse's shoes. How would I feel if my deceased husband's children wanted me dead so that they could have what they think is their money? As one second wife said to me, "I don't talk to my husband's children, and they don't communicate with me. But just knowing that there are people out there who cannot wait for me to die . . . it's making my remaining years so miserable."

Based on these thoughts, I changed the way I deal with the second spouse in the Living Trust. I decided that I would advise clients (and you) to insert a clause in your Living Trust that would enable the second spouse and the first children to disassociate themselves from one another forever. After you die, if the only connection between your first children and your second spouse is the money and property in your Living Trust, then that connection should be terminated, and the parties should go their separate ways.

I used to call this the John Wayne approach to estate planning, because John Wayne didn't fool around when it came to solving problems. But now I call it the Colin Powell approach, because during Gulf War II he said that the way to win the battle on the ground in Iraq was to "cut off and kill" the enemy troops on the ground. And that's the solution in this family context—cut off and kill the economic connection between your first children and your second spouse.

As your Living Trust advisor, I warn you that if you remarry and you love your second spouse, you need to take steps to alleviate and perhaps even eliminate the battle that I have described in this chapter. This will require that you amend the inheritance instructions of the survivor's trust portion of the Living Trust to incorporate one or more of the following plans to terminate the economic connection between your first children and your second spouse.

Option 1: You can change your survivor's trust to leave a lump sum to your second spouse and a lump sum to your first children. With this method, both parties receive an immediate inheritance.

Option 2: You can change your survivor's trust to leave all of its assets to either the first children or the second spouse, but have an insurance policy that leaves the other party with roughly equal benefits that pay out after your death.

Option 3: If the assets include your house, you can limit the time your second spouse may occupy the house. After the expiration of that term, you can require that the house be sold and the proceeds divided among all parties. Your second spouse can do whatever he or she chooses to do with the spouse's portion of the sale, such as developing an estate for his or her own children, or possibly purchasing another residence.

The first children may be aware that with this "sell and divide" plan, the dollar they receive today could, through appreciation and investment, be worth five times more at your second spouse's death. However, your first children would rather have the certainty of that dollar in their pockets today than the possibility of five dollars after your second spouse's death untold years later. It's certainty versus speculation; sooner rather than later.

However, it may be that the economics of your situation are not enough to provide for termination of the economic connection between your first children and second spouse after your death. For example, if your survivor's trust consists of only a portion of a house and some cash and brokerage assets, and you insist that your second spouse have the right to live in the house for the rest of his or her life, your first children's lump sum will not be enough to remove the edge that comes with the waiting game.

If there are not enough assets to make everyone happy, there is only one solution, which is: Hope for the best that all parties will get along if you die before your second spouse.

This is not a facetious statement. It's a sincere wish that common ground can be found to the extent that your second spouse's life will not be interrupted by first children who will be hard-pressed to wait for their ship to come in, meaning the death of your second spouse. To that end I suggest that all parties—you, your first children, and your second spouse—meet with your lawyer, who will explain the problem of having insufficient assets to successfully terminate the economic connection between your surviving second spouse and your first children. In my experience, there is some salutary effect for the parties to know what to expect beforehand, even if it is a small one.

13

Dealing with the Estate Tax Return, Splitting the Living Trust Assets, and Other Tax Stuff That You Would Rather Just Ignore after Your Spouse Dies

OR,

AS MUCH AS YOU WANT TO, DON'T SKIP THIS CHAPTER! TO PREVENT ESTATE TAXES AFTER YOUR DEATH, YOU MUST DEAL WITH ESTATE TAX MATTERS AFTER YOUR SPOUSE'S DEATH

The mere words *estate tax* may make you run screaming for the hills in boredom. Well, perhaps I should not assume what accounts for your running and screaming. For me, it's boredom. For you, it may be anger that comes from having to deal with tax stuff after your spouse has died. For others, perhaps it is fear of the prospect of having to tangle with the Internal Revenue Service (IRS) in the estate tax arena, a completely different venue than the normal income tax area with which you have some familiarity.

The estate tax stuff is one of the reasons you established your Living Trust in the first place. Even though there is usually no estate tax due on the death of the deceased spouse, there still may be estate tax stuff that needs to be done so that little or no estate tax will be due when the surviving spouse dies. Put another way: You paid for it. You might as well become familiar with what you paid for.

What Is the Estate Tax?

The estate tax is a federal tax on the after-death transfer of your assets and wealth to your Living Trust beneficiaries and the beneficiaries of your assets outside your Living Trust such as insurance policies, individual retirement accounts (IRAs), "pay over on death" accounts, and so on. The estate tax is sometimes referred to as the "death tax," which is quite misleading, because it gives one the impression that there is a tax on death. The government does not mandate that you pay taxes as a result of your death. If that were the case, then the government would be constantly reaping profits and be able to retire the insanely high federal deficit, because thousands of people die in the United States every day.

Again, this is a tax on the transfer of assets from the dead to the living. If this transfer took place during your lifetime, the tax imposed on that transfer would be a gift tax. So, if you think you can escape estate taxes by transferring what you own before you die, think again. If you could do that, then everyone would do that, and the IRS would never get its share on the transfer of your money and property. Thus, under current law, the IRS will nail you with a gift tax if you transfer assets worth more than $5,450,000.

After the death of your spouse, there are three aspects about the estate tax in the context of your Living Trust that you must know. Why? Because if you're rich enough, tending to these matters now—after the death of your spouse—will save your Living Trust beneficiaries thousands of dollars in estate taxes after *your* death. In other words, the estate tax training you put in now will pay off after you die.

I can hear your footsteps now as you are running away. As I grab you by the collar to prevent your escape (which causes you to run in place like Snagglepuss in the old Hanna-Barbera cartoons), let me give you some helpful perspective. In my practice, I have to slog through what seems like an interminable amount of estate tax treatises, updates, and periodicals that discuss the latest estate tax concepts and tax court cases. They are so dry and monotonous that I actually have to steel myself just to pick them out of my mailbox. But for you, all you have to know is these three concepts that, once implemented, will have the practical effect of saving money for your Living Trust beneficiaries. The three estate tax concepts that you need to know are:

1. A basic and simple understanding of an estate tax concept called the "lifetime exemption."
2. Preparing your deceased spouse's *death inventory*—otherwise known as the federal estate tax return.
3. Allocating your spouse's half of the Living Trust assets to a separate subtrust called the exemption trust.

So get back here, and let's begin!

The lifetime exemption

Right now, as you read this sentence, you can transfer money or property to whomever you wish without you incurring one penny of gift tax. This is called the *lifetime exemption.*

Think of the lifetime exemption as $5,450,000 of money or property in a barrel. While you are alive, you can dip into this barrel and give away some or all of its assets—up to $5,450,000—to anyone you want and whenever you want, tax tree. However, this barrel is not renewable. Once the barrel is empty, it's empty forever. Once the $5,450,000 in the barrel is gone, it's gone.

Whatever remains of your $5,450,000 lifetime exemption at your death can be used after your death. Say your barrel has money and property in the amount of $5 million. During your life, you dole out from the barrel $1 million to whomever you wish. The remaining $4 million in the barrel will pass estate tax free to whomever you name as the beneficiaries of your Living Trust.

It's just that simple. As long as the total amount of your lifetime gifts and after-death bequests does not exceed $5,450,000, you don't need fancy and expensive estate planning to beat the estate tax. For all but 0.5 percent of the American population whose net worth will not come close to exceeding $5,450,000, this is not a problem.

This is easy so far, yes? It gets a tad more complex in the context of a marriage. Stay with me.

If you are married, you and your spouse each have a barrel of $5,450,000. Each of you can give away during your lives $5,450,000 apiece (for a total of $10,900,000) tax free. *But,* when your spouse dies and you inherit your spouse's half of the Living Trust assets, you do *not* automatically "inherit" your spouse's remaining unused lifetime exemption. You only have *your* $5,450,000 lifetime exemption.

Why are you not allowed to automatically combine your deceased spouse's lifetime exemption with your lifetime exemption? Because that's just the way it is according to the rules. When your spouse ceases to have a lifetime, she ceases to have a lifetime exemption.

Since your spouse's lifetime exemption does not "live on" after death, only your lifetime exemption remains—which means that you can leave "only" up to $5,450,000 of the family money to your children (or other heirs) tax free. If you own less than $5,450,000 on your death, this is not a big deal. But if you own more, there will be an estate tax on the excess.

Using Your Deceased Spouse's Lifetime Exemption

In the last section, did you notice my careful placement of the word *automatically?* I said, "When your spouse dies and you inherit your spouse's half of the Living Trust assets, you do not *automatically* inherit your spouse's remaining unused lifetime exemption."

Using that word allows me to conduct this near-seamless segue to this point: There is *nonautomatic* method you can put in play to preserve *both* the lifetime exemptions of you and your deceased spouse. The end result: You and your spouse can leave up to a combined $10,900,000 to your children (or other heirs) without any estate tax.

Nonautomatic means, of course, that you must "do something" within certain deadlines after your spouse dies. Easier said than done—especially if you are in the grip of emotional upheaval after your spouse's death. But if you do that certain something, you will have accomplished all the estate tax reduction planning that you need to do for the rest of your life . . . unless you are really *really* loaded.

What is this "something" that you must do after your spouse's death to preserve your deceased spouse's lifetime exemption? Actually, there are two "somethings."

One something has nothing to do with your Living Trust and simply involves you checking a box on your spouse's federal estate tax return. The other something is your "trigger" of a complex mechanism already contained in your Living Trust.

The "Simple Something" You Must Do to Preserve Your Deceased Spouse's Lifetime Exemption— the Federal Estate Tax Return

The federal estate tax return is nothing like your income tax return. It's a completely different animal. Let me put it this way: I could not prepare my own income tax return to save my life, but I have prepared over 400 estate tax returns.

The estate tax return does *not* report income earned by you and your spouse. Rather, the estate tax return reports what your spouse *owned* at the time of his or her death. In essence, it is a death inventory—that is, a 40-page document prepared by a Living Trust attorney who is relying on you to provide him or her with the values of all the assets that were owned by your deceased spouse.

In my mind, the death inventory preparation is truly an arduous task that your attorney asks you to do during a particularly emotional time. During the grieving process, you may not feel like doing anything that requires energy and acumen. But now, if you are required to file the estate tax return, you have to make the effort to fish around for information that your attorney needs to file the estate tax return. You have to hire an appraiser to obtain the value of your real estate. You have to contact your brokerage representative to get statements that show the value of the stocks and securities on the exact date of death. You have to go to your bank to get bank statements showing date-of-death balances. You have to make lists of all the personal property in your house—clothes, furniture, jewelry, antiques—and have those items appraised. You have to call your insurance companies to find out the cash values of the policies. You have to get in your car, find parking, and meet with your attorney several times.

As you can see by this exhaustive list, compiling an inventory for your deceased spouse's estate tax return is a lot of work. Moreover, this list must be compiled relatively quickly. The IRS deadline to file the return is within nine months after the death of your spouse, which is certainly not a lot of time given that you may be emotionally debilitated to the point where you cannot handle dealing with such business matters. Your attorney can obtain a filing extension of six months, but it must be applied for within that nine-month period. However, I can tell you that the 15-month filing deadline will be here (snap of the fingers) like that.

Financial Advisor Alert

Is it your job to prod your surviving spouse client into doing this homework? Not really—but do it anyway, with a phone call or email about every three months. Even though your client is likely receiving the occasional reminder from her estate planning attorney, you cannot assume that task is being performed. When you make that communication, make sure she knows that she can call on you to render assistance with the gathering of the information needed for the estate tax return.

After your spouse's death, you will be faced with the issue of whether you are legally required to file your deceased spouse's estate tax return. There are two situations that require you to file that return:

1. You must file the return if your deceased spouse's half of all assets—whether or not in the Living Trust—exceed your deceased spouse's lifetime exemption. As I stated before, under current law, the lifetime exemption is $5,450,000.
2. You must file the return if there is an estate tax due. An estate tax will be due if (a) the assets of your deceased spouse pass to people other than you—the surviving spouse—and (b) the assets of your deceased spouse passing to people other than you—the surviving spouse—exceed the spouse's lifetime exemption of $5,450,000.

(Why is there no estate tax on the transfer of *any* assets from your deceased spouse to you, the surviving spouse? Because of an IRS rule called the marital deduction. This means that there is a dollar-for-dollar estate tax deduction for any transfer of assets from a deceased spouse to a surviving spouse. The IRS is not being nice. It is just waiting to impose an estate tax on those appreciated assets when *you* die.)

Chances are, you won't see yourself in either of those two scenarios that require you to file your deceased spouse's estate tax return. Your deceased spouse's half does not amount to $5,450,000—and your Living Trust does not leave anything to anyone other than you, the surviving spouse. As a result, you will likely not be legally required to file it, which, of course, will not require you to do the asset information gathering homework. Such a relief, yes?

Still . . . I, your Living Trust advisor, now *instruct* you to endure the hassle and cost of getting this return prepared. Why? Because following changes in the estate tax law enacted in 2013, the estate tax return now contains a new "Magic Box" that *allows you to "pick up" whatever remains of your deceased spouse's lifetime exemption.* It's as simple as it sounds. By simply checking this Magic Box, you have made certain that your Living Trust beneficiaries will not pay any (or if you're really rich, minimal) estate tax when you die and your estate is transferred to your children or other heirs.

I can hear your objection now. "Condon! Why should I spend good money for that return when the combined assets of my deceased spouse and I don't come close to $5,450,000? Everything together is worth maybe $2 million. When I die, that entire $2 million will fit nice and snug in my $5,450,000 lifetime exemption, and my kids won't have to pay any estate tax. Are you trying to sell me something I don't need?"

Well, to that I say this: The estate tax is a political football. Nothing in the tax world has changed with the political tide in the last 10 years more than the estate tax. Its status, effect, and impact are entirely dependent on who runs the congressional and executive roosts. (A separate book could be written on all of its recent permutations that would sell maybe eight copies.) If you don't capitalize on this opportunity to pick up your deceased spouse's lifetime exemption, that opportunity might be swept away forever with ensuing federal elections and actions. And if the political tide brings us a new and lower lifetime exemption, you will find yourself regretting your decision to forgo the return after your spouse's death.

So, from a net worth perspective, perhaps your current numbers do not rise to the level of requiring you to prepare the estate tax return. Which is good news. You won't have the expense of the legal work necessary to prepare the return. And you won't have the hassle of the hiring real estate appraisers, pestering your stock broker representative to get a list of stocks as of the date of your spouse's death, inventorying every asset you and your deceased spouse owned together. *Still . . . do all of this anyway.* You—rather . . . your children (or other heirs)—may thank me later.

This is how the Magic Box works in action. You and your spouse are alive. Your combined net worth is $8 million. That's $4 million for each of you. Your spouse dies and her $4 million goes to you.

Now you, the surviving spouse, own the entire $8 million. If you die with an $8 million estate, your $5,450,000 lifetime exemption will shelter the first $5,450,000 from estate tax. But there will be an estate tax on the remaining "unsheltered" $2,550,000 at a top estate tax rate of 40 percent, which would be $1,020,000.

But, within nine months after your spouse's death, you go to your Living Trust attorney and say the following:

> "Hi there! Long time no see. My spouse died and I would like you to prepare whatever documents are necessary to transfer her $5,450,000 lifetime exemption to me."

Those three sentences (well, just the last one if you want to skip the perfunctory pleasantries) will have saved your family an estate tax of $1,020,000. Because with that marching order to your attorney, he will then prepare your spouse's estate tax return which has a box that, when checked, essentially says, "Yes, in fact, I *would* like to take my poor deceased spouse's $5,450,000 lifetime exemption, or whatever amount of it that remained at his death."

With that one-time action, you will have picked up your deceased spouse's lifetime exemption (which is $4 million in this case because your spouse only had $4 million of assets) and added it to your own $5,450,000 lifetime exemption. This gives you a total of $9,450,000 lifetime exemption! And with your $8 million estate being less than your full $9,450,000 lifetime exemption, your total $8 million estate will transfer to your Living Trust beneficiaries without a single penny of estate tax.

Financial Advisor Alert

Is it just that simple to pick up the deceased spouse's lifetime exemption? Just checking the Magic Box on the estate tax return? Well—let's not forget we are talking about our government tax law. In other words . . . it ain't easy. There are a few other considerations at play when your surviving spouse client attempts to capitalize on the opportunity to pick up her deceased spouse's lifetime exemption. As the surviving spouse's financial advisor, it is incumbent upon you (and expected) to be aware of, at least, the broad strokes of those factors. Here are the greatest hits:

1. Your surviving spouse client must file her deceased spouse's estate tax return within nine months after his death. If she needs more time, she can get a six-month extension.

2. It is common knowledge that the IRS has, in general, a three-year limit to examine an income tax return. Well, that does not apply to an estate tax return where your surviving spouse client elects to pick up her deceased spouse's lifetime exemption. Why? So the IRS can change that return to adjust to any changes in the death tax law—including a reduction in the $5,450,000 lifetime exemption! In other words, by electing "portability" of your deceased spouse's lifetime exemption, you give the IRS "forever" to examine your deceased spouse's estate tax return.

So . . . say your married clients own a combined $6 million—$3 million each. Husband dies and wife inherits her half. Wife now owns $6 million.

Wife files her deceased husband's estate tax return to pick up the maximum amount of his $5,450,000 lifetime exemption—which is $3 million because the husband's half is only $3 million. Wife now has her $5,450,000 lifetime exemption and husband's $3 million lifetime exemption, for a grand total of $8,450,000 lifetime exemption. When the wife dies, her estate of $6 million will fall under her $8.45 million lifetime exemption. So—your client's beneficiaries escape all death taxes. Everyone wins!

But . . . while wife is still alive, the death tax becomes, once again, a political football. The congressional and executive branches reduce the $5.45 million lifetime exemption to $2 million. Well . . . you may not believe this, but the new death tax rules say that no matter how many years pass after the first spouse's death (husband, in this example), the IRS has the option to go back to husband's return and retroactively adjust his $3 million lifetime exemption pick-up to $2 million.

Can the IRS do that? Yes. And I can hear your screams of obscenities from here . . . but stay with me to finish this example.

This (for now) hypothetical reduction in the lifetime exemption from $5.45 million to $2 million thrusts your clients' beneficiaries into the estate tax world. Specifically, the wife would be left with a $4,000,000 combined lifetime exemption, which would subject the $6 million estate to a $800,000 estate tax. Using the only math equation you will find in this book (because it was my inability to do math that drove me to law school), that's the $6 million estate minus $4,000,000 combined lifetime exemption = $2 million net taxable estate × 40% tax rate = $800,000.

3. There is a serial remarriage prevention clause in the new death tax law. Say the wife (the surviving spouse in this example) files her deceased husband's estate tax return to pick up his $5.45 million lifetime exemption. Subsequently, wife remarries—and wife's second spouse dies. In such a case, the IRS will cancel wife's pick-up of her first husband's lifetime exemption, even though she timely filed her first husband's estate tax return.

But, don't go full-blown yet with your anti-IRS tirade. Even though the wife lost the pick-up of her first husband's lifetime exemption, the IRS will permit wife to pick up her second husband's lifetime exemption . . . assuming she has not used up her lifetime exemption by making gifts before she met her second husband. And in the midst of wife's mourning her second husband's death and lamenting her fate of having two spouses die on her, she has to engage in yet another inventorying process for yet another estate tax return to pick up that lifetime exemption.

The "Complex Something" You Can Do to Preserve Your Deceased Spouse's Lifetime Exemption Trust

Your Living Trust's inheritance instructions may provide that on the death of the first spouse, his or her half of the assets in the Living Trust bucket will be allocated to a separate subtrust. For now, let's call it the "smaller bucket."

Don't worry—the smaller bucket is not described in some other document that you signed at the time you established your Living Trust. In your Living Trust, there is a section that details what creates the smaller bucket after the deceased spouse's death and discusses how it functions.

Basically, this section states three functions of the smaller bucket during your life:

1. You receive the income from the smaller bucket, which you keep, invest, and spend on anything and in any way you desire.
2. You get to spend the principal from the smaller bucket for your health and support, which is usually defined as the amount of assets necessary and reasonable to provide you with a comfortable standard of living.
3. You get to wheel and deal with the smaller bucket assets (buy, sell, trade, refinance, invest, borrow against—whatever) in any way you wish.

With all of your power and control over the assets in the smaller bucket, it appears that you own those assets. That's what it sounds like to me. However, in a complete betrayal of your confidence in me and my assertions, you are, in fact, *not* the owner of the assets in the smaller bucket. Yes, you get the income, principal, and managerial power—just like any owner of property. But the real owner is still your deceased spouse.

In other words, your deceased spouse is the owner of the assets in the smaller bucket, and you are merely the authorized user of those assets for the rest of your life.

Let me say this more succinctly. For all practical purposes, you are the owner of the assets in the smaller bucket. But from a legal perspective, your deceased spouse is the owner of those assets.

Why engage in this charade? In one word—taxes. As your Living Trust advisor, I don't necessarily want you to be considered the owner of the assets in the smaller bucket. If you own them, the IRS will impose an estate tax on them when you die. But if you don't own those assets, the IRS cannot tax them on your death—because you don't own them! How's that for circular reasoning? You cannot be taxed on what you don't own. In legal parlance, this is called "reducing your taxable estate."

The Real Name of the Smaller Bucket Is ...

In your Living Trust, the smaller bucket may be referred to by any one of a number of names. I call it the *exemption trust* because the assets in that subtrust will be exempt from estate tax on your death. Another reason I call it the exemption trust is it preserves the lifetime exemption of your deceased spouse. This estate tax reduction method has existed for as long as the estate tax has been around. You might have heard this referred to as the A-B trust, the credit shelter trust, the credit trust, the bypass trust, or something of similar nature.

When you allocate your deceased spouse's half of the Living Trust assets to the exemption trust, you are transferring assets that are "painted" with your deceased spouse's lifetime exemption. What is the effect? The assets in the exemption trust do not belong to you, and they are not distributed to the children or other Living Trust beneficiaries. Instead, those assets stay in the exemption trust for the rest of your life, providing you with income and principal for your support and health in the event that your half of the Living Trust assets is insufficient to provide for those needs.

When you—the surviving spouse—die, the assets in the exemption trust will pass to the children with no estate tax whatsoever. In effect, the exemption trust has preserved your deceased spouse's lifetime exemption while allowing you, the surviving spouse, the ability to use those assets for the rest of your life.

So one more time—with feeling! The exemption trust preserves your deceased spouse's right to leave his or her half of the Living Trust assets to the children, or other Living Trust beneficiaries, free of estate tax.

Here is another benefit of having assets in the exemption trust. If those assets appreciate, the appreciation will also pass to your children tax-free. For example, after your spouse's death, you allocate $250,000 of stocks to the exemption trust. You are the greatest investor of money the world has ever seen—Warren Buffett is nothing compared to you. You invest that $250,000 to the point where it is worth $5 billion on your death. Guess what? If the root of the tree is tax-free ($250,000), the fruit of the tree is tax-free ($5 billion). In other words, the children won't have to pay any taxes on that $5 billion!

Is there a downside to allocating your deceased spouse's assets to the exemption trust? Of course there is. Why would the IRS give you this break without some type of catch? And here it is: The assets in the exemption trust will *not* get a stepped-up income tax basis on *your* death.

You will not understand this downside until you have, at least, a basic understanding of the concept of basis, which you shall now receive with this example. You and your spouse purchased your house in 1970 for $10,000. That $10,000 purchase price is your "basis" in your house. For tax purposes, *basis* is generally the amount you pay for an asset. Fast-forward to 2016. Your house is worth $500,000. If you and your spouse sell your house for $500,000, your profit will be the difference between the sale price ($500,000) and your "basis" ($10,000). Thus your profit will be $490,000, which will result in an income tax (called a capital gains tax) on that profit. That's a lot of dough.

Is there a way to get around his income tax? Yes. You or your spouse simply have to die. The current federal tax law provides that when the first spouse dies, that spouse's one-half share of the house's basis ($5,000) "steps up" to the date-of-death value of one-half of that house. So, if you sell the house after your spouse's death for $500,000, and with your deceased spouse's basis in the house stepping-up to $250,000, the profit on sale becomes $245,000 because we only count the gain on your half of the house, which is the $250,000 sale price minus your $5,000 basis.

(By the way, if you live in a community property state, the gain on sale would be zero because the *entire* property receives a stepped-up basis when the first spouse dies. So if this sale took place in, say, California, the $10,000 basis would jump to the house's value as of your spouse's date of death. And if you sell the house for that date-of-death value, there is no capital gain and no capital gains tax.)

Now that you understand stepped-up basis, let's get back to this downside of exemption trust allocation. When you, the surviving spouse, die, all of your assets will receive a stepped-up income tax basis. If your children sell your assets after your death at or below those assets' value as of your date of death, they will escape any capital gains taxation. Sounds great! But remember, you don't own the assets in this "smaller bucket" called the exemption trust. They "belong" to your deceased spouse. As a result, the assets in the exemption trust will not receive a stepped-up income tax basis on your death, and the sale of those assets will result in a capital gains tax if the sale price is greater than their value as of your deceased spouse's date of death.

Financial Advisor Alert

The purpose of the exemption trust is to preserve the lifetime exemption of the deceased spouse. But since exemption trust assets do not receive a stepped-up income tax basis on the surviving spouse's death, your clients' family could be looking at a boatload of capital gains taxes if they sell those assets. Nonetheless, because estate tax rates are way higher than capital gains tax rates, and because sales of exemption trust assets after death are never a given, I believe the estate tax to be the greater of the tax evils, and the exemption trust allocation should proceed. (However, whether an exemption trust allocation should *ever* take place in our present world of "portability" is discussed later in this chapter in the section "Do You Have to Do the 'More Complex Something' (Exemption Trust Allocation) When the 'Simple Something' (the Magic Box) Works Just Fine?"

The Magic Trick

As your Living Trust advisor, I must say that this is a really nifty trick. The exemption trust will, like magic, prevent your deceased spouse's share of the Living Trust assets, and its appreciation, from being estate taxed on your death. But, like any magical illusion, there is some effort the magician must make in order for it to work and look so easy.

What a fabulous analogy! You are the magician who must engage in a number of steps in order to achieve the illusion (estate tax avoidance) that is the goal of the trick (the exemption trust). And if you, the magician, do not make the required effort, the trick (estate tax avoidance) will not work, and you will be booed (taxed) by the audience (the IRS). (This is good stuff. I am finally using the writing skills and devices I learned as an English literature major at UCLA.)

So, what is the effort you will have to make for the trick to work? It's the kind of effort that gives the IRS the distinct impression that the exemption trust is a separate and viable entity. If the trick works, the IRS will say that the exemption trust assets are not owned by you and, thus, are not part of your taxable estate on your death.

If the trick does not work, then the IRS will "pierce the veil of separateness" and will proclaim that you, and not your deceased spouse, are the owner of the exemption trust assets and, therefore, those assets are part of your taxable estate on your death.

But before I tell you how to make this trick work, I must first pose this question: In light of your shiny new ability to pick up your deceased spouse's lifetime exemption with a mere check of that Magic Box on her federal estate tax return (which is the "simple something" I discuss in the previous section), why resort to this seemingly archaic and fairly complex method that accomplishes the same result?

I must admit, I did not initially have a good response to this inquiry, and was about to eliminate this entire section about the exemption trust. After all, why confuse you with ancient history of a complex method that has almost been rendered extinct by a new method that only requires you to check a Magic Box? But as I was about to delete this section, I thought of two decent reasons to keep this stuff in.

The first is . . . maybe you and your spouse are really rich. Say you and your spouse have a combined $15 million estate (which, if that is the case, means you're not reading this book because you have your own hot-shot inheritance attorney on retainer to handle this stuff for you). Your husband's half is $7.5 million and your half is $7.5 million. Your husband dies first and you complete and file his estate tax return to preserve his $5,450,000 lifetime exemption. You then allocate the portion of his half in excess of his lifetime exemption (which is $2,050,000) to the exemption trust. Because you picked up your deceased husband's entire $5,450,000 lifetime exemption by filing that return, the remaining portion of his half ($2,050,000) will be part of your taxable estate on your death— even though it's in the exemption trust. *But,* any appreciation on that excess between your husband's death and your death will not be included in your taxable estate when you die.

This method is what we inheritance lawyers call "freezing" your assets. Meaning, any appreciation realized on assets in the exemption trust is not subject to an estate tax on your death. For estate tax purposes, that appreciation is frozen.

The second reason I did not delete this section is what I previously discussed about the volatility of the estate tax law. The estate tax law is only permanent until Congress decides to change it, which, of course, means that it's impermanent. As the struggle in Washington, D.C., continues to keep incoming revenues up to speed with the insane amount of government spending, Congress may very well be forced to once again lower the lifetime exemption. If that occurs, then the exemption trust becomes *very* relevant yet again.

So, with those two justifications in mind, let's take a look at what I call the *seven steps for exemption trust validity.* You must take these seven steps to successfully perform the magic trick of preserving your deceased spouse's lifetime exemption with the exemption trust:

1. File a separate income tax return each year for the exemption trust if the assets in the exemption trust generate income (e.g., investment real estate, brokerage assets, certificates of deposit). The exemption trust, like any corporation or other business entity, for tax purposes is considered a separate person. And like any person, it files its own income tax returns . . . for the rest of its life.

   Don't allow this income tax concept to confuse you about the estate tax training you are receiving. For the most part, and for the purposes of this book, income tax has *nothing* to do with estate tax.

   Also, you may be somewhat confused by my statement that you need to file exemption trust income tax returns because of my previous statement that the exemption trust is tax-free. Don't be. The exemption trust *is* tax-free. When you die, the assets in the exemption trust and the appreciation on those assets will pass to your Living Trust beneficiaries without any *estate tax*. But, it's not quite the free lunch you wanted. During your lifetime, if those exemption trust assets generate income, the IRS still wants to impose an *income tax* on that income. That is why you will need to file a separate income tax return for the exemption trust and pay income tax.

2. All exemption trust assets must be vested in the name of the exemption trust. This means you have to retitle the bank accounts and brokerage accounts that you allocate to the exemption trust. If you are transferring all or a portion of real estate to the exemption trust, the deed to that property must reflect that new ownership.

3. All income generated by exemption trust assets cannot be allowed to sit in the exemption trust accounts. Rather, the income must be taken out of those accounts and transferred to your accounts. Why? Because even though the exemption trust assets, and their appreciation, are exempt from estate tax on your death, the income from those assets is not so exempt. If the income is allowed to stay in the exemption trust accounts, somebody (your after-death agent) will have to go through tons of statements to re-create a separation of taxable income and nontaxable appreciation. Not a fun prospect. As a result, you have to arrange with your bank or brokerage officer to have all income and dividends from the exemption trust automatically transferred to your accounts.

4. Trace exemption trust assets from one form to the next. In other words, you have to keep the exemption trust assets in the name of the exemption trust at all times—no matter what form those assets subsequently take.

For example, say you allocate your deceased spouse's one-half share of your home to the exemption trust. You sell the home for $300,000 and put the proceeds in the bank. You have to open up two accounts—one for $150,000 in the name of the exemption trust, and the other in your name (or the name of your Living Trust). If you then apply the $150,000 in the exemption trust account toward the purchase of securities, the securities must be purchased in the name of the exemption trust. You can wheel and deal all you want—but you have to maintain the exemption trust status of the new assets.

5. You cannot give away exemption trust assets. Sure, you can wheel and deal with them as often as you want, and you can use them for your health and support (defined as the amount necessary to maintain your comfortable standard of living), but you cannot make gifts of them.

   For example, say you meet the person you desire as your next spouse. You are smitten with this person to the extent that, to show your love, you wish to give him or her all the assets you own. Certainly, no one can legally stop you from foolishly giving away your share of the Living Trust assets. But, if your generosity includes dipping into and giving away a portion of the exemption trust assets, the entire tax-free status of the exemption trust is seriously jeopardized. If you give any of them away, the IRS will say that you exercised too much control over those assets and, as a result, will deem you to be the owner of those assets. And if you own them, they will be taxed on your death.

6. You cannot use the exemption trust assets for anything other than your support or health. This is huge. If you are caught using exemption trust assets for any purpose other than your support or health, the IRS will take away the exemption trust's tax-free status.

   What is considered a violation of this standard for invasion of exemption trust principal? Look again at the definition of *support*—the provision of funds sufficient to maintain your comfortable standard of living. What makes you comfortable? It's a very subjective standard, but it is still subject to a standard of reasonableness. Is it reasonable to use principal for food? Of course! Food would be considered a reasonable support expenditure in any context. But would it be a reasonable expenditure to travel to Thailand on a monthly basis for some amazingly authentic kang ka ree chicken? Clearly not.

The IRS does not give any guidelines as to what constitutes a reasonable expenditure of exemption trust assets for support. It defines support on a case-by-case basis. I suppose the only guidance I can give you on how to recognize an infraction of this standard is this: Does it pass the smell test? If an expenditure looks wrong, and you harbor doubt about whether it is wrong, it is probably wrong.

7. You cannot use exemption trust assets for your support or health *until* you have exhausted your own Living Trust assets. Your share of the Living Trust assets is deemed to be part of another subtrust described and created by your Living Trust, called the *survivor's trust.*

Whew! Those seven steps for exemption trust validity sound like a lot of work. Well, they are! But, if you have done the job right, and if your net worth is more than the combined lifetime exemptions of you and your spouse, you will save your family tens of thousands—maybe hundreds of thousands—of dollars in estate taxes on your death.

Financial Advisor Alert

The biggest quandary in my practice comes when the Living Trust *mandates* an exemption trust allocation after the first spouse dies, but there is no reason to do so. Once again, I refer you to this discussion later in "Do You Have to Do the 'More Complex Something' (Exemption Trust Allocation) When the 'Simple Something' (the Magic Box) Works Just Fine?"

The Other Subtrust: The Survivor's Trust

This chapter thus far has focused only on allocating your deceased spouse's half of the Living Trust assets to the exemption trust to preserve your deceased spouse's lifetime exemption. But to give you the complete picture of what happens to your Living Trust assets when your spouse dies, I need to discuss the other "shoe"— the survivor's trust, which is your half of the Living Trust assets.

When your deceased spouse's half of the Living Trust assets goes to the exemption trust, your half is automatically considered part of the survivor's trust. The survivor's trust contains your assets—your half. They are owned by you. You get income, principal, managerial authority to wheel and deal . . . whatever you want. Like the exemption trust, the survivor's trust is also listed in the provisions of your Living Trust in the section dealing with what happens upon the death of one spouse.

Because you own the survivor's trust assets, they *are* included in your taxable estate on your death. But, if your survivor's trust assets do not exceed your lifetime exemption, there will be no estate tax on those assets. Since the exemption trust is not taxable on your death, and since your survivor's trust *is* taxable on your death, all of the expenditures for your support and health should be taken from the taxable survivor's trust. If you run out of survivor's trust assets, then at that point, and *only* at that point, you can resort to exemption trust assets to provide for your support and health.

The Emergency Paragraph

Hang in there. I am almost done about the exemption trust. You have probably been to insurance seminars more exciting than this.

It is entirely possible that your Living Trust does not have provisions that create an exemption trust upon one spouse's death. If this is the case, then all the assets in your Living Trust—your deceased spouse's half and your half—will be part of your taxable estate on your death. As a result, you have lost an opportunity to prevent your Living Trust assets from being depleted by the estate tax. But don't panic just yet. I am here to make sure that doesn't happen.

Welcome to the emergency paragraph. If your Living Trust does not have exemption trust provisions, and the combined net worth of you and your deceased spouse is more than $10,900,000, you can still prevent your deceased spouse's half of the Living Trust assets from being counted in your taxable estate with an emergency procedure called a "disclaimer." However, the rules of the disclaimer process are, in my opinion, even more onerous than the rules about maintaining an exemption trust. Perhaps the cure is worse than the disease. But what else should you expect in such a last-resort method of preventing your Living Trust assets from being taxed on your death?

In essence, the disclaimer is a document that says that you do not want your deceased spouse's half of the Living Trust assets. Remember, you do not want them because if you get them, and you do not spend them prior to your death, they will be included in your taxable estate upon your death. Hence, the disclaimer prevents you from getting them.

That's just as bad as it sounds. If you draft and sign this disclaimer, you do not get the assets you disclaim. And unlike the exemption trust assets, you do not get any use or authority over the disclaimed assets. No income. No principal. No wheeling or dealing. Instead, the disclaimed assets go to other people. Who? The ones you and your deceased spouse named as the backup beneficiaries in your Living Trust, such as your children and your siblings.

The disclaimer must be signed within nine months of your spouse's death. If you don't make the deadline, the disclaimer will be invalid.

Furthermore, you cannot validly disclaim any asset of which you have accepted the benefits prior to the disclaimer. In other words, after your spouse dies, if you gain access to any portion of the assets in any Living Trust bank or brokerage account, you disqualify that *entire* account from being part of the disclaimer process. Harsh, but true!

For example, let's say that after your spouse died you went to the bank and withdrew some money from the Living Trust account to pay for your new membership on Match.com. That entire account is rendered ineligible for disclaiming because you used a portion of that account.

You will notice that I explained the disclaimer using examples involving financial assets. Intentionally so. One of the rare breaks given by the IRS in the estate tax arena is that you can disclaim your deceased spouse's half of the Living Trust real estate (like the home) without you having to skedaddle from the home. You can reside in the house and disclaim half of that home both at the same time.

Putting All of This Estate Tax Stuff Together

Although I have presented you with an overwhelming amount of information in this chapter, the estate tax essentially boils down to the following.

What Estate Tax Stuff Happens after Your Death If You Are Unmarried and Die with Less Than Your Lifetime Exemption?

If you are an unmarried person and your net estate is less than your $5,450,000 lifetime exemption on your death, the beneficiaries of your estate will not pay an estate tax when your estate is transferred to them. There is nothing that you need to do during your lifetime to make sure that your beneficiaries can claim that $5,450,000 lifetime exemption after you die. No fancy tax planning is needed. You get that lifetime exemption without doing anything.

And because your estate is under your lifetime exemption at your death, your after-death agent does not need to file your estate tax return.

What Estate Tax Stuff Happens If You Are Unmarried and Die with More Than Your Lifetime Exemption?

If you are an unmarried person and your net estate is more than your $5,450,000 lifetime exemption, on your death your beneficiaries will pay an estate tax when your estate is transferred to them. They will be required to file your estate tax return so the IRS can see how much you are over your lifetime exemption—and impose the appropriate amount of estate tax.

What Estate Tax Stuff Happens If Your and Your Spouse's Combined Worth Is Less Than $5,450,000 When the First Spouse Dies?

Say you and your spouse have a combined worth of $4 million—which is $2 million each. When your spouse dies, his half transfers to you . . . and now you own the entire $4 million. Now what?

When your spouse dies, his $5,450,000 lifetime exemption expires with him. You have "only" your $5,450,000 lifetime exemption.

There is no estate tax when your spouse's half passes to you, the surviving spouse, because of the marital estate tax deduction.

There is technically no requirement for you to file your deceased spouse's federal estate tax return because his half is well under his $5,450,000 lifetime exemption. *Still*, because I operate on a "you never know" belief system, I insist that you file your deceased spouse's estate tax return so you can check the Magic Box that adds your deceased spouse's lifetime exemption to your lifetime exemption. By doing so, your $4 million estate will pass to your beneficiaries estate-tax free because it falls well under your now-combined $10,900,000 lifetime exemption.

Because you've successfully beaten the estate tax by checking the Magic Box in your deceased spouse's estate tax return, there is no need for you to allocate your deceased spouse's half to an exemption trust. But, what if your Living Trust says that such an allocation is mandatory? Do you have to allocate anyway? What a waste of time, money, and effort that would be! This is discussed later in this chapter.

What Estate Tax Stuff Happens If Your and Your Spouse's Combined Worth Is More Than $5,450,000 When the First Spouse Dies?

This is the only scenario where you have to do something to make certain that your beneficiaries will not pay any, or minimal, estate tax when both you and your spouse have died and your estate is transferred to your children or other heirs.

If your deceased spouse's half of the family wealth (whether or not in the Living Trust) exceeds the $5,450,000 lifetime exemption, you will need to run around and get information for your attorney so he or she can file an estate tax return. On the estate tax return, you will check the Magic Box, which allows you to pick up your deceased spouse's $5,450,000 lifetime exemption. Now you have a combined lifetime exemption of $10,900,000.

As long as your deceased spouse's half is allocated to either one or more of you (the surviving spouse) in a marital trust, which is exclusively for your benefit, and an exemption trust, there will not be any estate tax due upon his death.

Do you have to allocate your deceased spouse's half of the estate to an exemption trust even though you picked up your deceased spouse's lifetime exemption by checking the Magic Box in your deceased spouse's estate tax return? If it seems that both accomplish the same result, you are correct. But, you may have a Living Trust, which actually requires you to perform an exemption trust allocation no matter what. Can you get out of this? This is discussed in the next section.

What Exemption Trust Stuff Happens after Your Spouse's Death?

Your Living Trust probably contains provisions that, after your spouse's death, establish two subtrusts: the exemption trust and the survivor's trust.

The main purpose of the exemption trust is to preserve your deceased spouse's lifetime exemption., While the assets in the exemption trust are used for the benefit of you—the surviving spouse—those assets that remain in the exemption trust on your death will be distributed to your Living Trust beneficiaries without any estate tax. Moreover, the appreciation on the exemption trust assets will also be tax-free.

There are seven formalities in the maintenance of the exemption trust that must be followed (which are discussed above with the seven steps of exemption trust validity). If those requirements are not met, the possibility looms that the IRS will disregard the exemption trust and consider those assets to be included in your taxable estate upon your death.

The assets that are not allocated to the exemption trust are considered to be in the survivor's trust. Whereas the exemption trust assets, for estate tax purposes, belong to your deceased spouse, you are the owner of the survivor's trust assets, and, as a result, they are included in your taxable estate upon your death.

However, the exemption trust allocation only becomes necessary if the combined wealth of your and your deceased spouse's half of the family assets (whether or not in the Living Trust) exceeds your combined lifetime exemptions—which is more than $10,900,000. Otherwise, to preserve your deceased spouse's lifetime exemption, you really only need to check the Magic Box on the federal estate tax return and send it to the IRS.

Still . . . even though all you need to do to preserve your deceased spouse's lifetime exemption is check the Magic Box, you still have your Living Trust that mandates and "commands" you to allocate your deceased spouse's portion of the Living Trust assets to the exemption trust. Overkill? Unnecessary? You bet! So we turn to the next section with the heading.

Do You Have to Do the "More Complex Complex Something" (Exemption Trust Allocation) When the "Simple Something" (the Magic Box) Works Just Fine?

The exemption trust accomplishes the same goal as checking the Magic Box in your deceased spouse's estate tax return—which is preserving your deceased spouse's lifetime exemption. Certainly, the exemption trust sounds great, but if the same result can be accomplished with the Magic Box, do you still have to go through the time, expense, effort, and hassle of the seven steps of exemption trust validity for the rest of your life?

This is the most burning issue in my estate planning practice today. I have drafted hundreds of Living Trusts for clients, which command the surviving spouse to allocate the deceased spouse's half of the Living Trust assets to an exemption trust. When those clients die, their surviving spouses come to my office and give me the usual "what happens now" question—to which I give this somewhat unprofessional response: "I don't know! I hate to put you through the complexities of exemption trust allocation and maintenance when an easier solution is available. But your Living Trust was drafted before that easy solution existed! And so your Living Trust requires you to do an exemption trust! I'm sorry!"

Can the surviving spouses simply ignore those mandatory exemption trust allocation provisions? Just pretend they don't exist? Let me give you the legal answer . . . then the real-world answer.

In the legal world, the answer is . . . no. Every state's trust law has a statute that says, in essence, that when a trust becomes irrevocable (meaning, after the death of a person who established the trust), the after-death agent must faithfully carry out the terms of that trust. As a result, the surviving spouse (who typically serves as the after-death agent) must comply with those exemption trust allocation provisions. Bummer!

However, in the real world, the answer is not so clear-cut. If I said it was "fine" to ignore those exemption trust allocation provisions, I run the risk of the state bar and/or the IRS swooping down on me for dispensing law-breaking advice. So . . . my cop-out answer is this question: If you don't perform a mandatory exemption trust allocation, is anyone going to chase you down and force you to do it? Is there any agency "out there" that is going to force you to comply with those mandatory exemption trust allocation provisions? The answer to THAT question is no. There is no "Trust Enforcement Department" anywhere that forces surviving spouses to carry out their obligation to set up the exemption trust. And the IRS does not, and may likely never, assume that role.

In reality, there is only *one situation* that creates a "class" of people who will hold the surviving spouse to the task of complying with a compulsory exemption trust allocation. This class is created when the following elements occur:

1. You and your spouse are both on your "second time around." Your spouse has children from a previous marriage. (You may also have children from a previous marriage . . . but that is not a relevant consideration for purposes of explaining this situation.)

2. You and your second spouse set up a community property Living Trust—and both of you transfer your pre–second marriage separate assets to this community property Living Trust. This means that the respective separate property of you and your second spouse has been "transmutated" to you and your second spouse's community property.

3. The Living Trust set up by you and your second spouse provides for the usual mandatory exemption trust allocation. That is, when the first spouse dies, the half of that deceased spouse shall be allocated to the exemption trust, and the surviving spouse's half shall be allocated to the survivor's trust.

4. That Living Trust further provides that after the surviving spouse's death, all the assets in the exemption trust will be distributed to your deceased spouse's children, and all assets in the survivor's trust will be distributed to "your side."

5. Your second spouse dies first. You do nothing to allocate your deceased spouse's half of the Living Trust assets to the exemption trust because you said that your Living Trust advisor (moi) can simply check the Magic Box in your deceased second spouse's estate tax return to pick up the lifetime exemption.

Do you see the problem here? If you (the surviving spouse) do not allocate your deceased spouse's half of the Living Trust assets to the exemption trust, then ALL of the Living Trust assets will be deemed to be in your survivor's trust—which will go entirely to *your side!* And what's more, your survivor's trust is completely revocable and changeable by you! You can change the survivor's trust to leave everything to anyone you want. To *your* children. *Your* siblings. *Your* nieces and nephews. *Your* bowling instructor. *Your* dance teacher. *Your* charitable cause. To anyone *other* than your deceased spouse's children.

So, to protect your deceased second spouse's children's ultimate distribution from the exemption trust after your death, they will literally follow you around to make sure you see your Living Trust attorney to engage in the exemption trust allocation process. If you forgo or forget this step, I guarantee you that your deceased spouse's children will hire an attorney to force you (via litigation, if necessary) to allocate their deceased parent's half to the exemption trust.

But, other than that specific scenario, there is simply no reason to obey your Living Trust's command to perform an exemption trust allocation if you and your deceased spouse's net worth falls under your combined lifetime exemption amounts. But, at the same time, this is still a legally binding command in your Living Trust.

Financial Advisor Alert

Actually, there is another scenario (which is relatively uncommon and beyond the scope of this book) that requires your surviving spouse client to fulfill the Living Trust's exemption allocation commandment. In an oversimplistic nutshell. The surviving spouse must perform that function if the Living Trust provides that on the death of the surviving spouse, all or a portion of the Living Trust assets shall be allocated to special subtrusts for their grandchildren's benefit called generation-skipping transfer tax trusts. The generation - skipping transfer tax (GSTT) is a separate federal tax on transfers of property to those subtrusts. However, each spouse has a GST exemption—presently $5,450,000—which can be allocated to those subtrusts. If the surviving spouse elects not to allocate the deceased spouse's portion of the trust estate to the exemption trust, the deceased spouse's GSTT exemption of $5,450,000 cannot be carried forward to the surviving spouse. Consequently, if the exemption trust is not established, the GSTT exemption of the deceased spouse would be lost, which leaves only the surviving spouse's GSTT exemption available.

So, what to do? There is only one "legal" solution—get a court order that modifies your Living Trust. That is, have your Living Trust attorney file a petition with your county's probate court, which requests an order removing your Living Trust's mandatory exemption trust allocation provisions. With this modification order, the court "boots" the Living Trust's exemption trust allocation command from that document—and all the assets will be considered to be in your survivor's trust.

Will the court grant your modification petition? I believe there is a high degree of success, but *only if* your state's trust laws allow judicial modifications of irrevocable trusts (because the exemption trust is, well, an irrevocable trust), *and only if* your own children, who may be skittish about you having the power to change the survivor's trust's inheritance instructions (to cut them out in favor of newfound friends?) don't file objections. But putting those provisos aside, once that modification order is made, you can legally ignore those pesky exemption trust allocation provisions.

Let this head-twisting exemption trust allocation discussion serve as a cautionary tale to you. If your Living Trust contains these command provisions and your spouse is deceased, you have no choice but to address it. BUT, if you and your spouse are both still living, you have the opportunity to run to your Living Trust attorney and amend your Living Trust to make those exemption trust allocation provisions *optional.* That is, your Living Trust can provide that after the death of the first spouse, the surviving spouse has the *option* to allocate the deceased spouse's portion of the Living Trust assets to the exemption trust. Then, when the first spouse dies, the surviving spouse and the Living Trust attorney can discuss whether to exercise the option.

Financial Advisor Alert

If you take nothing else away from this book, take away this: Go through your married clients' Living Trusts to see if the exemption trust allocation provisions are mandatory! If those provisions are mandatory, and your clients' combined net worth is less than $10,900,000, get them running to their estate planning attorney, so they can discuss whether to amend to incorporate an optional exemption trust allocation!

As the estate tax stuff relates to the Living Trust, this is all you really need to know—for now! Just wait until the IRS actually imposes an estate tax. When is that? When you die! If you cannot wait for this other shoe to drop, jump ahead to Chapter 22, which discusses estate tax stuff that takes place after your death.

THE FOURTH QUARTER

DYING WITH YOUR LIVING TRUST

It's the start of the Fourth Quarter of the Big Game. Unfortunately, that means that you and your spouse or co-trustee are no longer participants in the Big Game. The playing field is Inheritance Arena. The combatants are your Living Trust beneficiaries. The object of the game is the smooth flow of Living Trust assets from one generation to the next. What kind of game will it be? If you remember the training you receive in this Fourth Quarter, the match will go smoothly. But, if you fail to do your reps, it will deteriorate into an organized riot.

So what does this mean for you? Since both you and your spouse are dead and your inheritance instructions are set in stone, not a lot. But, through the magic of absurdist fiction, I have invented a time machine that will transport you back to when you and your spouse were alive and sitting in your Living Trust lawyer's office. Armed with the chapters in this section that deal with many harmful scenarios that could befall your children in the Inheritance Arena, you will be able to bring to your lawyer's attention a particular problem that is of consequence to you. From there, you can incorporate special provisions into your Living Trust that will prevent these scenarios from rearing their ugly heads in the Inheritance Arena after both you and your spouse are dead.

Ninety-five percent of the solution to any problem is recognizing the problem in the first place. This takes on a new sense of urgency when you strive to resolve the most common problems that arise in the Inheritance Arena. By looking at these problems, you will help keep peace in your family and shield your Living Trust assets from risk of loss once they are in the hands of your children.

After all, you did not work your entire life just so the fruits of all your labors could pass so far afield from your family bloodline or cause family disputes.

14

Distribution of Your Living Trust after Both You and Your Spouse Are Dead

OR,

THE INHERITANCE ARENA IS NOT FOR THE FAINTHEARTED

This will sound so obvious that it should not need saying. But since I am charging you for every word you read in this book, I am going to say it anyway: When you die and both you and your spouse are gone, the Living Trust no longer serves to benefit you. You no longer get the income or principal. You are no longer in charge of the Living Trust assets, whether it's your half, your deceased spouse's half, the exemption trust assets, or the survivor's trust assets. You are no longer the wheeler-dealer of Living Trust assets. You are no longer the surviving lifetime agent. You no longer have standing to sue your lifetime agent if he or she screws up the management of the assets.

While it may seem that your Living Trust in essence died when you died, it does just the opposite—it actually springs to life when you both pass away. In fact, your Living Trust lives on to become one of the last lessons you leave to your children and other heirs.

It is the lesson of passing on your lifetime of accumulations—your house, brokerage assets, businesses, bank accounts, personal possessions, pedigreed dogs and cats—to them in a way that preserves family harmony in the inheritance arena.

Financial Advisor Alert

Following your clients' deaths, their children may approach you for information about the process of transferring to them the Living Trust's bank and brokerage assets. Which is fine. Since they are likely the successor trustees (whom I refer to elsewhere in this book as the after-death agents), they should have some idea about the mechanics involved to obtain their inheritance.

But while most inheritors maintain an even and patient keel about this process, you will encounter those who want their money yesterday and want you to pressure the estate attorney and the account representatives to "hurry up" with the distributions.

What do you do when you encounter beneficiaries who are in a rush to get their share? You give them the facts of life, which are as follows:

1. There are no tanks rushing down the street forcing the successor trustee to make fast distributions. Nothing has to be done overnight—nor can it be. While the Living Trust avoids the lengthy distribution delays of probate, the postdeath administration and distribution of Living Trust assets still involve care and deliberation.
2. There are several matters that the successor trustee must attend to before making any distribution. These include inventorying the Living Trust assets, searching for documents evidencing creditors, commissioning appraisal reports of real property, ascertaining if any assets are not contained in the Living Trust, preparing the final income tax returns, and possibly preparing the federal estate tax return.
3. The successor trustees must ascertain the total value of the Living Trust assets and non–Living Trust assets and subtract the debts, taxes, and administration expenses from that number. Perhaps there are thousands of dollars in noncovered medical expenses. Or maybe their parents incurred a large amount of outstanding credit card debt. Or there are past-due income taxes or property taxes. Then there are attorney fees to be incurred for services rendered in the distribution of the Living Trust assets. And accountant fees for the

filing of the final and/or fiduciary income tax returns. Whatever those subtractions are, the resulting number is the *net estate* or *remainder;* and only when that number is ascertained does the successor trustee know the amount of each beneficiary's portion.

4. Distributing the Living Trust's bank and brokerage assets is not the simple process it used to be. In the olden days, the successor trustees gained access to the assets simply by showing the settlor's death certificates and the portion of the Living Trust that names them as successor trustees. But these days, in light of all the post-911 bank regulations, the successor trustees will have to additionally show two forms of identification and the entire Living Trust document. Then, in most cases, the documents assembled will require scrutiny by the branch manager and the institution's legal department. About 10 days later, the successor trustees will be told that they cannot access the funds directly from the Living Trust accounts; rather, they must open new accounts in their names as successor trustees. Of course, a new Living Trust account requires a new taxpayer identification number, which you (or the accountant or attorney) will obtain. Once that new taxpayer identification number is received, the successor trustees must complete forms to open the new accounts—which will require your help, due to the numerous questions that the successor trustees don't have the wherewithal to answer. ("Is the Living Trust revocable or irrevocable?" "Is the date of the Living Trust the date that the amendment was signed?" "Does the Trust give us powers to make investment decisions?" "Who are the settlors?" "What's a settlor?") When the new account is finally established, the assets from the old account must be transferred to the new account, which sometimes can take a while. After that entire maddening process, the successor trustees can access the accounts and make distributions in accordance with the Living Trust's inheritance instructions.

The Grim Reality

The deaths of both you and your spouse spark the inheritance instructions that are stated in your Living Trust into action. These instructions are now set in stone. No more revocations. No more amendments. This is it. Your death becomes the time when we see if the inheritance instructions in your Living Trust constitute a good inheritance plan—or a bad one.

Don't panic—if you have been implementing my advice thus far into your Living Trust, and if you have taken to heart the training you've received thus far, then I am sure you have developed a good inheritance plan. However, if you have been ignoring my advice, some of the following scenarios may arise after your death:

- Your daughter, who loves her husband, puts his name on her inherited assets. As a result, your daughter loses all of her inheritance or one-half of her assets to your son-in-law after he files for divorce.
- Your financially overextended son loses his inheritance to his bankruptcy creditors.
- Your combative son engages in a legal battle with his siblings over some de minimis aspect of the postdeath Living Trust administration to even some personal score.
- Your daughter mismanages her share of the inheritance into the ground.
- Your compulsive gambler son liquidates his share so he can put it all on one spin on the green double-zero at the roulette table in Las Vegas.
- The board of directors of the off-brand charity you named as a beneficiary in your Living Trust uses its gift to buy a Cadillac for each board member.
- Your flower-child daughter hands over her entire share to the crazy cult in Santa Cruz in which she finally finds herself.
- One of your sons demands that his siblings give him a portion of their shares of the Living Trust assets because he perceives, whether justified or not, that he did not receive an equal share.
- Your normal son, who holds and manages your problem daughter's share, is incessantly bombarded with demands from your daughter to give her money.

These are but a few of the scenarios that I have seen after both spouses die and the inheritance plan comes to life—not quite the picnic you envisioned of the smooth transition of wealth from one generation to the next. You may think your children, daughters-in-law, sons-in-law, and grandchildren are perfect. And you know, maybe they are! But, when it comes to dividing the inheritance, and handling and managing the windfall, you do not really know your children.

Why this doom-and-gloom projection of the picture of your family after you die? Because after dealing with the children of deceased clients for 30 years, I can tell you with all confidence that even in the most perfect of families where everyone . . . *everyone* . . . loves each other, there is no family loyalty in the inheritance arena. Not to you, their deceased parents, and not among themselves, your children. Why? Because in the inheritance arena, your children are no longer your children, and they are not siblings. They are simply people dividing and handling money. Family loyalty goes out the window, and it's a whole new ballgame.

Money does funny things to people. It's as if a special DNA—an inheritance gene deeply recessed in the human body—is activated when an inheritance is divided. The way a person perceives, acts, talks, walks, smells, and thinks can all change dramatically when immersed in the inheritance arena.

If you have ever shared an inheritance with a sibling, or lent money to a family member, or gone into business with a sibling, you may have experienced a taste of what I am talking about. You wanted your end, your fair share, the benefit of your bargain. If what was supposed to come to you did not, you took the appropriate remedial measures. What were those steps? Did you scream at your family member to own up to the deal? Did you hire a lawyer to threaten litigation? Did you take your family member to court? Did you get other family members involved to bring pressure on the deadbeat? Whatever those steps were, you did not let the family relationship stand in the way. You did what you needed to do in order to get yours.

Lawyers like myself don't learn about the inheritance arena in law school. We are not schooled in family dynamics, nor do we learn about how human nature responds to the death of a family member and how the children behave when they divide and manage the family money. Therefore, we do not know if the inheritance instructions we draft in our clients' Living Trusts will, oodles of years later, result in harmony or upheaval between their children. The only way we learn about what makes an inheritance plan a good one or a bad one is through on-the-job training of seeing what happens when clients die.

Have you heard the term "Monday - Morning Quarterback"? This is a football player who, on Monday morning, reviews his Sunday performance and comes up with all kinds of excuses for his team's loss, which usually start with "I coulda," or "I shoulda," or "I woulda." Well, we Living Trust lawyers are the ultimate Monday-morning quarterbacks. When clients die and the inheritance instructions come to life, and we witness chaos and conflict erupt over the division of the inheritance, or see the inheritance rapidly dissipated, or learn that the inheritance was used to fuel destructive vices, we can gauge what advice we gave or provisions we wrote that directly or indirectly resulted in those scenarios. We then bring those experiences to new clients to ensure that their Living Trusts do not wind up as cautionary tales for their successive generations. In other words, when we see Living Trusts go bad after the death of both spouses, it's our turn to say "I coulda," or "I shoulda," or "I woulda," and then we learn from those mistakes.

Beating the Odds

Rest assured, as your Living Trust advisor, I have provided you and will continue to provide you with various ways to ensure that you do not become a Monday - morning quarterback. After all, once you pass away, there is nothing you can do to rectify the problems you might cause because you did not think about all of the possible scenarios that could happen after you and your co-trustee die. Having seen the worst-case scenarios throughout my 30 years of practice, I can assure you that if you take the practical advice that I offer, then you will effectively and peacefully distribute your Living Trust and avoid the awful situations that I have witnessed over the years.

CHAPTER

15

Don't Intentionally Leave Your Children Unequal Inheritances

OR,

SO WHAT IF ONE NEEDS IT MORE THAN THE OTHER?

I have demonstrated to you throughout this book that I am a master of stating the obvious. Such mastery will be quite evident in this chapter. Let me start off with two facts that you already know about leaving your money and property:

1. Your money and property are your money and property. You can do whatever you want with them during your lifetime, and you have the unfettered authority to decide who shall receive them after your death.
2. There is no law in the United States that requires you to leave any of your assets to your children.

Having made these bold and unequivocal assertions, it is, nonetheless, highly likely you will name your children in your Living Trust as your beneficiaries. Of course, if you have no children, or if you have cut your children out of the inheritance, you will not be caught up in this sweeping generalization. But for the purposes of this chapter, you are in the vast majority of fairly conventional people with children who will be the beneficiaries of your Living Trust assets.

When it comes to leaving your Living Trust assets to your children, the best advice that I can offer you is to leave them each an equal inheritance. Even though you can divide your assets among your children as you wish, the goal of preserving family harmony in the inheritance arena, to my mind, trumps that particular exercise of free will. I can guarantee discord and conflict among your children if you treat them differently in your Living Trust.

That's the long and short of it. If you care about your children and their relationships with each other, do not leave them unequal inheritances. That's pretty simple stuff.

But It's Not So Simple

If the answer is that simple, you may be wondering why I haven't already concluded this chapter. Even though I am certain you agree with this advice, there is a significant possibility you may disregard it and tell your lawyer to leave more Living Trust assets to one child and less to others because you, like most of my clients, may believe that your Living Trust should factor in the differing financial needs of your children. You may feel that your more financially successful child needs your money less than the child with greater financial requirements, and you want to use your Living Trust to create equity between them.

You do not have the experience of seeing what happens when parents die and this unequal inheritance plan comes to life. If you did, you would seriously reconsider any plan to render what you consider to be economic justice. Let me tell you about one such occasion, which I have seen repeated in one form or another during my 30-year practice.

After the death of the second parent, the children met at my office for advice on the administration of their parents' Living Trust (which was prepared by another attorney). I was surprised to learn that the children had no idea of the terms of the Living Trust, because usually the children have already torn through it to learn what they receive.

Like a scene out of a movie, I read the inheritance instructions to the children. This was the first time the successful businessman son discovered that his parents had left him a one-third share of the Living Trust assets, with his struggling schoolteacher sister receiving a two-thirds share. The Living Trust contained an explanation for the unequal treatment, which was, in a nutshell, that the parents thought that their son did not need the money as much as their daughter did.

The son became apoplectic when he heard this news, and the scene turned into quite a frenzy, with four people—me, his sister, his wife, and my secretary—trying to get him to calm down. I picked up the glass of water on my desk and prepared to throw it at him. Finally, he calmed down (without the dousing) and I was able to glean these words from him:

"You just don't get what this has done to me. I worked in high school. I worked to get money to go to college. I put myself through college. I busted my butt at an entry-level position in the company. I worked my butt off to become vice president of the company. I am a respected person. I am self-made. I made my parents proud. I brought honor to my parents. And what did my parents do? They punished my success and rewarded my dingbat sister's failure! Backstabbers! Backstabbers my parents are!"

From the parents' perspective, they thought they were doing justice. But they neglected to solicit the opinion of their successful son. Maybe they purposely left him out of the loop because they knew how vituperative his reaction would be and wanted to avoid that whole scene. One thing is for certain, though; they left the mopping up to their son and daughter and their lawyer (me).

In any event, the last I heard, the son and daughter, who I understood had been very close, had ceased talking to each other. Using my best bedside psychology, the son apparently transferred the blame he assigned to his parents to his sister. Since they were backstabbers, his sister, who played no part in the parents' decision to leave her more, was a backstabber as well.

Financial Advisor Alert

Your clients' children will, most likely, be equal beneficiaries of the Living Trust assets. These terms will be quite evident in the section titled "Distribution of Trust Estate After Death of Surviving Spouse" or some variation thereof. (If the Living Trust is for a single person, substitute the word *settlor* for *surviving spouse*.) In that section, you will see a specific reference to each child and a specific reference to the share to which each child is entitled. For example, if there are three children, it will say one-third to Jessie, one-third to Jossie, and one-third to Jussie. Very simple.

Or you may have to hunt for this provision because the drafting attorney inserted a one-size-fits-all instruction that doesn't use any names, such as this: "The balance in equal shares, of the trust estate shall be distributed to the issue of the Settlors, by right of representation." This means that each living child of the settlors (your clients who set up the Living Trust) shall receive a one-third share; and a share for a child of the settlors who is not living shall be distributed to that deceased child's children in equal shares. Nice shorthand, yes?

An unequal inheritance distribution, however, will be as plain as day regardless of the language used. If you see such a plan, then it's time to play the part of concerned financial advisor and warn your clients of the emotional fallout that often derives from unequal inheritances. They will either tell you to mind your own business or confide in you their reasoning for the inequality. If the latter, what is that reason? Are they estranged from the child who receives less? If so, your clients must realize that by dumping that child from an equal distribution, they are possibly dumping that child into the lives of their other children. The child who receives less often financially imposes himself on his siblings because, in that child's view, they received "his money" . . . and now they "owe" him.

If they are leaving less to one child because that child doesn't need it as much as their other children, make them aware of the main point of this chapter—that from the successful child's view, the parents are punishing success. And that child will demonstrate his resentment toward your clients by cutting off all communication and interaction with his siblings. Sure, it's not their fault . . . but so what? This is the stuff of transference.

By sparking your clients' awareness to the adverse consequences of these (and other) unequal inheritance distributions among their children, they can make an informed decision on whether they want to keep their Living Trust as is . . . or change it for the sake of avoiding postdeath volatility and upheaval.

Touchy-Feely Advice: Talk to Your Richer Child Before You Leave Him Less

If you are of similar mind to leave less of your Living Trust assets to your more financially successful child, I recommend that you tell that child your plan. You may be surprised at that child's response. Perhaps your successful child will be in agreement with your plan to leave him or her less. If so, then all is well.

However, really examine your successful child's response to see if any agreement is genuine, because the child may be telling you what you want to hear in order to not appear greedy. Listen to the tone of voice. Is it facetious or sarcastic? Look at body language. Are his shoulders slumped? Did she need to sit down after you gave her the big news? Is he giving you a beau geste where he gladly offers to make the sacrifice but secretly hopes that you do not take him up on his offer? It may be a tough read, but it's a read you must make. Remember, your goal is to preserve your children's relationships in the inheritance arena. If you determine that your plan to punish your child's success will make him resentful of you and his siblings, abandon that plan and leave your Living Trust assets to your children equally.

Quite often, however, you do not have to work so hard to make that determination. Your successful child may have no problem telling you what she really thinks of your plan to leave her less. This happened in my own family. Yes, we lawyers are not immune from human nature in the inheritance arena. Quite contrary to popular opinion, lawyers are people, too.

When my then-wife's parents wanted a Living Trust, they called me, saying, "Jeff, it's good to have a Living Trust lawyer in the family! Now get over here so we can tell you what we want." Ultimately, I prepared a Living Trust for Ben and Florence in which they left all of their assets, which consisted of only a small house and some cash, to all of their eight children in equal shares.

When Florence died, I was summoned to Ben's house, where he instructed me to prepare an amendment to his Living Trust to cut out one of his sons, Craig. As Ben said, "Craig does not need the money. Everyone else needs it. Everyone else can split his share."

Ben was certainly correct. Craig lives an upscale life, and he made it all himself with no leg up from anyone. He has a fabulous home in Scottsdale, Arizona. He is a partner in one of this country's largest accounting firms. He has first-rate seats for almost every college and pro sports event in Phoenix. On the Sunday after his daughter's bat mitzvah, he took the entire extended family to a Phoenix Cardinals game at ASU Stadium. Craig is an ardent follower of all Arizona State University sports. If ASU had a tiddly-winks team, he would show up and cheer it on. I miss Craig and his wife and children. Divorce sucks. When a divorce is imposed on you, you can lose an entire family.

But I digress. Back to the story. I told Ben about the destructive consequences of the "punishing success/rewarding failure" plan that I had witnessed in my practice, but he was not to be swayed. So, I told Ben two things.

First, an amendment cutting out Craig would increase the share to my then-wife, which, in turn, would result in Craig perceiving me as an opportunistic piece of crap.

Ben said, "That won't happen. Craig knows you are not like that. If you were interested in making money that way, then you would be making more and my daughter wouldn't have to work."

Okay. I then said my second piece.

Ben should talk to Craig just to see what his reaction would be. To that, Ben responded, "Craig won't care. I think I know him better than you. I'm not going to make that call."

So, I asked Ben if I could call Craig to give him the big news. Ben gave me the go-ahead, and I went home to make that call.

My telephone call with Craig lasted all of three minutes. The first minute was pleasantries. For the next minute and 55 seconds, I engaged in an uninterrupted monologue in which I described the Living Trust, Ben's power to change the inheritance instructions after Florence's death, and Ben's plan to change those instructions to cut Craig out. The remaining five seconds consisted of Craig saying to me, "I'll talk to Ben."

A few minutes later, I got a call from Ben, who said, "Just leave the Living Trust as it is." I never asked Craig about the contents of his phone conversation with Ben. But you don't have to be a genius to surmise that Craig told his father what he really thought of the proposed change in the Living Trust.

I do not judge Craig's adverse reaction to the plan to leave him less simply because his father perceived he did not need as much of an inheritance as his siblings. Nor do I cast aspersion on the son whom I almost drenched or any of the other successful children who let me know, in one way or another, how slighted they felt when they learned that their parents had punished their success. This is simply human nature when faced with such circumstances. I would probably feel the same way if my parents left me less. How would you feel?

Then again, you may not care about how leaving your children an unequal inheritance based on need will affect their relationships with each other . . . or how it will impact on their memory of you. I have many clients who profess "After me, who cares?" and then proceed to do it their way.

One of my favorite client quips came from such a gentleman who was hell-bent on leaving almost nothing to his very successful daughter. My father explained to him the adverse impact this plan would have on his children's sibling relationships, but to him, consequences be damned. Finally, my father said to him in an exasperated and sarcastic tone, "When you die, your daughter will s— on your grave." The client calmly responded, "Then I'll tell you what, Mr. Condon. I will just be buried at sea."

16

The Accidental Unequal Inheritance

OR,

IF YOU THINK YOU HAVE TREATED YOUR CHILDREN EQUALLY BY LEAVING THEM EQUAL INHERITANCES, I HAVE SOME NEWS FOR YOU!

You have three children. Your Living Trust leaves all of the assets to them equally. With the preservation of family harmony in the inheritance arena being dependent on equal treatment of your children in your Living Trust, you have done your job. It doesn't get more equal than one-third apiece.

However, from your children's perspective, you have not treated them equally in your Living Trust if you made unequal gifts to them during your life.

I know this does not make sense, because, from your viewpoint, the gifts you make to your children during your life have nothing to do with the inheritances they receive after your death. And you are correct. By all objective standards, the money you give to your children has no direct connection to or correlation with the bequests you leave to your children.

In the inheritance arena, though, objectivity becomes secondary to perception, whether or not the matters perceived are real or imagined, reasonable or unreasonable. And as unreasonable as it may seem, your children will perceive a connection between life-time gifts and Living Trust bequests.

When you make a gift to a child, you are not keeping a scorecard. You simply help a child who needs financial help. A wedding. A car. College tuition. A down payment on a house. Seed money for a new business. A medical payment. Whatever. But there are people out there who *are* keeping score—your children.

Your children will not tell you they have kept mental score of lifetime gifts, because they do not want to come across as selfish or greedy. When you and your spouse are both gone, if the Final Scorecard is not roughly a tie among all the children, the child with the short end of the stick may put pressure on the children who received more to pony up with a portion of their shares of the inheritance to equalize. Will those children concede a portion of their equal shares of the inheritance to preserve family harmony?

Let me answer that question with another question: Would you?

The Family Scorecard

My first brush with this concept came during a meeting in my office with the four children—three sons and one daughter—after their last parent died. Their Living Trust left all of the assets equally to each child. At some point during that meeting, their daughter produced a computer printout of the significant gifts their parents had made to them: $10,000 for one child's wedding; $7,500 for one child's care; $25,000 attorney fees for one child's divorce; and so on. My mouth went agape at the detailed recollection of these expenses.

After this recitation of expenditures, the daughter announced that after tallying all the gifts, she had received the least amount by about $125,000.

The daughter turned to me and asked if I had advised her parents to factor these lifetime gifts in determining whether their inheritance was truly equal for each child. I admitted I had not given that advice because I did not see the connection. Gifts are gifts. Inheritances are inheritances.

But the daughter said something to me that profoundly changed my thinking in that respect: "Mr. Condon, I don't think your firm did a good job on my parents' Living Trust. My parents were very fair people, but the disparity of the gifts to their children is significant. Had this disparity been brought to their attention, I am certain they would have taken steps in their Living Trust to equalize those gifts. But it wasn't brought to their attention, was it? So the opportunity they had to equalize fell by the wayside."

This woman spoke the truth. As an inheritance planning attorney, one of my chief functions is to create a Living Trust that does not cause harm to a client's family. This function cannot be achieved unless attention is cast on matters outside the Living Trust that matter to the children. If unequal lifetime gifts are important to the children—and they absolutely are—those matters become relevant to the Living Trust.

We live . . . we learn. Now, whenever I meet with a new client, I always bring up the subject of lifetime gifts. But unfortunately for the daughter, this on-the-job training came too late. Dad and Mom were dead, and the only solution to equalize the unequal lifetime gifts was an agreement by all the children to apportion the inheritance in a manner other than equal. I meekly suggested this course of action to the three sons, but their only response was to silently notice the decor in my office.

The daughter made one last shot in an attempt to get her siblings to give her a portion of their shares to equalize the lifetime gifts. She stood up and addressed her brothers: "Guys, if Mr. Condon had done his job correctly, Dad and Mom would have equalized. You know this. I know this. We are a family. So as a family, we should do what our parents would have done if Mr. Condon had brought it to their attention in the first place. Just give me a portion of your shares to make me whole."

Silence.

"If you won't do this for me, do it for Mom and Dad."

More silence. I could almost hear the crickets chirping. Personally, I was moved by that little speech and I would have tossed some part of my share her way. But her brothers just did not say anything, and the room grew icy cold. One of the brothers finally said, "Let's discuss this later." With all that had transpired in my office, it was obvious to everyone that there was no substance to that statement. It was just something to say to break the silence and placate the daughter.

What I know of the family today is that they did not equalize, and the daughter, once close with her brothers, has no meaningful contact with them.

Financial Advisor Alert

As I have stated throughout these Alerts, I believe that engaging with your clients about Living Trust matters is part of your job description. Such inquiries constitute a valuable service and show your care and commitment beyond the numbers. By raising your clients' awareness on the potential adverse impact of unequal lifetime gifts to their children, you fulfill that duty in spades. There is almost zero chance that your clients have expended any brainpower on equalizing lifetime gifts among their children because, like most people, they don't consider it an inheritance issue.

So when you notice that your clients' Living Trust leaves the trust estate to their children in equal shares, you *must* ask them whether they made unequal gifts to their children and, if so, is that unequal treatment likely to be recalled after their deaths? Not every gift disparity will trigger a "less-gifted" child's reaction of "Dad and Mom always liked you best." When each child's equal inheritance share is in the millions, a gift disparity of a few hundred thousand dollars will likely not generate any family upheaval. But when the inheritance dollars are significantly less, each dollar becomes more precious—and the stage is set for family infighting.

You Live, You Learn

In retrospect, I should have asked Dad and Mom whether they made any earlier lifetime gifts to their children, determined the extent of the disparity of those gifts, and discussed solutions that could be incorporated in their Living Trust to equalize among their children, which could have included the following:

- In the Living Trust, Dad and Mom provide that an extra amount goes to the children who received less in lifetime gifts, and that all their children receive the rest of the Living Trust assets in equal shares.
- During their lives, Dad and Mom arrange for the children who received less in lifetime gifts to own a life insurance policy on the joint lives of Dad and Mom in an amount equal to the disparity. Then, in the Living Trust, Dad and Mom provide that all Living Trust assets go to their children in equal shares.
- During Dad's and Mom's lifetimes, they give cash to the children who received less in lifetime gifts in an amount needed to bring rough equalization of all lifetime gifts among the children. Then, in the Living Trust, all assets are left to the four children in equal shares.

Now that I have raised your awareness of this problem, you should tell your attorney about it and incorporate the appropriate solution in your Living Trust . . . but only if you care. You may be the type of person who, like many of my clients, thinks their children are lucky to get anything during their lives or after their deaths. As one client said to me, "Mr. Condon, what planet did you come from? My kids should be bowing to me in gratitude on a daily basis for all the things I've paid for them. And now you think I should care that they will get mad after I die because I gave more to some and less to others? If they become that ungrateful, they can go screw themselves."

If this client speaks for you, then fine. There is no law that says you need to care about creating equity among your children. However, based on the vast number of times I have raised this issue with clients during my 30-year practice, this "I don't care" viewpoint is in the vast minority. Indeed, whenever I point out the insurmountable chasm of conflict that unequal lifetime gifts create among children in the inheritance arena, the typical reaction is, "I never really thought about that before. Let's explore this further."

However, even when we go exploring, it sometimes appears that no solution exists to equalize lifetime gifts. This is typified by a parent who makes a gift to a child that the child uses to purchase an asset that appreciates substantially by the time of the parent's death. The parent's other child wants equalization. But what amount will satisfy the other child? Not an amount equal to the value of the original gift, but an amount equal to the value of the appreciated asset! Unreasonable, but true!

Examples of this scenario abound. In one situation, my clients had two children, a son and a daughter. They told me that about 20 years before, they had given their son $50,000 to purchase a home for him and his wife. When I gave them the routine about how unequal lifetime gifts can adversely impact their children's sibling relationship, the husband said, like clockwork, "Gee, I never really thought about that before." Eventually, they agreed to leave their daughter $50,000 "off the top" with both their children splitting all their other Living Trust assets equally.

So far, so good.

Ten years later, both clients died and their son and daughter came to my office for advice on the administration of their parents' Living Trust. All was well until I said, "I just want to make sure you know that the daughter gets an extra $50,000 from the Living Trust. I advised them to put that provision in to make sure that she has the same amount that your parents gave to the son 20 years ago."

I remember how puffed up I was when I made that statement. I was very impressed with myself that I, like some superhero, had come to the aid of this family by resolving an otherwise elusive issue that could have insidiously destroyed that family had it not been recognized . . . by me!

But that balloon of pomposity was burst by the daughter, when she said to me: "Mr. Condon, what the hell were you thinking? My getting an extra $50,000 doesn't come close to making it fair. My brother took that $50,000 and used it to buy a $250,000 home. That's one-fifth of the purchase price. Twenty years later, his home is worth $750,000. That gift of $50,000 is now worth $150,000. If you had really thought it through with my parents correctly, you would have advised them that I should get an extra $150,000."

Once again, I stood corrected. Or rather, I sat there red-faced and corrected. Giving the daughter $50,000 20 years later was not equalization. If the daughter had also received $50,000 20 years before, she too might have had appreciated equity of $150,000.

The daughter attempted to prevail upon her brother the wisdom of giving up $100,000 of his inheritance to her to increase her specific bequest to $150,000. You can imagine what her brother said to her as he gesticulated to his sister with his middle finger. That was the end of a formerly close sibling relationship.

There is usually no difficulty in equalizing relatively small gifts that are used to fulfill a temporary need—wedding, medical emergency, automobile repair, attorney bills, and the like. However, equalizing gifts that are used to purchase appreciating assets is a completely different animal. As my father used to say, not every problem has a solution.

An Easier Pill to Swallow

Of course, you can resolve a disparity in lifetime gifts by leaving an extra amount of Living Trust assets to your "less-gifted" child. But, if you are not rich enough and the disparity is significant, it will be hard to stomach that attempt at equalization. In fact, I cannot recall any client who has been willing to leave a substantial sum to a "less-gifted" child to equalize the significant disparity that results when lifetime gifts are used to purchase assets that become highly appreciated.

In my mind, the only viable solution to this problem is the use of life insurance. That is, you arrange for your "less-gifted" child to own, and be the beneficiary of, an insurance policy on your life in the amount of the disparity. When you die, that child receives the death benefit, which will not be reduced by any tax. For many of my clients in circumstances similar to the son and daughter I have discussed in this example, equalization through life insurance has been an easier pill to swallow than simply an outright bequest of extra funds from the Living Trust to the "less-gifted" child. But for this son and daughter, no such solution was offered because the lawyer who advised their parents (me) did not recognize the problem.

Financial Advisor Alert

You probably have "pitched" life insurance to your clients as a way to ensure that the surviving spouse can maintain a comfortable standard of living . . . and to provide their children with sufficient funds to pay the federal estate tax (or replace the family wealth used to pay that tax). Now I have raised another use of life insurance you may not have previously considered—maintaining post-death family harmony. If you find your clients in this boat of significant gift disparity, make them aware they can use life insurance as the life preserver; that is, to equalize that disparity.

Separate but Unequal

Do you feel depressed? Have you had enough of the tales of spoiled children who you may feel have no right to squawk over unequal lifetime gifts? Have you had your fill of how your Living Trust can unintentionally create a chasm of conflict between your children? Too bad. I need to make you aware of one more common scenario in the inheritance arena that can effectively kill the relationship between your children.

And once again, it involves an inheritance that you thought was equal, but ultimately turns out not to be.

One of my clients had two sons and two apartment buildings of approximately the same value. I advised my client to leave the buildings to her sons in equal shares. But my client informed me that her sons never really got along and it would be a good thing for them not to co-own each property. That sounded good to me. Each would receive a roughly equal inheritance, and each would not require the involvement of the other in the management of their respective buildings.

I drafted a Living Trust that left Building One to one son and Building Two to the other. At the time of my client's death, both properties were of approximately equal value, and both sons were relatively happy with the allocation made by their mother's Living Trust.

The peace did not last long. Within a few years after their mother's death, Building One had escalated in value while the value of Building Two remained flat. Prior to this development, the brothers had a relationship that was, at best, lukewarm for the sake of their respective children. After the disparity occurred, it was all-out war between them. Even though the brother with Building One had no influence on the inheritance plan, the poorer brother with Building Two transferred his anger to his richer brother. Today, the children of both brothers do not really know each other, even though they live within blocks of each other.

The road to hell is paved with good intentions. What started off as my client's good intent resulted in intense jealousy. The ensuing battle was the last thing my client wanted for her children.

Take a lesson from this cautionary tale. Do not leave separate properties to separate children in your Living Trust. The economic circumstances that arise following your death could drive their values up or down, leaving your children with unequal inheritances, which will add nothing but conflict to their lives. Instead, leave your properties to your children in equal shares so they will share the upswings and downswings of each property equally.

17

Don't Make a Child Who Owes You Money a Debtor to Your Other Children

OR,

AN UNFORGIVEN AND UNPAID LOAN TO A CHILD CAN WREAK HAVOC AFTER YOUR DEATH

If you are like most of my clients, you have lent—or you will lend—money to one of your children. After all, it is very nice to help your children financially when they need money to better their lives by going to school, starting a new business, or buying a home. I speak from experience, because if my parents had not lent me money for law school, you would not have the pleasure of having me as your Living Trust advisor.

In most cases, however, a loan to a child becomes a gift to that child. Deep down, you know this. Why do you know this? Because every time you raise the subject of repayment with your debtor child, you receive a convenient excuse why he or she cannot come up with any money.

- "I had a bad month at the office."
- "The kids' orthodontist bills came in."
- "We needed to go on vacation." ("Needed"?)

- "I will have it for sure next month."
- "If I pay you, I won't have enough left to buy groceries, and I don't think you want your grandchildren to starve."

Then again, your debtor child might be the kind of person who has no problem telling you how it really is. I will never forget one family inheritance meeting with my clients and their three sons. My clients had lent $25,000 to one of their sons to help him dig out of a financial hole he had created. They had their son sign a promissory note that evidenced his promise to pay them back.

During that meeting, I presented the note to the debtor son and reminded him that his parents fully expected repayment of the loan. The son leaned closer to me and said, "That's not going to happen. I don't have it. I may never have it." With that, the debtor son got up from the table, walked to the office door, put his hand on the doorknob, opened the door, turned to us, and said with all the drama he could muster, "You want your money? Sue me!"

Are you going to sue your debtor child and become your child's judgment creditor? After you discover the long road to attain that status, you may not. To be a judgment creditor, you have to hire a lawyer; file a complaint; propound and respond to discovery requests (depositions, written questions); proceed with a trial; and win at trial. At that point, you have to collect on the amount the judge awards you, which involves more demands for payment and more lawyering. Ultimately, if you are not paid, you can force the sale of your child's house and get the ordered amount from the sale proceeds.

Aside from the fact that this process may take two to three years, can you actually see yourself foreclosing on the house in which your grandchildren live? If you value your relationship with your children and grandchildren, you will not.

What Else Can You Do to Get Your Money Back?

However, maybe you are like one client who wanted to sue his daughter-in-law. He lent money to his daughter-in-law to purchase a business, a boutique in a cutesy part of Los Angeles called

Larchmont where the patrons park diagonally to the curb. The business went belly-up because she did not treat it like a true business. For her, it was an expensive hobby.

Nonetheless, my client was of the mind that a deal was a deal. (Actually, he believed his daughter-in-law had snookered him from the beginning with her sincere-sounding promises to return the seed money to him.) He pressured his son to get his wife to pay him back. Days passed without any repayment. There was complete silence from the debtor camp, which gnawed at my client to no end. Ultimately, he came to my office to hire me to write threatening letters to his daughter-in-law.

Knowing that such letters would destroy that family, I came up with advice to help resolve the matter. I had previously established a Living Trust for that client in which his three children were left equal inheritances. I advised that he treat the loan to the daughter-in-law as an advance on the inheritance of her husband, the client's son.

The client adopted this advice, and I prepared an amendment that reduced the share of the Living Trust assets that would be distributed to the son after the client's death, and increased the shares to each of the other two children in an amount equal to the reduction. With this solution, the client's tension over the unpaid loan was alleviated and he dropped his threats of litigation.

I saved the family relationship. But enough patting myself on the back. Let's get back to the main point. Whether your debtor child gives you a transparent excuse or a bold statement, the fact remains that the loan you made to your child is not being repaid. And nonpayment of the loan will adversely impact your relationship with that child during your lifetime. If you insist on repayment in the face of a debtor child who just cannot—or will not—pay you back, you will no longer have a meaningful relationship with that child because, to him or her, it becomes too awkward to visit you, call you, or even take your calls.

Yes, you want your money, but your nonpaying debtor child dreads even the prospect of you mentioning repayment. If you insist on repayment, you will lose any substantive contact with that child, and your grandchildren from that child as well. In other words, when you lent money to your child in the first place, you may have imagined that you might not get paid back; but did you ever think it would lead to not seeing your grandchildren?

So what do you do? Quite simply, stop asking your debtor child about when payment will be forthcoming. Forget about being repaid. In my mind, your relationship with your child vastly outweighs your need for repayment. Of course, if you do not care how the loan affects your parent-child bond, you will disregard this advice. As my high school English teacher once said when describing the differences we occasionally had with one another: That's what makes a horse race.

You may also dismiss my advice of forgetting the loan if you are relying on those funds for your support. Fine. Go after it. But in your quest to get the money back, you will be met with busybodies butting into your private business, wagging their fingers, and saying to you with a self-righteous tone, "What were you thinking when you made the loan? If you couldn't afford to lose the money, you shouldn't have made the loan!" But truthfully, you should not have to withstand such admonishment. You are a parent. Helping your child is what you do. It's instinctive. It's hard to say no to a child who truly needs the financial assist.

Okay. Let's say you take my advice and stop mentioning the loan to your debtor son. He starts coming around again with his kids, and you consider yourself lucky to have dodged a bullet that potentially could have harmed your relationship with your child. Good for you.

However, I must make you aware that not mentioning the loan is not forgiving the loan. When you forgive a loan, you are canceling it and saying, in essence, the debtor does not have to pay you back. There is a tax consequence to forgiving a loan, which is that the amount of the loan you have forgiven is considered taxable income to the debtor, and the debtor will have to include that amount as income on his next income tax return.

Nonetheless, if you are planning to stop mentioning the loan, you might as well forgive the loan, because you will not be paid in either event. Although the forgiven amount is taxable income to your debtor child, I would rather a few extra income tax dollars be paid than see what happens to your family if you die with an unforgiven loan in your mix of Living Trust assets. Therefore, make sure that you sent the message, loud, clear, and in writing, that you consider the loan forgiven.

Consequences of the Unforgiven Loan

If you do not forgive the loan and you die with a child owing you money, that loan is an asset of your estate. It is a Living Trust asset. It is divided between your children just as your home, stocks, personal property, and cash are divided. The result is the somewhat absurd proposition that your debtor child ends up being a creditor to himself on his equal share of the unpaid loan. Your debtor child may be a nice guy, but he is not going to go through the motions of paying himself back.

However, guess who does want to be paid? Your other children! Your other children are now creditors to their debtor sibling. By not forgiving the loan, you have inadvertently created a money relationship between your children. It's no longer just a blood connection, but a blood *and* money connection.

Your creditor children may love their debtor sibling, but not to the point where it's going to cost them money. After the dust of administration of your Living Trust has been settled, your other children will inform their debtor sibling that the loan exists and they expect repayment of their shares. If payment is not made, they will casually remind him about the loan on occasions when they happen to get together. If payment still proves elusive, then comes the peppering of gentle reminders through phone calls and letters. If that fails to trigger payment, perhaps litigation will be the next step.

Put aside the issue of whether payment is forthcoming. Instead, focus on the harm this unpaid and unforgiven loan has caused to the family relationship. They are no longer siblings. They are litigants.

I will never forget the words spoken by one daughter as she berated her brother in my office after the deaths of their parents. She told him in no uncertain terms that she expected to receive from her brother her one-half share of the $50,000 loan owed by him to their parents under a promissory note he signed about 25 years earlier.

The brother did his best to ward off his sister's entreaties for payment. He said that his parents had forgiven the loan, but his sister pointed out that there was no evidence to back him up. The sister added, "If Dad and Mom had forgiven the loan, they would have ripped up the note. But here it is! It's a little dusty, but it's right in front of you." I noted that as she made this statement, she slid the promissory note on my desk directly in front of her brother.

The daughter was right. A claim by the debtor child that a loan was forgiven by parents' inaction, or by the simple lapse of time, means little to the creditor child who just wants her share of the outstanding obligation.

After the daughter had kindly pointed out that her brother's promissory note was right in front of him, he snapped and yelled, "Forget it! The statute of limitations has run out. It's over. You will never get a court to enforce that note!" The sister calmly responded, "We're not talking courtroom justice. This is family justice. You borrowed the money. You had use of that money for 25 years. If I had received $50,000 25 years ago, it would be worth something more than $50,000, but I didn't. And there is nothing to show that Dad and Mom forgave this note."

The son stormed out of the office, and the siblings never spoke to each other again. In no way is this scenario an isolated incident, as I have seen similar exchanges take place between debtor and creditor children over the issue of unforgiven loans, although not every situation ends with someone storming through the door.

Financial Advisor Alert

You will never know whether your clients are creditors to their children unless you ask. So ask away! Remember . . . recognizing the solution to any inheritance problem that can undermine family relationships is recognizing that problem in the first place. If your clients confirm that such a relationship exists, make inquiry as to whether their child will ever satisfy that debt. Don't settle for an opinion of optimism ("I'm sure he will one day"). If they "get real," they will likely conclude that they will never get paid back. Yes, there are exceptions with debtor children who faithfully repay their parents, but I have found them to be few and far between. Be prepared to discuss the family fallout that will likely occur over the unpaid debt—and the solutions that appear in the next section.

Resolving the Family Fallout over the "Forgiven" Loan That Wasn't Really Forgiven

Now that I have made you aware of the harm that can come to families in the inheritance arena over the issue of unpaid loans, what should you do to ameliorate that harm? Here are a few simple solutions.

- Forgive the loan you made to your debtor child during your lifetime with a written statement of forgiveness, and give each of your other children an amount equal to the forgiven loan.
- Forgive the loan you made to your debtor child during your lifetime with a written statement of forgiveness. Then, arrange for your other children to be the owners and beneficiaries of an insurance policy that will, when both you and your spouse are dead, pay to each of them an amount equal to the forgiven loan.
- In your Living Trust, provide that the unpaid balance of the loan to your debtor child is forgiven and leave each of your other children an amount equal to that unpaid balance.
- If you do not have sufficient assets to give (during your lifetime) or leave (after your death) an equivalent amount to your other children, then engage in the "That's Life in the Big City" plan, which is:

    First, forgive the loan you made to your debtor child during your lifetime with a written statement of forgiveness.

    Second, at some point conduct a family inheritance meeting where you announce that you are unable (or, if applicable, unwilling) to equalize with your other children.

Third, sit back and listen to your other children regale you with their opinions as to how unfair that treatment is.

Fourth, and finally, tell them that you would rather they be angry with you now than allow the unpaid loan issue to fester after your death in the inheritance arena to destroy their relationship with one another.

18

Do Not Leave Your Child an Outright Inheritance

OR,

I'M NOT KIDDING! DON'T LEAVE YOUR CHILD AN OUTRIGHT INHERITANCE

Your children do not want you to read this chapter, because it talks about putting controls on their inheritance. I don't blame them. No one wants to be limited in how they manage and spend their own money. You wouldn't want such control imposed on you. I certainly wouldn't want my parents to restrict the use of my inheritance.

Nonetheless, as your Living Trust coach, I am instructing—nay, demanding—that you never leave any child an outright inheritance of your Living Trust assets. I know that you have noticed such sweeping generalizations throughout this book, but you have never before heard me use the word *never*. But that's how adamant I am about this point, which I will make again, this time with capitals, bold type, and an exclamation point: **NEVER LEAVE ANY OF YOUR CHILDREN AN OUTRIGHT INHERITANCE!**

Financial Advisor Alert

DO NOT ALLOW YOUR CLIENTS TO LEAVE ANY OF THEIR CHILDREN AN OUTRIGHT INHERITANCE! If your clients' Living Trust leaves their child's inheritance share "outright and free of trust," then throw the book at them—this book, and as it flies from your hand, instruct them to read Chapter 18.

The reason that you do not want to leave your children an outright inheritance is this: If you leave your children an outright inheritance, the money and property in your Living Trust—the family money that took you a lifetime of hard work to acquire—will be lost to the problems your children face in their lives.

What kind of problems? I ceased long ago being surprised at the number of problems your children have, or will have, that pose a risk of loss to their inheritance:

- Divorce
- Remarriage
- Addiction
- Bankruptcy
- Income tax trouble
- Creditors
- Financial immaturity
- Squandering
- Mismanagement
- Malpractice claims
- Psychological illness
- Incompetency
- Eccentricity
- Incapacity
- Compulsory tithing to charity
- Contribution to crazy cult
- Shrewish/nagging spouses
- Medical bills
- And many more

Here's the deal. When you and your spouse are dead and your after-death agent transfers your Living Trust assets to your children, your money and property are no longer your money and property. They are your children's money and property, and they become subject to the winds of your children's fates.

You did not work 40 or 50 years so that all that you have been blessed with ends up with your son's bankruptcy trustee, your daughter's ex-husband, your son's drug dealer, or your daughter's judgment creditors. That would kill you . . . even though you are already dead. No, you want to be certain that your lifetime's accumulations ultimately end up with your grandchildren.

I'm not one to presume how you feel about your grandchildren, but I am going to do so anyway. I am treating you just like the judge in my divorce who said to me, in essence, "Mr. Condon, I'm not holding you to a higher standard of knowledge simply because you are an attorney who should know better, but I am."

Your grandchildren are the lights of your life. You like your children, but you love your grandchildren. You may see your grandchildren every day, intermittently, not as much as you'd like, or never. They may be golden to you, or a royal pain in your butt. Whatever the feeling, you cannot deny that you quietly take some pride—a modicum or a lot—that they'll walk the earth for you long after you're in the earth. Your bloodline continues with them, and you want your assets to continue with them as well.

I know this sounds like the sickly-sweet romantic musings of a former UCLA English literature major (class of 1983—go Bruins!), which may completely turn you off. However, this is how the vast majority of my clients feel about leaving their Living Trust assets. They, and by extension, you, want the Living Trust assets to ultimately end up with the ultimate dividends of your life. I almost dare you not to think about your grandchildren when putting together your Living Trust.

But your grandchildren will not receive your Living Trust assets if they are diverted from your bloodline because of some problem that arose in your children's lives, which is the point of this really huge chapter.

So what is the solution to this significant issue in the inheritance arena? You cannot leave your children their inheritance outright. Instead, you have to incorporate protection into your Living Trust to shield their inheritance from their problems. Haven't you taken steps to protect your money and property during your lifetime? Now you need to think about taking measures to protect your money and property once it's in the hands of your children, without unnecessarily limiting their use of those assets.

The protection I am talking about is the protection trust, a term that my father and I coined that swept the nation for about 12 minutes when our first inheritance planning book was published way back in 1996. The concept of the protection trust can best be conveyed with this very clever analogy using medieval terminology.

Your children's inheritance is the *castle*. They can live in the castle. They can sell the castle and buy a new castle. They can pretty much do what they want in and with the castle.

Your children's problems are the *invaders*. The invaders want to burst in and take over the castle.

The protection trust is the moat surrounding the castle. The moat prevents the invaders from overrunning the castle so your children still have the castle to use and enjoy for the rest of their lives.

When your children die, the castle will be delivered—intact—to your grandchildren.

There are several types of protection trusts. There are those that offer maximum protection and completely control your child's inheritance, and those that provide minimum protection and allow your child unfettered access and management. The type you should use in your Living Trust depends on the kind of problem your child has now, or may have in the future, that poses a risk of loss to the inheritance.

For example, and continuing with the castle analogy, if the invaders are your daughter's alcoholism or drug addiction, it is a lock that the castle will be overrun. It's guaranteed. As your children peer through the windows, they can see the invaders waiting and hovering, ready to invade the place at any moment. That's what invaders do—they invade. So, the moat you build is going to be seriously wide enough to ensure that the invaders never, ever get over the drawbridge to ransack the castle.

But, what if your daughter is a normal person with no substance abuse problem? In that case, your children do not see any invaders when they look outside the castle. They're not there. They don't exist. Yet, there is the concern that, someday, they may show up and do their waiting, hovering, and invading thing. They are *possible invaders*: the possibility that your Living Trust assets will end up out of your bloodline because your daughter's excellent marriage may one day turn into a heated divorce where every issue is a battle; the possibility that your now-responsible daughter may turn out to be a ne'er-do-well whose only job in life is waiting for you to die so she can inherit. In such cases, the expense and hassle of building a wide moat to protect the castle from possible invaders seems extreme and unnecessary when a smaller moat may suffice to do the job.

Enough of this medieval analogy. My children are fond of saying that I often take something that I find clever or amusing and run it into the ground with overuse. The point is, there are many types of protection trusts, and the one you use is absolutely dependent on the type of problem you are protecting against. I can summarize them in four categories, starting with the type that offers the least protection and progressing to the one that guarantees protection.

Financial Advisor Alert

Nothing instigates an ostrich head-hiding response more than conversations about after-death wealth transfer issues. Sure, people intellectually understand they won't live forever and can't take their money with them. Still . . . the idea of their hard-earned assets ending up with their children? The same children they may barely trust with the family checkbook? That can be a tough one for even the most practical and business-minded people to wrap their mind around.

So never assume that your clients have given much (or any) thought to their children owning and managing the "family wealth." It's your function to help your clients move past the death horizon. You have to point out to your clients that their assets will one day be in their children's hands and they have to take protective measures now in their Living Trust to ensure that those assets don't slip through those hands. And that is what this chapter is all about.

Category One: The Protection Trust That Offers Only a Hope of Protection—the Transparent Trust

I call this protection trust *transparent* because the protection it offers is, theoretically, zero. In fact, it's like not having any protection trust at all.

This is how the transparent trust works. Your Living Trust, in the part that says who gets what, should state that when you and your spouse are both dead, the Living Trust assets will pour into another trust. This trust is not established by some separate document that exists outside your Living Trust. It is a trust within your Living Trust—a bucket within your bucket.

The bucket that receives the Living Trust assets is the transparent trust. The transparent trust is like your Living Trust. It states who gets the income from the assets that are poured into it, who gets the principal, when the principal can be dipped into and for what purpose, who can wheel and deal with the assets, who gets the assets when the beneficiary dies, and so on. Except . . . the transparent trust is not for you; rather, it is for your children. Stated another way, the transparent trust becomes a Living Trust for your child's inheritance that shall be held, managed, and distributed for the benefit of your child in accordance with the instructions set forth in the transparent trust.

So how liberal are these instructions? Very liberal. You will now see why we call it the transparent trust.

Who gets the income from the assets generated by the transparent trust? Your child.

Who gets the principal of the assets in the transparent trust? Your child.

Who is the trustee—the manager, the wheeler-dealer—of the transparent trust? Your child.

For what purpose may the trustee (your child) dip into the principal? For any purpose whatsoever: support, health, education, maintenance, comfort, entertainment, travel—you name it.

When may the trustee (your child) dip into the principal of the transparent trust? Any time, any day, any season.

Who gets the unused principal of the transparent trust when your child dies? Anyone whom your child selects; but if no selection is made, then to his or her children (your grandchildren).

Are there any limitations on how the trustee (your child) can wheel and deal with the assets? No. Sell them. Manage them. Exchange them. Throw them in the street.

Is there any restriction on your child from giving any of the assets of the transparent trust to any person at all? No. Your child can give away the assets to, if he or she wants, the next person he or she sees walking down the sidewalk.

Don't these instructions sound familiar? They should, because they are the same type of extremely liberal instructions found in your Living Trust, which speak to your ability to spend and manage your assets any way you see fit. Remember when I said the Living Trust is you . . . you are the Living Trust? The same can be said for the transparent trust for your child. Your child is the transparent trust . . . the transparent trust is your child.

The transparent trust is as close to outright ownership as ownership can be. In fact, it is just like outright ownership. Okay, but now your big question is: What good is it?

Funny you should ask. Even though the transparent trust is like not having any trust it all, I advise my clients on a daily basis to incorporate it in their Living Trusts, because it accomplishes five important goals.

1. On your child's death, the transparent trust assets will automatically go to your grandchildren without probate (if your child has not done anything to change the inheritance instructions).
2. Leaving your assets to your child's transparent trust serves as a constant reminder of your wish to keep the family assets in the family, and not commingled in the joint assets of your child and his or her spouse.
3. The transparent trust provides your child with an excuse to say no to a spouse who insists that the inheritance be placed in their joint names. (Your daughter-in-law: "Honey, if you love me, you'll put your inherited property in our joint account."

Your son: "Gee, honey, I would do it in a second, but I can't because my parents left it in trust for the grandchildren.")
4. The transparent trust becomes a Living Trust for your child's inherited separate property. As a result, you have saved your child the expense and hassle of hiring an attorney to establish an Inherited Separate Property Living Trust.
5. If the assets in the transparent trust include real property, and if your child sells or refinances that real property, the title company will not require the signature of the spouse on any sale or loan documents before issuing a title insurance policy.

This fifth reason is such a great benefit of the transparent trust that it requires a bit of exposition so I can make sure you understand it. As your Living Trust coach, that's my job.

The function of the title company is to insure title to real property. The issuance of a title insurance policy is required before any bank or other financial institution will lend money to an owner or purchaser of real property. Let me say it this way: There are three certainties in this life: death, taxes, and no sale or refinance of real property without a title insurance policy.

Before the title company issues the policy, its advisory title officer (ATO)—the head title guy—will want to be 104 percent certain that the owner of the property is, well, the owner of the property. Fine. The ATO looks at the history of all the recorded documents relating to the property to make sure that the person selling or refinancing the property is the real and true owner of the property.

The ATO determines that the person doing the selling or refinancing is the owner of the property. Lovely. There should be no problem getting the title company to issue the title insurance policy. **But, if the seller is married, the title company will not issue that policy unless the spouse of the seller signs all the selling or refinancing documents**—even if the spouse is not on the deed, and even if the spouse's name does not show up anywhere in the recorded documents in the property's chain of title!

When the seller approaches his spouse for her signature, will she sign? Perhaps they just had a big argument that morning. Perhaps she relishes the idea of road-blocking the transaction out of some warped notion of vengeance. Perhaps she wants to have an attorney review all the documents of the transaction. Whatever the reason, it is entirely possible that she may not sign. If she withholds her signature, good-bye sale or refinance.

Why is the seller's spouse's participation necessary? Because the ATO always presumes that the spouse obtained some interest in the property through the marriage laws of the state in which the property is located. For example, in California, it is entirely possible that a spouse's separate inherited property can be "transmutated" into the community property of both spouses, under certain circumstances, which gives the owner's spouse an interest in that property. Does the ATO know if such circumstances exist? No, and unless he becomes a fly on the wall in their house, he will never know. So, the ATO will want the spouse's signature on the documents, just to be on the safe side.

As the third-grade teacher of my daughter, Hayley, pointed out to her so many years ago: Life is not fair. Your child will echo this refrain when he learns that he cannot sell or refinance his inherited separate property without first getting his spouse to sign the documents. But, if he inherits the property in a transparent trust, his spouse's participation is rendered moot. For this reason, as well as the other four reasons cited, the answer to your big question that you asked two pages ago ("What good is the transparent trust?") is: plenty good!

If your children are normal, you should use your Living Trust to leave their inheritance to them in their respective transparent trusts. In the context of the inheritance arena, a normal child is one who is not mired in addiction, divorce, financial immaturity, creditors, or any of the other problems that I alluded to earlier in this chapter that pose a clear and present risk of loss to the inheritance. You know, the child you boast of as a "good kid" to your tablemates at your community's annual dinner dance.

Financial Advisor Alert

For the reasons given previously, advise your clients that their Living Trust inheritance instructions should create, at the bare minimum, transparent trusts for each of their children. Will you get resistance? Probably.

Allocating an inheritance share to a trust implies a need to prevent a "problem child" from blowing the dough—and they likely don't have such a problem child. That may be true; but still . . . don't cave! Blow past that defense with a recitation of the benefits of the transparent trust as set forth above. If they are truly listening to you, they will easily realize that their child is in full control of the transparent trust's assets . . . and there is absolutely no downside to leaving their child's share in that form.

Category Two: The Protection Trust That Is Just a Tad Less Liberal Than the Transparent Trust—the Self-Directed Irrevocable Protection Trust

The self-directed irrevocable protection trust (SIPT) has such a boring acronym. It does not even form a word that can be used to help remember this concept.

I need an acronym for the self-directed irrevocable protection trust that, for me, serves as a shorthand way to refer to this type of protection trust and, for you, creates an amusing mnemonic device to help you steer through this discussion. A little bit of cheating by transposing two of the letters and . . . voilà—you have the SPIT.

This SPIT is similar to the transparent trust, but only up to a point.

Like the transparent trust, the SPIT is created in the "who gets what" portion of your Living Trust. It is a bucket that receives your Living Trust assets after your death. The assets in the SPIT will be held, managed, and distributed for the benefit of your child in accordance with the instructions set forth in the SPIT.

Like the transparent trust, the instructions in the SPIT give your child liberal use and access to the assets in the SPIT. Your child gets all the income and principal, can dip into the principal at any time, and takes on the role of trustee, the wheeler-dealer who can manage and invest them in any way he or she sees fit.

Like the transparent trust, the SPIT is used for your child who, in the context of inheritance planning, is considered normal—that is, someone who does not possess any problems that automatically subject your child's inheritance to a significant risk of loss.

So much for the similarities. Unlike the transparent trust, you can build whatever limitations you wish into the matrix of the SPIT. Here are the five main differences between these two types of protection trusts.

1. In the transparent trust, your child may dip into principal for any reason. However, in the SPIT, you can forbid your child from using principal for any purpose you disapprove of. For example, if you do not want your child spending her SPIT assets on entertainment, travel, or other activities that you, the fuddy-duddy, consider frivolous and nonproductive, you can insert a provision stating that she cannot use the assets for those purposes.

2. In the transparent trust, your child can dip into the principal and give away any asset to any person at any time. However, in the SPIT, your child can make no such gifts, and can dip into the principal only for the specific purposes you set forth.

3. In the transparent trust, your child has the ability to control who receives the assets after her death. If she wants to leave them to persons or charities other than your grandchildren, she is free to do so. However, in the SPIT, you control who receives the assets after your child's death. When your child dies, the assets in the SPIT must be distributed to the persons whom you have named in the SPIT as the backup beneficiaries.

4. In the transparent trust, your child has the ability to revoke the arrangement. She can simply take the assets out of the transparent trust and own them outright. However, in the SPIT, your child has no power to cancel the trust. The SPIT is irrevocable and will last for the rest of your child's life.

5. The transparent trust and the SPIT send two different messages. The message of the transparent trust is: "Here you go. Enjoy. Do as you please. It is our hope you will use your inheritance properly and leave whatever remains on your death to your children. But that is up to you. We don't want to tie your hands as to how to use your money."

   All in all, this is a very lovely message that the transparent trust has been crafted for the sole benefit of your child. The SPIT, however, is created for the benefit of *both* you and your child. Your child benefits by having access to her inheritance as trustee. You benefit by obtaining some assurance that your child will not squander, mismanage, or divert your money and property. So, the message of the SPIT is this: "We trust you with your inheritance. . .sort of. We just can't die leaving you with unfettered control of your inheritance. We need to know that we've done all we can to nudge you into using your inheritance properly without tying your hands too much. So we are going to leave you in control of your inheritance with a few limitations so we can die with a bit more certainty that you will do the right thing."

The SPIT gives your child the same five advantages that are offered by the transparent trust. The SPIT avoids probate of the assets when your child dies; the SPIT ties a mental string around your child's finger to remind her that inherited property is precious property; the SPIT gives your child ammunition against her spouse who seeks to become a co-owner of her inherited assets; the SPIT becomes your child's Inherited Separate Property Living Trust; and the SPIT allows your child to sell or refinance her inherited real property without having to ask her spouse for his signature.

However, unlike the transparent trust, the SPIT gives you some assurance that your child will not improperly (as that word is defined by you) use and distribute the assets while still giving your child the use of, and access to, her inheritance. As trustee of the SPIT, your child is the one in charge of the assets, but must act in accordance with the limitations you have incorporated into its terms and provisions. The SPIT is your ghostly presence looking over your child's shoulder, making certain that she is not wasting or squandering her inheritance, not giving it away to her bully of a husband who, according to you, married her only for money (your money), and not having the assets go to anyone after her death other than her children.

However, a problem with the SPIT is that your ghostly presence may be the only factor keeping your child on the straight and narrow, and to your child, that may not be a very compelling factor. With your child as the only trustee of her SPIT, there is no police officer looking over her shoulder to ensure that she is not using the principal of the SPIT in a way that contravenes its prohibitions. Your child is her own SPIT police.

Financial Advisor Alert

Another problem is that the SPIT assets are subject to a higher income tax rate than assets left outright or in a transparent trust. Still, in my mind, the benefits of your clients' leaving the inheritance to a SPIT as described in this chapter greatly outweigh the extra tax dollars.

As trustee, your child is legally bound to adhere to the terms and provisions of the SPIT as you set them forth in your Living Trust. It is against the law for your daughter—or any trustee—to manage a trust in a manner that directly conflicts with the terms of that trust. The attorney that your child hires for advice on the distribution of your Living Trust assets will send this message loud and clear. In my experience, that warning is usually sufficient for most trustees to keep them on the straight and narrow. Nonetheless, with the child's knowledge that she is her own SPIT police, the temptation to deviate from the SPIT instructions is ever present.

There is, however, one group of folks who are interested in the SPIT activities of your child: the backup beneficiaries. These are the persons whom you have named in your Living Trust as the recipients of the SPIT assets after your child's death—most likely, your grandchildren. In legal parlance, they are the *remaindermen*. Your grandchildren inherit whatever *remains* in the SPIT after your child dies. With such an expectancy interest in the SPIT, they have a direct and vested connection to the goings-on of the SPIT during your child's life. The more your child deviates from the built-in limitations, the less your grandchildren will receive after your child's death.

Will your grandchildren monitor their parent's activities as trustee of the SPIT? Probably not. Chances are, your grandchildren will not become aware they have the right to receive information about their parent's administration and management of the SPIT until after the death of that parent.

In light of the possibility that your child will use the SPIT assets for prohibited purposes, what can you do to ensure that your child does stay on the right path? Really, the only solution is to name a co-trustee—a co-manager—of the SPIT. With a co-trustee, your child must obtain the co-trustee's signature on every transaction . . . every payment of income, every dip into principal, every deposit and withdrawal, and every wheel and deal. The co-trustee is your backstop from the grave to keep your child from going astray.

But, ask yourself: Do you really want your normal child to have to obtain a third party's consent to use her own inheritance when the only risk of loss to be minimized is your child's possible improper use of the inheritance? You know your child better than I do. Maybe she is the kind of person who does not show any backbone to pressure imposed on her by her spouse, and you project that she will succumb to his entreaties to give him a portion of her inheritance. Maybe your child has always thrown away paychecks in pursuit of wine, song, and shopping, and you conjecture that she will never become financially mature to the point where she uses funds only for her support, health, education, and other permissible purposes. If the risk of loss or diversion is legitimate and probable—even to the point of being tangible— then the co-trustee arrangement of the SPIT is an excellent tool to combat that risk.

Financial Advisor Alert

There is a compromise to this "one trustee vs. co-trustee" battle. A SPIT with your child and a third person as co-trustees can, in essence, provide that only your child's signature is required to engage in "minimal" transactions such as writing checks for normal day-to-day needs (e.g., rent payments, mortgage payments, grocery bills, physician co-payments) while "big-ticket" activities like investment decisions or house purchasing require both co-trustees' signatures. For your clients who are on the fence about whether to involve a third party in the co-management and control of their child's SPIT, this can prove to be an agreeable middle ground.

However, if the reason for a rule does not apply, then don't apply the rule. If your normal child has not shown any signs of problems that traditionally subject money to risk of loss, then the appointment of a co-trustee of the SPIT is too much control from beyond the grave. To involve a third party in the management and control of your child's inheritance is like punishing your child for bad behavior that she has not done. It's like Moe in one particular Three Stooges episode where he slaps Curly, who, by all objective standards, did not do anything to justify such abuse. In fact, Curly was just standing around. In complete shock and surprise, Curly yells, "What did you do that for? I wasn't doing nothing'!" With all confidence, Moe replies, "That was in case you do something wrong later and I ain't around to see it."

Never before and never again will you read a Three Stooges analogy in a book on the Living Trust. I should be feted for such an obscure and absurd reference—or, if you have no sense of humor, disbarred. Nonetheless, I willingly take that bullet for you, the reader, in order to drive home this point that you should not appoint a co-trustee of your normal child's SPIT out of the mere concern that she may possibly engage in behavior that is antithetical to the limitations you set forth.

Category Three: The Protection Trust That Gives Control of Your Child's Inheritance to a Third Party— the Third-Party Irrevocable Protection Trust

I require an acronym for the third-party irrevocable protection trust, because there is no way I am going to write "third-party irrevocable protection trust" ad nauseam. But, there is nothing fun and exciting that can be done with TPIPT. So, I will call it the PUPPET, for two reasons.

First, the word *puppet* has some of the same letters as TPIPT. Second, the word *puppet* aptly describes how your child may perceive herself in relation to the third party that you put in control of her inheritance. To your child, this means she is the puppet of the oppressive third-party puppet master who controls her (purse) strings.

As with the transparent trust and the SPIT, the PUPPET is an entity that you establish in your Living Trust. The terms and provisions of the PUPPET are just words on paper until you and your spouse are both dead. When that occurs, the PUPPET springs into existence and your child's inheritance from your Living Trust will funnel into the PUPPET, where it will be held, managed, and administered by a third-party trustee (manager) whom you've selected in your Living Trust.

The PUPPET states that income generated by the assets will be added to the principal, and that the third party must pay to your child, or apply for her benefit, so much of the principal as the third party determines is reasonable and necessary for any of the following:

- Your child's education
- The purchase or refurbishing of your child's principal residence
- The establishment of, or investment in, a business that will constitute your child's primary livelihood
- The development of a prudent personal investment program for your child
- Your child's support
- Your child's support in the event of her physical or mental incapacity
- Your child's health
- The health, support, and education of any of your child's own children

It is important to point out the words *must pay* in the paragraph preceding this laundry list of permissible payouts. That means the third party cannot randomly withhold the PUPPET assets from your child. If the third party determines that your child (or her children) has any of the needs described in the list, the third party *must* pay for those needs from PUPPET assets.

The third party can distribute the funds to your child, who will, in turn, use them to pay her supplier of goods and services, such as her physician, pharmacist, grocer, or landlord. However, if the third party determines there is a significant risk that your child will not properly apply the funds for those needs, the third party can pay your child's suppliers on her behalf.

The PUPPET may last for the rest of your child's life, unless you build in certain conditions that, if presented, will operate to terminate the PUPPET and cause the third party to hand over the PUPPET assets directly to your child. I discuss these conditions further on in this chapter.

When your child dies, the PUPPET assets will be distributed to the backup beneficiaries whom you named in your Living Trust. Your child has no power to instruct the third party to leave the PUPPET assets to any other beneficiary.

Your child has no right to dictate terms to the third party. She cannot make any demands on when the third party makes distributions to her and how much those distributions will be. The third party will conduct an independent investigation of your child's needs and make an objective determination of what those needs are—and what they are not—and then pay accordingly.

As you can see, the PUPPET is fairly restrictive. I say "fairly" because it is way less limiting than the protection trust I discuss in the fourth category, which, to me, is the neutron bomb of protection trusts. But that comparison is of little consolation to your child who, for all she knows, must capitulate to third-party control of her inheritance for the rest of her life.

In the understatement of the year, the decision to incorporate the controlling PUPPET into your Living Trust is not a casual one. We need to carefully examine the circumstances that justify the PUPPET. In other words, let's take a look at your child and talk about whether the problem she possesses justifies such a restrictive measure.

As you read the remainder of this section, it will be readily apparent that the success or failure of the PUPPET is seriously dependent on the person or entity you select as the third party who holds, manages, and administers the PUPPET for your child's benefit. I discuss the issues and factors that should govern your decision on the selection of the third party in Chapter 20.

Your Underage Child

Your child cannot receive an outright inheritance (not even in a transparent trust or a SPIT) if she is a minor at the time of your death. What were your money-managing skills like when you were in your teens? Nonexistent? So were mine.

It is self-evident that your minor child cannot manage and control her inheritance. Perhaps she will not have any financial maturity until she is in her late 20s or early 30s. As a result, you need to incorporate a PUPPET into your Living Trust that appoints a third party to control and manage your child's inheritance until she reaches an age that you designate. When she hits that designated age, the third party will turn over the PUPPET assets to your daughter outright either in a transparent trust or in a SPIT, depending on which device you choose.

What age should be the designated age when the turnover takes place? This decision is not based on any legal standard. It is whatever age you determine.

So again, what age? If I am drafting your Living Trust, I will put down whatever age you tell me. But if you are like most of my clients, you will not have a clue as to which age to select, so you will ask for my opinion, which is this: Usually age 25 seems appropriate. Why? Because as I get older, the young seem younger, and I cannot help but equate youth to financial immaturity. And to me, 25 seems to be the time of life when the young put away the spoils of youth and focus on the conventional lifestyle of career, family, and service to community. Thus, I will recommend that 25 be the age that you designate as the turnover age.

However, here comes another big question: What happens when your child reaches the designated age and the third party determines that, by all objective standards, she has a problem that poses a significant risk of loss to the PUPPET assets?

For example, when you established your Living Trust, your child was 16 and, by all accounts, a model child. Good grades. Fairly popular, with nice friends. Productive. Active in athletics. She was the type of young person others look at with envy and say, "I wish she was my kid." Then, the unthinkable happens and you and your spouse die in a common accident, leaving your now 20-year-old child with a substantial inheritance. Pursuant to your Living Trust, her inheritance is funneled to a PUPPET that will be held by a third party to spend and manage on her behalf until she reaches the designated age of 25. So far, so good (not that your untimely death is a good thing).

Your death, however, becomes the catalyst for your child's tragic downfall. She becomes aimless and directionless. Her grades decline. She withdraws into a shell. She suffers an emotional pain that she finds paralyzing. She attempts to mask that pain just so she can walk out the door. She begins with alcohol, then resorts to drugs. By the time she reaches 25, she is an addict. She calls the PUPPET third party and demands that she receive outright control of her inheritance.

The third party will not want to turn over the PUPPET assets to an addict. But will he have a choice? Yes he will, but *only* if the PUPPET gives the third party the power to postpone distribution of the assets if the third party perceives a compelling reason for that postponement.

In the Living Trusts I prepare, I always include such a provision, which states, in essence, that the third party shall have the power to postpone the distribution of any part of the principal or income to your child if the third party determines that there is a compelling reason to postpone distribution, such as your child's addiction to illegal drugs, alcohol, or any controlled substance; your child's serious disability, pending divorce, potential financial difficulty, or apparent inability to wisely manage the funds to be distributed; a serious tax disadvantage in making such distribution; or similar substantial cause.

Accordingly, the termination of the PUPPET may be postponed, and a postponement of any distribution may be continued from time to time, up to and including the entire lifetime of your child.

Without this safety net, the third party would have no choice but to turn over the PUPPET assets to your now-addicted child. I have encountered many situations where third parties had to sign over the PUPPET assets to beneficiaries despite knowing that the funds were at serious risk of dissipation, but still had no power to withhold or defer distribution, because the beneficiaries had reached the designated ages.

Although I am spending many pages discussing the PUPPET in the context of protecting your minor child's inheritance, I also want to reassure you that this discussion will, most likely, never apply in your situation. In the 20 years I have practiced law, and in my father's 45-year practice, I do not recall any occasion where both parents died simultaneously leaving minor children. More typical is one parent dying and leaving a surviving parent. Nonetheless, if you have children who are minors, I do not discourage you from pursuing the PUPPET plan in your Living Trust so that you have made the proper arrangement for the protection of your children's inheritance in the unlikely event that they are still minors on your death.

Financial Advisor Alert

The PUPPET should also include a provision that dictates what happens to the PUPPET's assets if your client's child dies before she attains the "turnover" age (which I have assumed in this chapter to be 25). It's difficult for your clients to think of their child dying young; but you and I both know that tragedies befall. The typical backup beneficiary provision names a "backup" trustee to manage the PUPPET assets for the children of their deceased child; and if that deceased child dies without children, then the backup trustee distributes the PUPPET assets to backup beneficiaries, such as your clients' other children.

Your Addicted Child

During the life of you and/or your spouse, I cannot help you alleviate the burden imposed on you by your addicted child, as you are probably the person walking this earth who has the most motivation to protect him from himself. I can only advise you on how your Living Trust assets should be utilized after your death for your addicted child so they are protected for him, and from him.

The most clear-cut of all problems in the inheritance arena is planning for the addicted child. You love your addicted child; but you just don't love what he does. You don't want to deprive your addicted child of his rightful share. You simply want to ensure that his inheritance is not used to feed his addiction.

For certainty that your addicted child's inheritance does not end up with his drug supplier, you must leave his share of the Living Trust assets in the PUPPET. With this method, your addicted child's inheritance will be held, managed, and spent by the third party for your addicted child's benefit for the rest of his life. When your addicted child dies, the third party will distribute the PUPPET to the backup beneficiaries you have named in the PUPPET.

There is only one issue about the PUPPET in the context of the addicted child that needs discussion. That is, should the PUPPET change if your addicted child changes? Although an addict is thought to be an addict for life, it is entirely possible that your addicted child, somehow, could miraculously kick his addiction after your death and sober up to the point that he no longer poses a risk to his inheritance.

This kind of miracle can happen. Out of my many clients who have an addicted child, I have witnessed the precious few occasions where the child cleaned up and became financially responsible after his parents' deaths. But these occurrences are, unfortunately, rare. That's why they are called miracles.

I have stated previously in this book that I am against the Tyranny of Unjustified Lifetime Control. I realize that, by all objective standards, your addicted child may never attain complete normalcy, and that he should never get his hands on his inheritance. In that respect, lifetime control of his inheritance through the PUPPET is justified. Nonetheless, I believe the third party should be allowed to terminate the PUPPET if your addicted child recovers, even if it would take a miracle for that to occur. Thus, I advise you to build hope into the PUPPET: a plan that can help in that recovery by offering your addicted child the opportunity to obtain control of his inheritance.

This inheritance plan of hope starts out with provisions that instruct the third party to use the PUPPET assets similarly to how you have spent money for your addicted child: making payment to the landlord for rent; making payment to the grocery store and restaurants for food; making payment for all other expenses for his necessities of life; and perhaps giving some money directly to your addicted child for pocket money, but not enough to provide a source to feed his addiction.

The plan then gives your addicted child the promise of acquiring more independent control of the PUPPET assets if he recovers. To your addicted child, the prospect of gaining access to his inheritance may become a powerful motivator to stop using drugs. Then again, perhaps he is so far gone that his entire motivation in life is just to do whatever it takes to get his next fix. No matter. This is the plan of hope, and hope is not self-executing. If you hope to achieve a result, you increase the odds of achieving that result by first laying down the appropriate groundwork.

Now for the hard part—laying down the groundwork. These are the standards in the PUPPET by which recovery is measured. These standards are completely dependent on the circumstances involving your addicted child and your attitude about how strict the standards should be. These standards of recovery must be drafted carefully, because a mistake could result in your still-addicted child gaining complete control of his inheritance. In fact, the specter of this kind of failure haunts me whenever I am charged with the responsibility of putting these standards on paper that someone, years in the future, must interpret and act upon. The standards could include one, some, or all of the following:

- Recovery is determined solely by the third party based on the third party's own observations.
- Recovery is determined by letters from two licensed psychiatrists who have no relationship, by blood or marriage, to your addicted child or to each other.
- Recovery is determined by a private investigator hired by the third party to investigate and examine your addicted child's addiction status.
- Recovery is determined by a judicial officer (a judge) sitting in a court of competent jurisdiction (in an area near where

your addicted child resides) who bases his decision on all or any of the aforementioned opinions or reports.
- Recovery is determined by the third party after receiving the results of drug tests commissioned by the third party that show that your addicted child has been drug-free for a required period of time that you designate in the PUPPET.

On a few occasions, I have drafted provisions that require that the third party shall turn over the PUPPET assets to an addicted child when he reaches an older or elderly status (e.g., 65, 70, 75). Although this seems antithetical to inheritance risk management, I assume that if an addicted person has not died before reaching those age categories, he has kicked, or at least controlled, his addiction. Perhaps this is too casual an assumption to make; but ask yourself: When was the last time you saw an old addict?

Your Financially Immature Child

The financially immature child is your child who is normal and conventional and who is beyond the age of majority or close to the age I would normally designate for receiving outright control of money, but you perceive that the child is not quite ready to take over and be put in control of her inheritance.

- You harbor some doubt about her ability to manage money based on an aspect of her lifestyle of which you disapprove or find distasteful.
- You feel lukewarm about the notion of her coming into control of the family money.
- You feel she is on the right track to financial maturity, but has not just yet arrived at the final station.
- You perceive she is simply too immature to handle money.

You may notice that each of these definitions of the financially immature child starts with the word *you*. *You* harbor. *You* feel. *You* perceive. I point this out because your definition of financial immaturity may be based on *your* standards that may not be consistent with the financial realities of modern-day life. The last thing you want to do is control your child's inheritance with a PUPPET if such control is unjustified.

For example, you come to me and say, "Mr. Condon, our daughter has a nice job, but she refuses to get married, and she spends all her money on the high life. My God, she just bought a new car, and my wife and I didn't get a new car until our 25th wedding anniversary. We've got to do something, or after we're gone she's going to spend our money into the ground!"

If I hear you make such a statement (which I hear all the time from my World War II/Greatest Generation clients), I am not hearing words that realistically connote financial immaturity that justifies the use of a PUPPET. That is not a description of someone who is out of control and frittering away money on frivolities. Using some very superficial and presumptive bedside psychology, you are looking at your daughter's spending habits through a window from another time . . . when you walked to school uphill in the driven snow and uphill again when you walked back home, and when spending money on anything other than the necessities of life was near-heresy. Your generational perspective has caused you to misinterpret your child's spending habits as those associated with a spendthrift.

And delving more into your psyche, which I am abjectly unqualified to do, are you not a little bit jealous of your child? Jealous of her early access to material things when you had to struggle to find money for those purchases? Jealous of her freedom from the shackles of conventional married life while you stayed on the oftentimes boring straight-and-narrow chamber-of-commerce path?

However, you may take offense at my attempt to assess your child's financial behavior from afar. That would not be an invalid response. You certainly know your child better than I do. I am not a psychologist or psychiatrist. All I can do is rely on the answers I receive during my interrogation of you and offer my opinion based on the sum total of my experience in dealing with families in the inheritance arena. If you persevere in your view of your child's character, I will concur and draft your Living Trust accordingly.

Financial Advisor Alert

You will be the one who ultimately determines whether your clients are correct in their assessment of their child's financial maturity. Why? Because the lawyer isn't going to leave his office to investigate the truth of your clients' child's level of financial savvy. The lawyer will simply accept your clients' judgment without any further scrutiny or examination. But *you*—with your business and investment background, expertise and acumen—are the expert in your clients' financial lives, and *you* are the one on the scene. In other words . . . it *has* to be *you!* And if you make the determination that your clients' child has a looooong way to go to becoming financially mature, then you must recommend that your clients leave the child's share in a PUPPET.

Regardless of whether you accept or dismiss my opinion of your perception, you can see that the determination of whether your child is financially immature depends on your perception of her just as much as it depends on her actual financial behavior. As these matters come into play, you can examine whether your child truly is financially immature to the point where a third party must manage her inheritance in a PUPPET, or is someone whose financial behavior is consistent with normalcy and reality.

But for purposes of making this section complete, let us assume that you have convinced me that your initial characterization of your child is correct and that you can trust your child with money only as far as you can throw her, which is not far at all. You have a financially immature child, and you must cast her share of the Living Trust assets into a PUPPET after your death to protect the money from being squandered into oblivion.

As you are now aware, I am against the tyranny of unjustified lifetime control. I do not believe that financial immaturity justifies third-party control of your child's inheritance for the rest of her life. Financial immaturity is not addiction, incompetence, or any other problem classification that poses a "forever" risk of loss to your child's inherited assets. Through the mere passage of time and occurrence of events (getting married, having children, obtaining employment), it is entirely probable that your child will eventually learn the financial facts of life. Children do mature—perhaps not as fast as you would like, but they do.

So, in your financially immature child's PUPPET, you should designate an age when the PUPPET ends and the third party must turn over the PUPPET assets to your child either outright, in a transparent trust, or in a SPIT. Or, if you want more certainty that your child's inheritance will not be ravaged by mismanagement and squandering, provide that the third party shall terminate the PUPPET when the third party determines that your child has exhibited financially mature behavior on a consistent basis. You can further provide that the third-party's determination must be based on objective factors and criteria, such as any or all of the following: private investigator reports; letters from psychologists who have met with your child; reviews of your child's bank and brokerage statements for a certain period; interviews with your child's significant other, siblings, employer, and friends; and monitoring your child's spending habits.

One last thing about the PUPPET for the financially immature child: The PUPPET holds and manages your child's *entire* inheritance until she reaches the designated age or until the third party determines that the risk of loss through mismanagement and squandering is minimized. My emphasis on the word *entire* is to help distinguish this plan from another concept of inheritance risk management subscribed to by many attorneys called *interval allocation*. This method instructs the third party to distribute, for example, one-third of the PUPPET assets upon attaining a designated age, one-half of the balance five years later, and the remaining amount five years after that.

The theory of interval allocation is that if a beneficiary blows through the first installment or loses it through inexperience, she will get another chance upon receipt of the next distribution. It assumes the beneficiary will gain experience and wisdom in dealing with an allocation, and that wisdom can be applied to later distributions.

Interval allocation was, and is, a popular trust allocation method, but not with me. When even one portion of the PUPPET assets is distributed to a beneficiary, it subjects that portion to the risk of loss through immaturity. Why put even that one portion at risk when the *entire* inheritance can be protected until the beneficiary reaches the age that, we assume, will prevent loss through immaturity? Also, the only thing a beneficiary may learn by blowing through the first installment is not to waste the next installment so quickly.

Thus, if your financially immature child is normal, I see no reason to distribute in increments. Forget about interval allocation, and use your Living Trust to create a PUPPET that protects your financially immature child's entire inheritance until she reaches the designated age or satisfies the conditions you set forth.

Your Mentally Ill Child

Not being a physician, I am acutely unaware of the panoply of non-congenital mental conditions that affect psychological and emotional well-being. What I can point out, however, is that for every 20 families that I deal with, there is a child or sibling who had a once-normal existence but was dragged down with a mental illness, usually schizophrenia or bipolar disorder.

If you have a child who developed a noncongenital mental illness that is possibly lifelong, you do not need me to tell you that her inheritance will need protection from that illness. When it comes to mental illness, the tyranny of unjustified lifetime control does not apply. You must leave her share to the PUPPET, where a third party will hold, manage, and administer it in accordance with its terms and instructions for the rest of her life.

I have had a brush with this area in the inheritance arena. I have personally seen, and may have been partially and indirectly responsible for, the inheritance loss and untimely death of Chris Cole, who was the brother of the woman who eventually became my girlfriend, Tristina (Tristina is now my ex-girlfriend, but we remain on friendly terms. That should satisfy anyone looking for an island of salacious gossip in this heavy-handed financial tome.)

After reading about this incident, you will wonder—as do I—why she stayed on board in the girlfriend capacity for as long as she did. Must have been the sex.

Throughout this book, I have regaled you with glimpses of my personal life in order to emphasize certain issues. Perhaps some of you may have found such a device unprofessional. My father certainly would. I can hear him now: "Dammit, Jeff, what client wants to know about the problems in his lawyer's life? It diminishes the lawyer in the eyes of the client. Just tend to the client and move on." While I understand this viewpoint, I have always disagreed with it. Sure, some folks might find my personal stories "oversharing." But what could drive a point home to the client more than sharing that point as it has arisen in the lawyer's own life?

With that disclaimer in mind, I want to tell you about my experience with Chris, a 34-year-old man who suffered from a permanent bipolar condition brought about, in part, by excessive drug use in his youth. Chris initially came to my office to oppose a conservatorship that he felt was unfairly being imposed on him.

As he sat in front of me, Chris appeared as normal as normal could be: Cogent. Articulate. Friendly. Humorous. Well groomed. He talked about his bipolar condition in the most objective of terms. He detailed his drug regimen. He explained that he wanted to live in Maui and establish there a video-production business, but that the financial restrictions of the conservatorship prevented him from gaining access to the funds necessary to make those moves.

I thought, what a nice, responsible guy. He's a man with a plan. Why would anyone think he needs to have his funds—an inheritance from his mother—monitored and controlled by a court-appointed conservator? Based on my observation, I agreed to represent Chris in his quest to be rid of his conservatorship and gain personal use of his inheritance.

Chris's conservator was his sister, Tristina. That's right—the same person as my girlfriend. It was through Chris that we met.

Tristina put up a small fight. She knew her brother could be as charming and reasonable as anyone, but that he became a completely different person when not on his meds: Erratic. Bizarre.

Rambling. Financially irresponsible. All the reasons why she obtained a convervatorship for him in the first place. However, in light of the most pleasant interview I had with Chris, I dismissed her warning as old news. The Chris I met was a new Chris, someone whom Tristina had not met and someone who no longer needed a third-party conservator to manage his inheritance.

The issue ultimately went to court. I did not convince the probate judge to terminate the conservatorship, but I was successful in getting the conservator, now a person other than Tristina, to free up more of Chris's inheritance for his personal use. I remember how happy Chris was with the result, and how much pride I felt in a job fairly well done.

After Chris came into possession of some of his inheritance, he nearly threw it all away. He paid for a multiple-night stay at the Ritz-Carlton that he did not use. He gave excessive amounts to homeless persons whom he befriended. He purchased a run-down and inoperable automobile for way more than its blue book value. He went to Hawaii, but he did not set up that video business. For the most part, he kept to himself, creating music that no one would hear, and engaged in behavior so erratic and bizarre that the authorities in Maui booted him off the island several times.

When Chris ran out of money, he came to my office. He was not the well-groomed and articulate person whom I had first met a few months before. Unshaven. Disheveled. Nonsensical. He did not appear to be any different from the homeless people who hit me up every day for change as I enter the corner 7-Eleven near my Santa Monica office.

Chris was also angry. He demanded that I file an action against his conservator to force him into releasing more of Chris's inheritance. Of course, having heard about his financial misadventures from Tristina, and seeing him then in his ravaged state, I refused, saying, "Chris, you really pulled a fast one on me. Fool me twice, shame on me." Chris responded with a 10-minute rambling monologue that was difficult to follow, but his main point was clear. To him, I was just like all the others who had refused to help him when he needed help the most.

I replied: "Chris, the biggest help I gave you was losing the opposition to the conservatorship. I didn't know that at the time, but I know this now. What a mistake that would have been for you to get all your money. There is no way I'm going to help you get more money, which you will only use to fuel your destruction." Chris did not like this admonition, so he fired me.

In my 30-year practice, I have been fired six times. Five terminations involved personality conflicts, which still amaze and disturb me. As my father said about me, "If you don't like Jeff, then you don't like anyone." But with Chris, for the first time, I had been fired for a strategic conflict. He wanted more money; yet he had displayed behavior that showed me that his mental illness posed a very real risk of loss to his inheritance—and to himself. But unlike the five prior terminations, this one did not cause me angst; I stood my ground on a firmly held principle, and I became free to date my former opposition, Tristina.

Chris went back to Maui and continued his routine of music making and bizarre behavior. In 2007, Chris went missing for several weeks. An island-wide search was made. Ultimately, he was found dead. He was 35. His partial remains were found in a small pond near the Maui airport. We will never definitively know whether his drowning was a suicide or the accidental result of a bipolar episode. However, I will always personally believe that having control of a portion of his inheritance fanned the flames of Chris's destruction, and that I unwittingly played a part in that process.

That should be the end of this section. Permanent control of your child's inheritance in the PUPPET is, well, permanent. What else is there to discuss? Well, maybe . . . just maybe . . . the PUPPET for the mentally ill child does not have to be a forever proposition.

If you live long enough, a lot can happen during that long time. Your child's mental illness may, through the miracle of modern medical science and technology, be wholly or partially remedied. Should not your child obtain control of his inheritance if such a medical breakthrough occurs after you and your spouse are gone?

You have wallowed in the misery of your child's mental illness for so long you may be emotionally incapable of mustering up the synapses needed to consider the possibility of your child attaining some semblance of normalcy. But now, your Living Trust coach is telling you to do just that. In your child's PUPPET, you should incorporate a provision that the third party will turn over control of the assets to your child in the event her mental illness is controlled to the extent that she can spend and manage it with relative fiscal responsibility. This determination can be made by the third party based on the opinions of medical doctors and psychiatrists who have examined your child.

There is, of course, always the possibility of error. If the opinion of the doctors turns out to be invalid, your ill child will have control of the inheritance and, in a fit of illness or mania, can run through it in the proverbial second. During my entire practice, I have witnessed two occasions when such misdiagnoses occurred. In both cases, the protection trust beneficiaries received the all clear to control their inheritances. Shortly after they received access to their former protection trust assets, they reverted back to their old selves, and the funds were used to feed their destruction.

If the possibility of error concerns you, then disregard my advice to build hope into that child's PUPPET. After all, you want certainty that your mentally ill child's inheritance is protected from herself, and your desire to obtain that certainty always trumps any other goal.

Category Four: The Neutron Bomb of Protection Trusts—the Discretionary Trust

The Discretionary Trust (DT) is just like the PUPPET in all respects, except for one key difference.

- Like the PUPPET, the DT is an irrevocable protection trust. After the death of you and your spouse, your child's share of the Living Trust assets will pour into the DT, which is designed to protect your child's inheritance from the problems that threaten a risk of loss.

- Like the PUPPET, the DT cannot be changed or amended by your child, unless it terminates by satisfaction of conditions that you build into the DT.
- Like the PUPPET, the assets of the DT are held, managed, and administered for your child's benefit by a third party.
- Like the PUPPET, the income generated by assets in the DT is added to principal, and your child receives principal for whatever purposes you set forth.
- Like the PUPPET, the DT dies when your child dies, and the assets of the DT will be distributed to whomever you name in your Living Trust as the backup beneficiaries.
- Like the PUPPET, your child has no right to direct the third party to give any of the DT's assets to any person, and cannot alter the DT's backup beneficiaries.
- Like the PUPPET, your child cannot demand that the third party apply the DT's assets in any way other than the purposes you incorporated into its provisions. Actually, I suppose there is nothing to stop your child from making the demand, but the third party is not allowed to acquiesce to that demand.

So what is the difference between the PUPPET and the DT? The difference lies in the usage of one word or the other: *shall* or *may*.

In the PUPPET, you provide that the third party *shall* use the PUPPET's assets for the benefit of your child. Certainly, the third party has the discretion to determine the amount of payments to maintain your child's day-to-day needs, and the power to decide whether those payments should be made to your child or directly to suppliers of your child's goods and services. However, the PUPPET's third party *must* make payouts of the principal. The third party has no choice. A third party who refuses to make any payments can be sued for breach of trust.

But in the DT, you provide that the third party *may* use the assets for your child. In other words, the DT's third party has the sole, complete, and absolute discretion to make payments of principal to or for your child. . . *or not!*

That is exactly as it sounds. The third party has the absolute power to, if he or she so chooses, *never* make any distribution of the DT's assets to your child. How about them apples?

So why would you do this to your child? What possible problem could your child possess that is just so huge and poses such an extreme risk of loss to your child's inheritance that it justifies this insane amount of control by the third party?

That problem is…creditors! Not small creditors, like the outstanding balance of a few thousand dollars on your child's Visa card. We're talking serious creditors, the ones that can potentially wipe out most or all of your child's assets, including the money and property he inherits from you. The bankruptcy creditors. The judgment creditors. The business creditors. The IRS. The State Board of Equalization to which your child has not paid sales tax in years. The malpractice action that is not covered by sufficient insurance. The loan shark to whom your child owes big—which really happens!

Even if you are the most casual person in the world when it comes to inheritance matters—the "I don't care what happens to my assets after I die" type—I guarantee that you do *not* want to die knowing that your child's creditors will swallow up the money and property it took you and your spouse 40 to 50 years to accumulate.

Financial Advisor Alert

What good is all the wealth that you have helped your clients create and manage if it ends up with their child's creditors? No good at all! So … in what is probably the most painfully obvious Alert in this book, find out from your clients whether their child is in bankruptcy, on the verge of bankruptcy, or is otherwise significantly debt-ridden. Maybe your clients cannot solve their child's creditor problems, but they can establish a plan that absolutely protects his Living Trust inheritance. And that is what the DT is all about. When your clients give the third party the complete discretion to never pay funds to their child, and the third party, in fact, does not pay out any funds, their child does not have control or ownership of those funds. And the child's creditors cannot go after funds that he does not control or own. It's that simple.

Can the creditors force the third party to choose to pay out funds to your child? Absolutely not! Again, with the DT, you give the third party complete decision-making power on the payout of the DT assets. The creditors cannot force the third party to do anything.

When your child's creditor problems disappear, and the third party determines that your child's creditor problems have, somehow, been resolved, the third party is free to distribute the DT's assets to your child in a transparent trust, SPIT, or PUPPET.

For you, this is the perfect solution. Your child will get his share, but it will be protected from his creditors in the DT. Your child, however, may not be as receptive, because his receipt of any portion of his inheritance is completely dependent on the whims of the DT's third party.

I have found that when the underage, addicted, mentally ill, or financially immature children learn that their inheritance will be funneled to a third party, they already had an expectation their parents would implement a plan for third-party inheritance control. But when the creditor child makes this discovery, stand back and watch the fur fly. Quite often, the creditor child has no idea— even though he should—what caused his parents to exercise such a restrictive inheritance risk-management device as the DT. As one creditor child screamed to me, "I'm a normal guy. I can handle my inheritance. I'm not going to spend it on drugs. I'm not going to spend it on stupid stuff. I'm not going to give it away. I'm not going to lose it in a divorce. I can handle my debt problems on my own. Why should I have to rely on anybody to decide whether I should get my own money? Condon, how could you let my parents do this to me?"

In Chapter 9, I discuss the use of the family inheritance meeting in the process of setting up your Living Trust. This meeting takes place with you and your children in your Living Trust attorney's office, where you open the lines of communication about the inheritance decisions you made and how your Living Trust will implement those decisions after your death. This meeting offers you the opportunity to gauge your children's reactions to your decisions and respond to them. This meeting is the best method I know to recognize and resolve any problems and conflicts over the Living Trust assets that could arise after your death; but, as I explained previously, it is a tool that is unfortunately little used.

However, if you are going to leave your child his inheritance in a DT, you had better damn well conduct that meeting to tell him about it. If you knew your inheritance would be subject to such repressive and seemingly outrageous controls, you would want to know that as well. After your creditor child has concluded the usual reactive process of shock and denial, you can help him with the acceptance portion, like, "We love you, but we don't feel the same way about your creditors. We know the DT is so intrusive, but can you think of any other way to prevent your creditors from getting your inheritance?"

If your creditor child is reasonable, he will recognize the wisdom of deferring control of his inheritance until his significant creditor problems are a thing of the past.

19

Using Your Living Trust to Force Your Child into a Conventional Lifestyle

OR,

IF THE TWIG IS BENT, WILL FORCE DO ANYTHING TO STRAIGHTEN IT OUT?

Financial Advisor Alert

Much has been made about the "ethical will," which is a free-form document that expresses the hopes, insights, and concerns by an older generation to its heirs. The principal limitation of ethical wills is their non-binding nature. If your clients have serious concerns about the impact of an inheritance upon their children, then they must go beyond the Ethical Will and adopt an approach that is legally enforceable . . . such as the incentive trust, which is the subject of this chapter.

My father and I used to constantly and facetiously pride ourselves on being the world's first (and only) father-son lawyers who wrote an inheritance planning book while perched on surfboards at Surfrider Beach in Malibu waiting for waves. No, we didn't balance laptops on our boards; but we did hatch a lot of the ideas and concepts that eventually became our first book, *Beyond the Grave*.

During the years that we surfed together, my father and I met several characters who loved and lived the sun-surf-sand lifestyle: Kemo, who lived in a van in the parking lot at Surfrider and sold shirts of his own design; Kathy Zimmerman, whose beach exploits became the inspiration for the series of Gidget movies screen-written by her father; Marty, who ran a marathon on the beach bike path almost every single day.

For me, the most memorable were the numerous folks we met on the beach every single time we showed up. The beach was not just their lifestyle—it constituted their entire existence. They spent entire days . . . weekdays, weekends . . . surfing and relaxing under makeshift cabanas just like the one the Big Kahuna built in *Gidget*. Forget college, higher education, employment, children, service to the community, and all the other trappings of the conventional lifestyle. For these beach dwellers, it was a continual hangout on the sand, with nothing more to do than chat up their fellow beach dwellers and bide their time until the next big swell.

My father went surfing more than I did, and he spoke with these beach dwellers frequently. One day, I asked my father how these people were able to sustain their alternative lifestyle. Did they have money? Were they trust-fund babies? I'll never forget my father's response: "Jeff, these guys don't have a pot to piss in. They live for the surf. The only job they have is waiting for their parents to die."

You, too, may have a child who marches to the beat of a different drummer. This is one who knows what work is by watching you go to work, but has decided that working is not for him.

How did your child get to that point? Perhaps you contributed to it by providing some financial support regardless of whether he made any productive effort. Or perhaps you never instilled in your child the sense of inner pride that comes from earning an honest wage. Whatever the reason, the fact remains that you have, metaphorically speaking, a bent twig—a child who never finished school or cannot or will not keep a steady paying job—and it appears that no outside force can straighten it out.

If you have resigned yourself to the fact that you are unable to do anything to bring positive change to your child's life, then join the club of the vast numbers of people who try to do something after they die. And that something is: to use the Living Trust to impose conditions on your alternative-lifestyle child's inheritance.

The Incentive Trust

This plan works like this. You provide in your Living Trust that your child's inheritance will funnel to a third party who will hold the inheritance in a separate trust, usually called an incentive trust. The terms of the incentive trust are built into the section of your Living Trust that deals with who gets what on your death.

The incentive trust's terms include conditions. These are hoops that your child must jump through to receive the incentive trust's assets. Such hoops may include getting a college degree, attaining a certain professional capacity, having a child, or keeping a conventional job for a certain period of time. When it comes to establishing inheritance conditions in your Living Trust, the world is your oyster.

Financial Advisor Alert

Read your clients' incentive trust provisions to make sure that its objective is not ambiguous. For example, if your clients want to encourage their children to work, what constitutes "work"? Is *work* defined in the provisions that constitute the incentive trust? If not, then it would be left up to the trustee to make the determination of whether your clients' child is working to the extent of qualifying for incentive trust distributions. Is that a traditional 40-hour work week? Working as an independent contractor? If it's not clear to *you*, then it's not clear and needs more definition. Otherwise, someone, whether the third party holding the money or your child who *wants* that money, will end up asking the probate judge (via a maddening and expensive petition procedure) for the conclusive and final interpretation.

When the third party determines that your child has satisfied the conditions that you established in the incentive trust, the third party will release the inheritance from the incentive trust to your child.

You can see why this plan is commonly referred to as an incentive trust. You treat your child's inheritance as the incentive for him to achieve the goals he did not want to attain during your lifetime. But to me, this plan should be called the carrot-and-stick trust, because that is exactly what it is. It's using the inheritance as the carrot that treats your child like a rabbit, leading him on and making him chase after a goal that may always be elusive.

I realize there are several schools of thought on the incentive trust. Some of my clients just love the idea of using their Living Trust as the last chance to lead their alternative-lifestyle child onto the more conventional path. But, by my use of that carrot and rabbit analogy, you can probably tell that I do not favor Living Trusts that contain incentive trusts. Unless inheritance conditions are necessary to prevent your child's inheritance from being squandered because of divorce, creditors, addiction, immaturity, mental illness, and the like, you should not try to control your child's behavior from the grave by placing conditions on the inheritance.

Why? Put yourself in the shoes of your child. What message do you think he receives from you with inheritance conditions? He is inadequate. He never measured up. He is like a recalcitrant schoolchild. He is a disappointment to his parents. Do you really want these to be your last messages to your child?

I also instinctively react against imposing inheritance conditions because I do not believe they accomplish the goal you attempt to achieve. When you and your spouse die, your child will probably be in his fifties, and his character and motivation will have long been established. Will the inheritance conditions help to undo that mind-set? Probably not. I realize this is an old and trite adage, but it's true: You can't teach an old dog new tricks. Don't attempt to coerce compliance with all-or-nothing conditions where compliance is unlikely.

The Incentive Trust That Creates a Real Incentive for Your Child to Find Employment

In most incentive trusts that clients have in mind when they come to my office, and in those I have seen in Living Trusts drafted by other attorneys, the conditions to the inheritances are all-or-nothing. These are the kinds of conditions that serve as plot points in inheritance-themed movies, like *Brewster's Millions,* where Richard Pryor's character had to spend $100 million in 30 days without owning any personal assets if he wanted to inherit $2 billion.

In the real world of the Living Trust, the all-or-nothing condition can be found in such examples as these:

- "If you want your inheritance, you will get a college degree."
- "You will receive your inheritance upon becoming a physician."
- "You will only get your inheritance once you have children of your own."
- "You will not get your inheritance unless you marry a person of the Lutheran faith."

I just do not like an incentive trust that potentially gives nada to your alternate-lifestyle child and that sends the message that it is "my way or the highway." Instead, I prefer a plan that gives that child some inheritance and an opportunity and incentive to get more.

For example, there is the dollar-for-dollar incentive trust. The effect of this plan is that your child shall receive some portion of the inheritance without any condition, with the rest of it passing to an incentive trust to be held and managed by a third party. The plan further provides that the third party will pay your child one dollar for every dollar your child proves that she has earned, such as with pay stubs or copies of receipts.

Another compromise is the "that's all you get" incentive trust. Your Living Trust provides that your child receives a certain amount of assets with no strings attached, and that's all she gets. This is considered an incentive trust plan because your child realizes that if she wants more money, she will have to find a way to get more money, such as getting and keeping a steady job.

A variation of the "that's all you get" plan involves your child's entire inheritance being transferred to an incentive trust with a third party holding and managing the funds. The third party is instructed to pay a certain amount to your child every month for the rest of her life. On your child's death, the incentive trust's assets will go to backup beneficiaries whom you name in the incentive trust. Once again, this plan may motivate your child to obtain employment to make additional money if, of course, she desires more income than the monthly stipend provided by the incentive trust.

Striking a Balance between Competing Desires

Although I have offered you a few alternatives to all-or-nothing inheritance conditions, I feel compelled to reiterate that they are middle-ground compromises between the extremes. On your end, you have your desire to control your child's behavior from beyond the grave and force him to live up to your standards. On my end, there is my instinctive negative reaction against lifetime inheritance controls that effectively coerce your child into a life he does not want. In my mind, all-or-nothing conditions belong only in the context of protecting inheritances from real risks of loss posed by such problems as addiction, immaturity, divorce, or mental illness.

But, with the compromise incentive trust plans I have just described, you do not leave your child the sour legacy of a perpetual reminder that he failed to attain goals and values you aspired to for him. Rather, and even if it goes against your grain, the message you send is productive and positive; it is that you accept your child's fate, you want to make his life a happy one, and you want to protect him by giving him access to a portion of his share while motivating him to get more

Financial Advisor Alert

The clients with inheritance incentives on the brain will likely disregard these compromise plans. Hell hath no fury like embittered parents ... who became embittered from the pain of witnessing their children engage in whatever lifestyle the parents find objectionable. Still . . . , if you see an incentive trust provision in your clients' Living Trust, you should advise your clients to make sure it, at the minimum, allows a degree of flexibility to accommodate changing circumstances and unintended effects, such as not punishing a child who chooses to be a stay-at-home parent or who pursues a lower-income profession. Also, the incentive trust should provide your clients' child with the ability to support a family even if the child fails to achieve some of the goals set out in that trust.

20

The Success of the Third-Party Irrevocable Protection Trust (PUPPET) Depends on Whom You've Selected as the Third Party

OR,

TRY NOT TO APPOINT ONE PRIVATE PERSON TO HOLD AND MANAGE MONEY FOR ANOTHER PRIVATE PERSON

In Chapter 18, I wrote a blue streak about the protection trust, a device incorporated into your Living Trust that is used to protect your child's inheritance from the winds of fate. Essentially, the protection trust forms a castle wall around your child's inheritance to shield it from whatever problems your child has that could waste and dissipate the inherited assets.

I also discussed several types of protection trusts that have clever acronyms attached to them for easier communication. In some of those protection trusts, you appoint your child to serve as his or her own trustee—the manager of the assets that you leave to the protection trust. However, there are two types that require the use of an independent third party as manager: the third-party irrevocable protection trust (which I dubbed the PUPPET) and the discretionary trust (DT).

In a nutshell, your PUPPET is a special subtrust that you write into your Living Trust. Generally, you create a PUPPET if you have a child with a problem or vice that poses a substantial risk of loss to the inheritance, such as addiction, youth, financial immaturity, or mental illness. Basically, this subtrust of your Living Trust states that after you and your spouse are dead, the Living Trust assets shall be funneled to a third party, who will hold them in a separate subtrust for the benefit of your child. The third party is required to manage, spend, and apply the funds for your problem child's benefit in accordance with the instructions you set forth in your Living Trust.

The success or failure of your child's PUPPET is seriously dependent on the person, or entity, that you name as the third party in your Living Trust.

Who Will You Appoint as the Trustee of Your Child's PUPPET?

As the heading of this section explicitly and boldly inquires, who are you going to appoint as the manager of your child's PUPPET? In a perfect world, you have choices. In that perfect world, you can be the rich, top-hatted Monopoly icon who can choose any option you desire. For the rest of us who live in the real world, though, our choices for the selection of our children's manager may be quite limited because, as you will soon see, you may have a very tough time getting someone to take the job of being your child's PUPPET manager. As such, your choices boil down to two categories:

1. Third-party private individuals, such as your other children; your child's uncles, aunts, or cousins; or one or more of your closest and most trustworthy friends.
2. A third-party professional corporate fiduciary, such as the bank trust department or professional private trustee.

Before we can address which category you should select from, we must address what the job of PUPPET manager entails. Quite simply, the PUPPET provides the management, application, and distribution of your child's inheritance for the benefit of your child. This involves basic duties of trust management, which, as you will see, are not exactly casual endeavors. These duties are:

- Preserve the PUPPET assets so they are not wasted or diminished by bad or risky investments.
- Protect the PUPPET assets so they are shielded from persons attempting to gain unauthorized access to those assets.
- Make the PUPPET assets productive so they maintain their purchasing power in the future when inflation has raised the basic costs of living.
- Monitor your child's life and needs, and use and apply the PUPPET assets for your child's benefit (such as providing the basic staples of food, clothing, and shelter) in accordance with the instructions you set forth in the PUPPET.
- Perform all the functions and tasks that typically comprise the active management of money, such as reviewing investments, keeping books, inputting financial information in some computer program, preparing PUPPET activity reports, and meeting with professionals such as certified financial planners, accountants, and attorneys.

If the PUPPET portfolio consists of real estate, add to these duties all the activities required for the management of property: dealing with the crazy tenants, collecting rent, filing unlawful detainer actions for nonpaying tenants, hiring and monitoring a property manager, and getting a handle on the wear and tear.

Whew! Is that all? Now that you know what the job is, let's take a look at the pool of potential candidates. As expressed earlier, your choices are a private individual or a corporate trustee.

Financial Advisor Alert

Many clients have asked me to be the trustee of their children's PUPPET. And I have politely turned down each request. Why? Because I am not a financial asset manager or advisor. I may have my own investment philosophy (which is *very* conservative because I freak out every time NASDAQ takes a downturn), but I am not skilled, experienced, or licensed to advocate that philosophy to others. Nor do I wish to have the homework of immersing myself into the financial life and personal welfare of my clients' children. *You,* however, with your asset management and investment expertise and background, may be perfect for the job.

But, if your clients approach you to serve as the trustee, keep in mind that it's more than just an investment gig. As trustee, you will become integrated and immersed in the financial and personal lives of your clients' children. You will have to respond to every e-mail and phone call. Visit their homes and places of employment. Talk to their neighbors and friends. Consult with their health care providers. Defuse family conflicts that arise over distributions. Respond to litigation filed by unhappy campers. Although each PUPPET administration is its own breed of cat with different players and scenarios, you have to expect to be pulled into the lives of your clients' children in some degree if you take on the trustee role. Certainly, you will be compensated for your trouble, but you have to ask yourself if the compensation is worth the potential aggravation and involvement.

Your First Choice: The Private Individual

If you are like most of my clients, your instinctive choice to be the PUPPET manager for your problem child will be an individual, particularly your normal child. You feel this is the most natural choice because you believe that blood watches out for blood and that only a sibling would be willing to assume the burden of helping out another sibling. Of course, these are very sensible reasons.

But, after having seen what happens when one child holds and manages money for a sibling, I must advise you to not make that choice. Why? Because you will make the life of your normal child a miserable one, with his or her daily life subject to the following prospects.

The Prospect of Being Sued

The trust law of every state in the United States provides that a trustee must keep the trust assets safe and productive. If your problem child perceives that the sibling PUPPET manager has not effectively discharged those duties with the PUPPET assets, even if that perception has no basis in reality, your normal child can find himself or herself being hauled into court to explain to the judge that all is well. We lawyers have a saying about any matter that goes to court: You may be absolutely and objectively in the right, but who knows what some crazy judge or jury is going to believe?

Moreover, the manager's financial activities are always subject to the child's scrutiny and judgment. For example, if the PUPPET assets take a nosedive, your problem child can accuse the sibling manager of breach of trust and sue for the diminution in value. On the flip side, if your problem child claims that the PUPPET assets would have skyrocketed had the sibling manager capitalized on particular investment opportunities, your problem child can sue for the alleged loss of profit.

And finally, your normal child may not be equipped, intellectually or emotionally, to fulfill the administrative and investment duties necessary to keep the PUPPET assets safe and productive. If that is the case, then by appointing your normal child as the PUPPET manager, you are practically inviting a lawsuit into his or her life.

The Prospect of Being Consumed

As I mentioned earlier in this chapter, it is not a casual endeavor to fulfill the duties of being a PUPPET manager, and your normal child will discover this firsthand. Bookkeeping. Filing. Meetings with professionals. Preparing reports. Dealing with your normal child and his possibly crazy antics. It requires *a lot* of time. If the PUPPET assets suffer any loss due to your normal child's inattention, he or she can be sued to pay back the amount of that loss from his or her own funds. And what's more, your normal child may not be skillful in investments and may not have the necessary tools to deal with daily details of managing the PUPPET assets.

Who needs that? When I leave my office after a long day, the last thing I want is to have to immerse myself in another job. Why would I want to drown myself at home in spreadsheets when I can go surfing, coach my daughter's softball team, watch reruns of *House* and *Seinfeld,* and engage in any other pleasurable out-of-office activity that does not require a lot of brain power? The loss of quality "me" time is not worth whatever fee I am allowed to take from the PUPPET for management services rendered.

The Prospect of Being Harassed

Your normal child also has to deal with your problem child, who can potentially make his life miserable. For example, your problem child wants a car. His sibling PUPPET manager agrees. Your problem child says he wants a Cadillac. The manager responds with, "How about a nice Hyundai?" Although today's Hyundai is miles ahead of the cheap model we used to drive when they were first introduced to the United States many years ago, your child still wants an Escalade. So, he presses the issue with his sibling PUPPET manager . . . a lot. Incessant daily telephone calls. Dozens of daily e-mail messages. Unannounced daily visits to the sibling PUPPET manager's home. Laying his body in front of his sibling PUPPET manager's car, vowing not to leave until the manager capitulates. Creating a scene with the sibling PUPPET manager and his family in public.

The Prospect of Misuse of the PUPPET Assets

Say that you have a disabled daughter and a healthy son. You provide in your Living Trust that your daughter's share of the inheritance will pass to a PUPPET with your son as the manager. What happens if your son needs money because he lost his job or his house is about to be foreclosed upon? What happens if your son or any member of his family suffers from an illness and they have insufficient health insurance? What happens if your son decides to send his children to private school and the tuition is above their means? There are so many what-ifs that could happen in your son's life, but they all lead to one significant prospect: Your son may use his sister's PUPPET assets to come up with desperately needed funds.

You may be thinking, "Wait a minute! Condon says that the PUPPET funds are to be used solely for the benefit of my daughter. My son is not supposed to use them for himself or for his needs. The second my son uses even one penny for himself he can be sued for breach of trust!" And you would be correct. A third-party PUPPET manager is legally bound to use the funds for your daughter's health, education, support, and all other purposes you set forth in your Living Trust.

The legal world and the real world, however, are two different concepts. Is there anyone around to ensure that your son is applying the PUPPET funds properly? Perhaps, but only if your disabled daughter has the mental capacity to protect herself. However, your daughter may not understand the financial workings of the PUPPET, leaving herself vulnerable to your son. And even if your daughter senses some mismanagement, will someone listen to her? Will she have the ability to seek legal redress, or will she be totally at the mercy of your son with none of the safeguards that normally protect a beneficiary from a trustee's abuse?

The Prospect of Loss of the Sibling Relationship

If you have one child hold, manage, and distribute for your other child, the sibling relationship will fade away and become supplanted by a money connection. When they get together, they are joined by an invisible elephant named "PUPPET." All your disabled child thinks is "You have my money, and I want it." At some point, the elephant's presence becomes more tangible and substantial, with pleasantries subtly melding into questions about money. ("What terrific pictures of my nephews. By the way, when can I expect the next payment?") Ultimately, the elephant fully emerges and tramps around the room with demands for money. ("Damn it, stop holding back! I asked you for payment a week ago! Where is it?!")

I don't know about you, but living with these five prospects does not sound like a good time. If your normal child is aware of these risks, he will probably decline to serve. And if he discovers them only after he begins service as the PUPPET manager, he might quit . . . and surrender the PUPPET assets to your problem child!

Of course, quitting and relinquishing the PUPPET assets to your problem child is not what you had in mind. In fact, such a turnover would be considered a breach of trust, and your normal child could be sued by anyone affected by that act. Also, perhaps the problem child's inheritance, and maybe your child, will be at risk as a result of having unfettered control of the assets. However, to your normal child, all those concerns would run a distant second to the joy and relief of getting his life back.

Your Second Choice: The Better Choice

For all of these reasons, from the perspectives of both your problem child and the person whom you might select as your problem child's PUPPET manager, you should select a third party who is in the business of managing the money of others. These are professional private fiduciaries, bank trust departments, brokerage firms, and certified financial planners, whom I shall lump together in one category as the professional manager.

Where do you find the professional manager? The same place you find any professional you desire to hire. Internet. Google search. Referral from a friend. Yellow pages. Also, since many banks have their own trust departments, you can simply walk into the bank you normally do business with and ask to speak to a trust officer. Is such a spontaneous visit an imposition? Believe me, it is not. Any bank trust officer will drop whatever he or she is doing and spend as much time with you as you need to satisfy whatever inquiries you have about the bank's services.

The professional manager treats the management of the PUPPET, well, professionally. It's a full-time job. The professional manager has facilities to manage PUPPET assets. The professional manager may be audited internally as well as by state and federal regulators. The professional manager has employees with sophistication and experience in dealing with investment decisions. The professional manager can withstand being hounded and pressured by a child intent on getting more control. Of course, the professional manager will charge a fee for services rendered; but you get far more for the dollar than the nonprofessional individual manager, who will not do as good a job.

When you are putting together your Living Trust that includes a PUPPET for your disabled child, you will need to find a professional manager who you believe will protect your child's assets and effectively work with your child, which means:

- You want the professional manager to know and adhere to your investment philosophy.
- You want the professional manager to distribute the PUPPET income and assets in accordance with your wishes.
- You want to know that the professional manager will have a good working relationship with your disabled child.
- And of course, you want to know how much the professional manager will charge for its services.

After you have selected the professional manager, you need to convey that information to your Living Trust attorney, who will incorporate that name into the document.

Financial Advisor Alert

If your clients elect the professional manager to be the PUPPET trustee, they may not know what to ask the candidates other than what are the trustee charges. You will score big points with your clients if you meet the candidates with them and ask suitable questions, such as the following:

- Do you see eye-to-eye with my clients as to how they want the PUPPET assets managed?
- What procedures are made or followed in making investment decisions?

- Who makes the investment decisions? If a committee, how often does the committee meet?
- How is the investment mix determined?
- Will you invest the principal entirely in growth assets, entirely in fixed income assets, or a mixture of both?
- Is your investment analysis done in-house or by an outside investment firm?
- What is your performance on your trust funds?
- Do you deal with trusts similar to the PUPPET trust, which is the subject of these questions?
- Will you telephone my clients' child occasionally to determine if everything is all right?
- How will you deal with pressure from my clients' child to be paid more money?
- How will you determine whether the distributions are meeting the financial needs of my clients' child?
- How will you discover if my clients' child is receiving more PUPPET income than he actually needs?
- Are you so "large" that you will not have a personal relationship with my clients' child?
- How do you typically handle a PUPPET of the size of my clients' PUPPET?
- Are there frequent personnel changes in your trust and asset management business?

CHAPTER 21

Who Are Your Grandchildren?

OR,

DO YOU REALLY WANT YOUR LIVING TRUST ASSETS TO ULTIMATELY WIND UP WITH YOUR SON'S SECOND WIFE'S KIDS FROM HER FIRST MARRIAGE?

We live in a soap opera world of multiple marriages, multiple divorces, domestic partnerships, same-sex unions, long-term relationships, and commitment ceremonies. We have wives, husbands, ex-spouses, lovers, significant others, partners, girlfriends, boyfriends, and cohabitants. All this sounds fine to me. Live and let live, as long as you don't smoke. Your right to enjoy an activity or endeavor ends when it directly and adversely affects my right to breathe air devoid of poisons. The last time I checked, living an alternative lifestyle is not carcinogenic.

With all these different types of relationships and characterizations, you may no longer know who you consider to be a grandchild for inheritance purposes. This becomes fairly significant because you have, most likely, named your grandchildren as direct or backup beneficiaries in your Living Trust. For example:

- You have provided that a certain amount of cash will go to each grandchild who is living at the time of your death.
- You have provided that if a child is not living when you and your spouse are both dead, the deceased child's children

(your grandchildren) will step into the inheritance shoes of that deceased child.

- You have provided that if your child is living when you and your spouse are dead, your Living Trust assets are funneled to your child's protection trust. No matter what type of protection trust you have crafted (transparent trust, SPIT, PUPPET, discretionary trust), it is likely that the protection trust assets will be distributed to your child's children (again, your grandchildren) when your child dies.

Who you consider to be your grandchildren to the extent that you wish to include them in your inheritance bloodline is more of a personal matter than a legal issue. In other words, you really are on your own with only your feelings as your guide. After all, there are no books on this subject. We lawyers are not taught "grandchildren recognition" in law school. However, this very short chapter mainly serves to bring your awareness to this overlooked issue.

Financial Advisor Alert

If your clients have "conventional" grandchildren (which typically means their married children's naturally born children), there is no need to raise the issue of whether they consider their grandchildren as the ultimate inheritors of their largess. But if your clients' children's children do not fit into that category, then you must ask your clients whether they should "count" as grandchildren for inheritance purposes. A crass and alienating inquiry? Actually, quite the opposite. You'll likely find your clients appreciating you for giving voice to an issue that they, for family political and diplomatic reasons, may never have brought themselves to discuss.

Grandchildren 101

Who are your child's children? Who are your grandchildren who are likely to be the ultimate inheritors of the money and property it took you a lifetime to accumulate? In all of inheritance planning, I believe this is the most subjective and personal issue that my clients grapple with. For example, do you consider your grandchild to be:

- The child of your unmarried daughter?
- The stepchild of your married son?
- The adopted child of your married daughter?
- The child born to your son and his wife "out of utero"?
- The child of your daughter's same-sex partner?
- The foster child of your unmarried son?
- The child whose only bond with your child is an emotional, not genetic, one?

There are probably more scenarios of grandchildren classification than I am aware of. But, you do not need a technical treatise on all possible strata of grandchildren to know that your family includes a grandchild in the nontraditional sense. This is a person who is at least two generations after you, is not a child naturally born to your child, and who has established a parental-type bond with your child.

My attempts at bedside psychology go only so far. Only you can gauge how you feel about whether the young person in your child's life is a grandchild for inheritance purposes. When you are able to make that intensely personal decision, you can tell your Living Trust attorney that you want that person included or excluded as a direct or backup beneficiary.

Two Certainties

As I mentioned, the decision about whether someone is a grandchild for inheritance purposes is a very subjective one. There is no right or wrong answer. It is all based on your feelings and perceptions. Unlike other issues in the inheritance arena, this is one where I am not going to impose my personal beliefs. But, there are two certainties that I believe should be considered when you face this issue.

First, I am certain that not including that young person as a beneficiary will result in estrangement between you and your child, the young person's parent. To your child, that young person, whether natural-born, conceived in a test tube, or brought into the fold by a new spouse or partner, is your grandchild. Your child will expect you to exhibit and engage in all the behaviors that loving grandparents demonstrate to their grandchildren: allowing that young person to call you "Grandpa" or "Grandma"; giving that young person holiday and birthday gifts; taking that young person to the movies and playground; showing up to that young person's Little League games and graduation ceremonies. You know . . . grandparent and grandchild stuff.

Welcoming that young person with open arms is one thing, but including him or her as an ultimate inheritor of your assets is a completely different animal. However, to your child there is no difference. As you ponder whether to include that young person as grandchild in your Living Trust, your child will wonder, "What the hell is there to ponder in the first place? That's my child. That's your grandchild, just as sure as if he was natural-born."

Those are the feelings of someone who is hell-bent on ensuring the acceptance of that young person into the family. If you do not include him as a beneficiary, then you have become, in your child's eyes, a narrow-minded traditionalist who cannot see how the world has changed.

However, I urge you to be honest with yourself and not be swayed by your child's opinion. Your child's feelings are not your feelings. You need to die knowing that your money and property will follow the path you want, and that your decision is not based on what your child forces you to accept by the threat of estrangement.

Here is the second certainty. However you define who your grandchild is, I am certain that you do not want that definition to include your child's significant other.

Why am I making this seemingly bizarre statement? Here is why.

My client left one-third of his Living Trust assets to his daughter in a protection trust. The protection trust provided that upon the daughter's death, the protection trust assets would go to the daughter's children; but, if the daughter did not have children, then to my client's other children (the daughter's brothers).

After my client died, the daughter's protection trust was funded with one-third of the Living Trust assets—just like clockwork.

Shortly after the protection trust was funded, the daughter made an appointment to see me. When she conferred with me, she told me four things.

1. She was suffering from a medical problem that was potentially terminal.
2. Her two brothers viewed her alternative lifestyle with disdain.
3. She had no children.
4. She was in a long-term relationship with her girlfriend.

Why was the daughter dumping her life story on me? Because she wanted to find a way to beat the protection trust. She wanted to know if she could do anything to leave her protection trust assets to her girlfriend after her death. This was my response: "No way. The protection trust says what it says. When you die, since you don't have children, the assets will go to your siblings. You can't change it. Your parents made it irrevocable. They wanted your share to stay in the family, not go to your girlfriend. Sorry."

The daughter died about two years after that meeting. After her death, I received a call from one of her brothers. This is how the conversation went, which I remember like it happened yesterday:

Brother: Mr. Condon, I see that my sister saw you about two years ago before she died. What the hell kind of crazy advice did you give her?

Me: None. I just gave her a run-down of her protection trust. She wanted the assets in the protection trust to go to her girlfriend. I said no can do. With no children, those assets would have to go to her siblings on her death.

Brother: Well, Mr. Condon, you must have said something, because we're not getting anything from her protection trust.

Me: Of course you are. I remember my meeting with her. She did not have children, so the protection trust provides that it all goes to you and your brother.

Brother: That's not happening.

Me: Why?

Brother: Because she went out and adopted her girlfriend!

I nearly fell out of my chair when I heard that bit of news. I was shocked by the daughter's scheming maneuver, and yet totally impressed by it. The definition of "grandchild" as it appears in the daughter's protection trust is this: A grandchild of the client is a person born to, or adopted by, the daughter of the client. So, the daughter simply adopted her girlfriend, who then became the daughter's child . . . and my client's grandchild . . . and the backup beneficiary to the protection trust assets.

The New and Protective Definition

You live, you learn. To prevent this type of unintended inheritance allocation from reoccurring, the protection trusts that I now draft define a grandchild as a person who is born to a child of the client, or adopted by a child of the client *prior to that adoptee attaining the age of majority*. With that simple alteration, your children will be unable to bust the trust to leave the protection trust assets to anyone other than their own children. Not that they will make the attempt. But, as I found out with the daughter who gamed the protection trust to leave the assets to her girlfriend, you just never know.

Financial Advisor Alert

The word "issue" appears in your clients' Living Trust in at least two places, and how that word is defined in the document can have a *huge* impact on the ultimate inheritors of their Living Trust assets.

First, your clients' Living Trust states that their child's "issue" shall inherit that child's share if that child dies before your clients. Meaning, their child's children (the grandchildren) step into the child's "inheritance shoes" if that child is deceased. Second, the word *issue* comes up in the context of a protection trust. If a child receives his or her share in a, say, self-directed protection trust (which I call a "SPIT" in Chapter 18), it states that the child's trust estate shall be distributed to that child's "issue" when that child dies.

In the "Definitions" section of your clients' Living Trust, there is a paragraph that defines who is their child's *issue*—their children's descendants who shall be the ultimate inheritors of your clients' assets. So look it up. What does it say? Does it include your clients' children's stepchildren whom your clients barely know? Does it include their children's foster children whom your clients never met? Does it include their children's adopted children whom your clients never really "cottoned to"? Well, a broad definition of *issue* may make those little (or not-so-little) kids the ultimate inheritors of your clients' largess. So you have to point out that their Living Trust's definition of *issue* might not be specific enough to exclude those categories of grandchildren and they should get over to their lawyer for a Living Trust fix.

CHAPTER 22

The IRS Is Back! And This Time, It's for Real!

OR,

"SORRY ABOUT YOUR PARENTS' DEATHS. THAT WILL BE $200,000, PLEASE."

I t was a huge effort to write this chapter for the first edition of *The Living Trust Advisor*. The state of the estate tax was in massive flux. Whether your children (or other heirs) paid estate taxes after your death involved seemingly endless factors and scenarios—and I felt compelled to address nearly all of them. And on top of that, nobody knew anything about whether we would have an estate tax after 2011. The ultimate estate tax planning advice I could offer was to facetiously instruct you to die during the one-year-only 2010 estate tax repeal.

To put it mildly, reading another chapter about estate tax stuff is not an especially thrilling prospect—especially after you survived the Chapter 13 slog-fest dealing with estate tax issues after the first spouse dies. But you'll hardly break a sweat reading this chapter about estate tax stuff that arises after the death of the surviving spouse. Why? Because you already did the hard estate tax work after your spouse's death to ensure that no estate tax will be paid after your death.

Financial Advisor Alert

If your married couple clients own way less than their combined $10,900,000 lifetime exemptions, then that hard estate tax work isn't really so hard. All they need to do is (1) put in provisions in their Living Trust, which give the surviving spouse the option of splitting the trust estate into an exemption trust and survivor's trust; and (2) check the "Magic Box" in the deceased spouse's estate tax return, which allows the surviving spouse to combine both of their lifetime exemptions. But if your married couple clients own way more than their combined lifetime exemptions of $10,900,000, then they (hopefully) will utilize any of the myriad estate tax reduction methods available, which may save their families hundreds of thousands (even millions) in estate taxes.

As I previously told you in Chapter 13, the estate tax is a tax on the transfer of assets after the death of the owner of those assets. Because this tax takes place after death, some folks call it the *death tax*. That is a completely misleading label, as it gives the impression that there is a tax on the act of death.

Let me be clear so you will never make this mistake again . . . or the first time. There is no tax because of death; there is only a tax on the transfer of wealth after death. So, the next time someone running for political office attempts to goad your vote by promising to abolish the "death tax," you can now interpret what he or she really means.

In Chapter 13, I discussed the estate tax in the context of the death of the first spouse to die, whom I call the deceased spouse. As a general proposition, there is no estate tax after the deceased spouse's death, because there is no tax on the transfer of assets from the deceased spouse to the surviving spouse. This is called the *marital deduction,* which is a dollar-for-dollar deduction for every dollar that goes to the surviving spouse, or to a trust for the benefit of the surviving spouse. There is also no estate tax on the transfer of assets that pass to the exemption trust, which is a concept I also discuss in detail in Chapter 13.

Just a quick review.

Although there is usually no estate tax due after the deceased spouse's death, the surviving spouse should still file the deceased spouse's estate tax return. The estate tax return (known in the vernacular as Form 706) is like an inventory of assets that the deceased spouse owned at the time of death. In this return, the surviving spouse describes the nature and value of all assets in which the deceased spouse had an interest. But again, the fact that an estate tax return may be due after the deceased spouse's death does not mean that an estate tax is due.

Why should the estate tax return be filed even though there is no estate tax after the deceased spouse's death? Because the estate tax return has a Magic Box that, when checked, allows the surviving spouse to "pick up" the deceased spouse's $5,450,000 lifetime exemption. The result is that the surviving spouse ends up with a combined $10,900,000 lifetime exemption. That means that the surviving spouse can leave up to $10,900,000 to the Living Trust's beneficiaries with nary an estate tax in sight.

Actually, was that really hard work for you? To call up your Living Trust attorney and say, "Condon told me to instruct you to prepare my deceased spouse's estate tax return so I can pick up my deceased spouse's lifetime exemption"? Assuming that calling your attorney is not a daunting prospect to you, then no.

Now that you are sufficiently reviewed about the estate tax stuff that happened after your spouse's death, you are ready and energized to tackle the estate tax stuff that happens when both you and your spouse are dead.

Which really isn't much—unless you're really, *really* rich. When the surviving spouse dies (that is, when both you and your spouse are dead), another estate tax return may be required. And this time, it's for real. If you are rich enough, the IRS will ask for a portion of your assets in the form of an estate tax. Who qualifies as "rich enough"? To the IRS, you are rich enough to pay estate tax if the net value of your estate exceeds your lifetime exemption (more on this later in this chapter).

The responsibility for preparing and filing the estate tax return belongs to the after-death agent you named in your Living Trust.

After the last spouse dies, your after-death agent must gather information about all the assets that have the surviving spouse's name on them.

What kinds of assets? All of them. Real estate. Stocks. Bonds. Treasury bills. Savings bonds. Brokerage accounts. Mutual funds. Checking accounts. Savings accounts. Certificates of deposit. Cash. Insurance. Promissory notes. Pedigreed dogs and cats. Jewelry. Antiques. Collections. Furniture. Automobiles. Oil and gas leases. Businesses. Limited partnership shares. Limited liability company membership interests. Mining rights. Time shares. If an asset does not fit into a category, it gets listed in the return as "Miscellaneous."

The IRS does not care how the surviving spouse owned the assets. In the Living Trust. Out of the Living Trust. In joint names with any other person. In a survivor's trust. In an exemption trust. In a marital trust. In an account with someone named as a beneficiary. In an IRA account. In a pension plan. In a 401(k). In a partnership. It just does not matter. If the surviving spouse's name is anywhere on that asset, your after-death agent must list it in the estate tax return.

How does your after-death agent go about getting this information?

For real estate, the after-death agent has to hire a real estate appraiser. I say "hire" because appraisers do not prepare those reports for free. Your after-death agent must pay a fee from your Living Trust assets in order to report the value of your real estate to the IRS so the IRS can impose an estate tax on that value. It's a nasty little circle.

For all your other assets, your after-death agent must obtain all the statements and documents that represent those assets. This means your after-death agent will root through your main financial workspace looking for bank statements, brokerage statements, income tax returns, and all other documents that will provide a clue as to the nature and extent of your non–real estate assets. If the surviving spouse has an asset that is not evidenced by a statement, such as a receivable not reduced to writing, your after-death agent may never know about it and will not list it in the estate tax return. Since the IRS imposes an estate tax on only the assets listed in the return, the omission of undiscovered assets may be just fine with you; but unknown assets also do not get transferred to your children or other heirs.

Financial Advisor Alert

You may be contacted by the after-death agent for help in gathering the date-of-death "numbers." If so, keep in mind that the date-of-death value of a brokerage asset is *not* its closing price; rather, it is the average of the high and low sale prices on the day of death. Also, if the surviving spouse died on a weekend or holiday, the high-and-low averaging will be based on the sale prices on the last day of trading prior to that date of death.

In addition, as incongruous as this may sound, the estate tax return must also list any transfer or gift made by the surviving spouse that exceeds the annual gift exclusion. What is the annual gift exclusion? It is the amount the IRS says you can give away each year to any person with no gift tax to you and no income tax to your recipient. Right now, the amount of the exclusion is $14,000.

If your clients give their son $50,000 right now for a down payment on a house, their after-death agent is required to list that gift in the estate tax return as the value of that gift over the $14,000 exclusion (or $36,000). Put another way, the value of that gift over and above your $14,000 exclusion ($36,000) is added back into the inventory and is counted for estate tax purposes as an asset that you owned at your death.

Again, I know it may be difficult to wrap your head around this concept. How can a gift before your death be considered an asset that you owned at your death? Here's how. The IRS does not want you to think you can avoid an estate tax by giving away what you own before your death. If you could do that, so would millions of others, and the IRS would never collect any estate tax dollars. So, the IRS says that any gift you make above a certain amount (the annual gift exclusion) is, from an estate tax reporting standpoint, put back into your estate.

At some point, your after-death agent will conclude the search for the assets that are owned by the surviving spouse at death. He or she will have the real estate appraiser reports, the bank and brokerage statements, the canceled checks from the insurance policy payouts, and all other relevant documents to show ownership and value, and will also have the information about all the gifts and transfers over the annual gift exclusion made by the surviving spouse to any other person. Your after-death agent will then feed that information to the Living Trust attorney, who will, in turn, input it into special software that adds it all up and calculates the estate tax.

After completing that task, the attorney will call your after-death agent to give the big news on the amount of estate tax to be paid.

The Good News

As the estate law stands as I write this sentence, there will be no estate tax if the total value of your death inventory is less than your individual lifetime exemption of $5,450,000. In English, this is the amount that the IRS says that the surviving spouse can transfer after death to anyone and in any manner without the imposition of any estate tax. So if your total net worth (including the gifts added back into your asset inventory) is less than $5,450,000, your after-death agent will not have to raid any of your assets to pay an estate tax. Lovely.

Even lovelier is the result if you checked the Magic Box in your deceased spouse's estate tax return. By checking that box and filing that return, you picked up your deceased spouse's $5,450,000. This means that there will be no estate tax if the surviving spouse dies with less than $10,900,000. Even lovelier.

Although it is somewhat difficult for me to know the wealth category of you, the reader, I don't believe it is too thin a limb to climb on when I say that you do not fall into the estate tax payment category. If that is the case, then there is nothing for your after-death agent to do in the estate tax world. Certainly, there are a few reasons why the Living Trust attorney may still advise your after-agent agent to file the surviving spouse's estate tax return: Perhaps as a preemptory strike against a possible future IRS inquiry about whether the surviving spouse died with more than her single or combined lifetime exemptions. Or perhaps to conclusively establish the values of the assets described in the return for capital gains tax purposes. But in the main, there will be no estate tax issues that require handling.

However, if the total net worth of the surviving spouse is more than the single or combined lifetime exemptions, there will be an estate tax on every dollar above those amounts. The rate of tax starts at about 33 cents on the dollar, with the top tax rate at 40 cents on the dollar.

The Estate Tax Return Process

Still awake? Yes, you are. How can you nod off while reading about estate taxes? It cannot be done. But, let's get back on track to the story of the surviving spouse's estate tax return.

If you lived in that rare multimillionaire air during your life and the Living Trust lawyer ascertains that an estate tax is due, your after-death agent will have to write a check from your Living Trust assets to cover that tax. If there are insufficient liquid assets to pay the tax, your after-death agent will have to sell something to generate those funds, most likely your Living Trust real estate. Of course, the sale of real estate incurs a number of costs and fees over and above the estate tax, such as broker commissions, escrow fees, installation of low-flow toilets, water-heater bracing, documentary transfer taxes, recording fees, and many miscellaneous charges. It's as if the estate tax is being paid at 105 percent of its value—that is, 100 percent for the tax and an additional 5 percent for costs needed to come up with the money to pay the tax.

After your after-death agent signs the estate tax return, the Living Trust lawyer sends the check and the return to the IRS. The return and check must be sent within nine months of the date of the surviving spouse's death. An extension of six months can be obtained to file the return, but the extension request (Form 4768) must be accompanied by a check for the estimated estate tax.

If your after-death agent cannot obtain the funds to pay the estate tax within that nine-month period, the lawyer can request an extension of time to pay the estate tax for up to one year (also on Form 4768). However, after the nine-month date, the IRS's interest clock ticks away on the unpaid estate tax. The interest rate is very high, typically from 9 percent to 12 percent.

The estate tax return and check are sent to the IRS estate tax return center in Cincinnati. Every single estate tax return is sent to this location regardless of the state of the surviving spouse's residence, because this is the only location in the United States set up for anthrax screenings for estate tax returns.

Here is another indignity suffered by your Living Trust beneficiaries. Your after-death agent will not make any distribution of Living Trust assets to your beneficiaries *until* the entire estate tax process is completed. "Completed" means more than just the writing and sending of the check for the estate tax. The estate tax process is not completed until the IRS has examined and *accepted* the estate tax return.

If the IRS accepts the return as filed, it will issue a "closing letter" to your after-death agent. This is like getting a "pass" on a test. However, if the IRS wants more information, or wants to contest some aspect of the return, it will issue an "examination letter" in which the assigned IRS officer, who will be an attorney, will state the issues he or she desires to address.

Playing the Waiting Game after Your Estate Tax Return Is Filed

In my experience, the time it takes for the IRS to issue a closing letter ranges from one to two years *from the date of filing*. Remember, the estate tax return is filed up to 15 months after the death of the surviving spouse. Applying my incredible math skills, this means your Living Trust beneficiaries may wait a long time for your after-death agent to distribute their Living Trust shares. Out of all the phone calls I receive on a daily basis at work, I would estimate that 20 percent of them are from Living Trust beneficiaries asking, in essence, "Are we there yet?"

Why does the IRS take its sweet time to examine the estate tax return? Unlike an income tax return, which has a 1 percent chance of audit, *every* estate tax return the IRS receives is audited. It's a 100 percent chance of audit. In addition, each person examining each estate tax return is an IRS attorney. As you may have experienced, it takes a long time for an attorney to do anything.

If the IRS contests a matter in the estate tax return, it will most likely concern the valuation of real property. In my experience, real estate valuation is the number one issue raised by the IRS during estate tax return examinations.

The IRS is always wary that the return may include a property valuation that is too low. If the IRS does not agree with the value of the property as contained in the appraisal reports that have accompanied the return, the IRS will obtain its own appraiser, who invariably will value the real estate higher than the appraiser retained by your after-death agent.

Usually, these disputes settle at the median value between the high and low appraisals, but don't count on that. While the majority of IRS attorneys I have encountered have been pleasant to deal with and will readily accommodate an expense-saving deal, I have also experienced the wrath of those few who refuse to bend at all. In such an event, the appraisal battle goes to the next level of scrutiny with that attorney's administrative superior. If a deal cannot be struck, the battle wages on to the Tax Court to let the judge decide.

However, rarely, if ever, will I let an appraisal battle or any other estate tax return issue go to the Tax Court level, as the legal costs can potentially eat up any estate tax savings that a favorable Tax Court ruling could offer. I would rather your after-death agent hold his nose, make the best deal possible, and walk away with hurt pride, but also with your Living Trust assets largely intact.

If the examination process results in the imposition of more estate tax, the IRS will charge interest on that extra amount. Certainly, that is to be expected. But what is truly unfair is that the interest will be deemed to retroactively begin from the nine-month date, not the date that the final ruling is made. This means that if the IRS has taken its sweet time examining the estate tax return and finalizing the case, interest is accruing during that entire time!

On one occasion, I dealt with an IRS attorney during an examination of an estate tax return where we engaged in an otherwise typical appraisal battle. About eight months into that examination, the IRS attorney quit and went into private practice. It took the IRS about 13 months to hire a new attorney and get him up to speed on a caseload that included my case.

When the examination was concluded, the new IRS attorney's report stated that additional estate taxes were due. Fair enough; but I was shocked to read that interest was charged for the 13-month hire-and-catch-up period! Although I try to keep my clients from IRS levels beyond the examination level, I was so incensed by such gall that I offered to take this issue to Tax Court . . . for free! Ultimately, I raised such a stink that the IRS attorney backed off on those charges.

But whether or not heroics are involved, at some point the issues raised for examination will be resolved and a closing letter will be issued, leaving your after-death agent to finally distribute the Living Trust assets to the beneficiaries you've named in your Living Trust.

Seek Out Solutions to Reduce Your Estate Tax

There are dozens of plans and techniques of which you can avail yourself to reduce your estate tax. Innumerable books have been written on this subject. While some are reader-friendly, most bring back nightmares of the most insufferably boring textbook of your school days.

If this were a book with the estate tax as its main subject, I would describe the menu of plans that you could implement to reduce or eliminate the estate tax on the death of the surviving spouse. However, such a discussion would turn this book into something it is not intended to be. This is a book on how to live and die with a Living Trust, and the vast majority of estate tax reduction plans have absolutely zero relation to your Living Trust. For such a discussion, I will take the easy way out and refer you to the reader-friendly laundry list of options that appears in my first book, *Beyond the Grave: The Right Way and the Wrong Way of Leaving Money to Your Children (and Others),* in Chapter 36, titled "How to Leave More to Your Children and Less to the IRS."

When you read that chapter or other books on how to reduce or eliminate estate taxes, you will notice that all estate tax planning techniques have one central common trait, which is: They all involve some element of giving up control of your wealth now, while you are alive. Why? Because the less you own when you die, and the lower the value of the assets you own on your death, the less the estate tax will be. For my estate planning attorney brethren reading this paragraph, I must add this little private message: Yes, ladies and gentlemen. Of course I realize that is a broad and sweeping generalization for which there are a lot of exceptions. But I'm attempting to convey, in plain English, an overarching concept in order to assist my readers with comprehending what can be a very complex subject. Back off, please.

If you have little or no problem conveying assets during your life to your children, grandchildren, or charities of your choice (whether or not above the annual gift exclusion), you are already ahead of the game. But, if the mere thought of releasing your kung-fu grip on your assets makes you weak at the knees, then forget it. My philosophy is: Never part with wealth that you feel you will need or that you feel you will miss. To your beneficiaries who end up paying more estate tax because of your inability to part with your money now, I say, tough! It's *your* money and property. You do or not do whatever estate tax planning you want. Your beneficiaries are fortunate to get what they get.

Having referred you elsewhere for your estate tax reduction training, I must add that there is one estate tax issue that is directly related to your Living Trust that is crucial in the context of payment of the estate tax following the death of the surviving spouse. But, I can almost guarantee that your Living Trust attorney has never discussed this issue with you. This issue concerns what your Living Trust says about who pays the estate tax, and it is covered in the next chapter.

CHAPTER 23

Who Pays the Estate Tax?

OR,

DON'T MAKE ONE PERSON PAY THE ESTATE TAX ON LIVING TRUST GIFTS THAT GO TO ANOTHER PERSON

After the death of the surviving spouse, your Living Trust's after-death agent will inventory all the assets owned by the surviving spouse at the time of death. If the total net value of that inventory exceeds the surviving spouse's lifetime exemption, (which I discuss at length in Chapter 22), the after-death agent will pay an estate tax to the IRS.

What is the source of the funds used to pay the estate tax? Your Living Trust assets! The beneficiaries whom you named in your Living Trust will have their respective shares reduced by the amount of Living Trust assets paid to the IRS by your after-death agent.

Now we come to the main point of this chapter. Here is the Big Issue: When the estate tax is paid, that payment will either reduce the shares of *all* of your Living Trust beneficiaries or reduce the shares of *some* of your Living Trust beneficiaries. And with this Big Issue comes the Big Question: Which beneficiaries in your Living Trust will have their shares reduced by estate taxes, and which ones will receive their full shares without any such deduction?

The Three Types of Estate Tax Allocation Provisions

In legal parlance, this is the area of the estate tax allocation, and it is probably the most overlooked subject in the inheritance arena. Ask yourself: Do you recall discussing this issue with your Living Trust attorney during any of your meetings? Most likely, you are in the vast majority of Living Trust clients who have never before encountered this subject. However, if your attorney took the time to raise the subject of estate tax allocation with you, I am pleased to tell you that you "did good" (or got lucky) in your selection of that attorney.

The concept of estate tax allocation is fairly simple. In your Living Trust, you have the power to decide which beneficiaries shall shoulder the burden of paying the estate tax. For purposes of this chapter, I will refer to the beneficiaries whom you select to pay the estate tax as the "chosen ones."

The chosen ones do not actually dig into their own pockets to come up with the money to pay the estate tax. Rather, the estate tax is paid from your Living Trust assets by your after-death agent. Later, when the estate tax process has been completed, the after-death agent distributes the Living Trust assets to your beneficiaries with deductions from the shares of the chosen ones in the amount of the estate tax. In effect, the chosen ones' shares are reduced by the amount of the estate tax payment.

You have three basic choices for determining who the chosen ones will be:

1. The chosen ones can be the beneficiaries of your Living Trust assets, in equal shares. This is the most common method of estate tax allocation. A provision in your Living Trust that calls for the estate tax to be borne equally by all your beneficiaries is called an "equal estate tax allocation provision."
2. The chosen ones can be the beneficiaries of your Living Trust assets in an amount that is proportional with each beneficiary's share of the Living Trust assets. This type of tax-sharing plan is called the "proportional estate tax allocation provision."

3. The chosen ones can be beneficiaries of your Living Trust whom you specifically name to be the persons who bear the estate tax. In essence, this plan allows you to pick and choose which lucky beneficiaries get their shares reduced by estate tax and which ones are allowed to receive their full shares without any reduction. Such a plan is called the "specific estate tax allocation provision."

It was math and word problems that drove me to law school. Nonetheless, I now must resort to those devices to drive home how these estate tax allocation provisions work, and their effect after you and your spouse are dead and estate taxes must be paid.

Equal Estate Tax Allocation Provision

Of the three estate tax allocation provisions just described, the equal estate tax allocation provision is the most straightforward.

- Your spouse died 10 years ago. You are the surviving spouse. You die. You are survived by your three children.
- Your after-death agent examines your assets and ascertains that your total net worth at your death is $6 million.
- Your Living Trust provides that your three children shall receive your Living Trust assets in equal shares.

Within nine months after your death, your after-death agent files your estate tax return along with a check for the estate tax in the amount of $250,000.

The IRS examines the return and accepts it as filed. Your after-death agent is now ready to distribute the assets to your children, in equal shares. But before that distribution is made, your after-death agent must look in your Living Trust to see whom you have appointed as the chosen ones—the beneficiaries who will have their shares reduced by the amount of the $250,000 estate tax!

If your after-death agent sees an equal estate tax allocation provision, each child bears the burden of the estate tax payment equally.

As a result, each child will receive the remaining $5,750,000 of Living Trust assets in equal shares, or $1,916.666 apiece.

Proportional Estate Tax Allocation Provision

We warmed up with a fairly easy example. Now, with the proportional estate tax allocation provision, it gets a bit more complex. But stay with me, and I'll get you through this. As complicated as this can get, it surely is easier to understand than the offside violation that I was required to know as a referee in my daughter's soccer league.

- Your spouse died 10 years ago. You are the surviving spouse. You remarry and you have a happy life with your second spouse. You die 17 minutes after reading this book. You are survived by your second spouse and your three children.
- Your after-death agent examines your assets and ascertains that your total net worth at your death is $6 million.
- Your Living Trust says that on the death of the surviving spouse (you), 10 percent of the Living Trust assets will be distributed to your second spouse, with the remaining 90 percent passing to your three children in equal shares.

Within nine months after your death, your after-death agent files your estate tax return along with a check for the estate tax in the amount of $250,000.

Eight months after the return is filed, your after-death agent receives a closing letter from the IRS, which gives the estate tax return a passing grade. Your after-death agent is now free to distribute the remaining assets of $5,750,000 to your beneficiaries. But before that distribution is made, your after-death agent must look in your Living Trust to see whom you have appointed as the chosen ones—the beneficiaries who will have their shares reduced by the amount of the $250,000 estate tax!

If your after-death agent sees an estate tax allocation section in your Living Trust, it will most likely have the standard boilerplate proportional estate tax allocation provision, which, in essence, says this: All estate taxes shall be borne proportionately by all beneficiaries. If so, then each beneficiary pays the estate tax in proportion to the value of his or her bequest as it relates to the entire estate.

If this proportional estate tax allocation provision is in your Living Trust, your second spouse will be responsible for 10 percent of the $250,000 estate tax, which is $25,000, and your children will be responsible for 90 percent of the $250,000 estate tax, which is $225,000. As a result, your second spouse's total net 10 percent of the remaining $5,750,000 is $575,000, and your children's total net 90 percent of the remaining $5,750,000 is $5,175,000.

Allocating the estate tax proportionately among the beneficiaries sounds pretty fair. With each beneficiary paying a share of estate tax in proportion to the amount of assets each beneficiary receives, who would kvetch about that? Well, if you did not want that allocation, the kvetcher would be you! Take a look at the next example to see what I am talking about.

Specific Estate Tax Allocation Provision

If I have not lost you yet, let's build on the previous example to explain the specific estate tax allocation provision.

Remember, your net total Living Trust assets are valued at $6 million. Your Living Trust leaves 10 percent to your second spouse and 90 percent to your three children. The estate tax paid by your after-death agent from your Living Trust assets is $250,000, leaving a balance of $5,750,000 for distribution to your second spouse and three children.

Your after-death agent looks in the tax allocation section of your Living Trust. Instead of a proportional estate tax allocation provision, he or she finds a specific estate tax allocation provision stating that your second spouse shall receive an entire 10 percent share free of estate tax. This means that the entire burden of paying the $250,000 estate tax specifically falls upon the 90 percent of the Living Trust assets passing to your three children.

You did not have to select your children as the chosen ones. You could have picked your second spouse as the chosen one.

When it comes to picking and choosing who bears the estate tax, the world is your oyster.

So, why did your specific estate tax allocation provision select your children as the chosen ones? Who knows? Perhaps you believed your second spouse requires the full 10 percent share to provide for basic needs. Or perhaps you wanted your second spouse to receive a full share as a reward for taking care of you during your incapacity when your children did not step up to lend a hand.

Financial Advisor Alert

Or perhaps this decision was made by the drafting attorney without any discussion with your clients. How does that happen? I'll tell you how! The drafting attorney made a specific estate tax allocation provision for another client's Living Trust and then used that other client's Living Trust as the format (or *boilerplate*) for *your* client's Living Trust. Unless this mistake is caught during your clients' lifetime, their Living Trust beneficiaries will be stuck with that estate tax allocation after their deaths.

Whatever the reason, you included this specific estate tax allocation provision in your Living Trust, which prevents your second spouse's share from being reduced by estate tax.

With this provision in your Living Trust, from the $6 million estate, your second spouse will receive a full 10 percent share of the $6 million estate ($600,000). As a result, your children's 90 percent share of your $6 million Living Trust assets is reduced by the full estate tax ($250,000) and by your second spouse's full 10 percent share ($600,000), for a grand total of $5,150,000.

Compare the results. With the proportional estate tax allocation provision, your children end up with $5,175,000. With the specific estate tax allocation provision that imposes the estate tax burden entirely on your children, your children end up with $5,150,000—a difference of $25,000.

Maybe you are in the wealth category where you do not consider $25,000 to be an overly significant amount of money. Then again, how do your children feel about it? How long does it take them to make $25,000? For some folks, like your children, that could be as much as one year's salary. By lowering their collective shares by $25,000, you may let them feel like they were robbed and you and your second spouse are the bandits—not with a gun, but with the specific estate tax allocation provision in your Living Trust that allocates the entire estate tax burden to them.

Do you care about your children's perceptions about imposing the entire estate tax burden on their share? Perhaps you do. Or perhaps you do not care one whit about how your children will react. But as your Living Trust advisor, I recommend that you explore these emotional and family issues that are part and parcel of estate tax allocation. Remember, this opportunity arises only if you are made aware of this tax issue in the first place.

Three Concepts You Must Know about Estate Tax Allocation

The area of estate tax allocation is very, very complex. Entire treatises have been written about this subject, which are beyond tedious. For you, though, I impose only this demand. When you walk away from this chapter, I want you to take away three main concepts.

The First Concept

The first concept is that you need to recognize the mere existence of the issue of the estate tax allocation. This is not just a boilerplate provision in your Living Trust; it is a substantive matter that will have a direct impact on the amounts received by your Living Trust beneficiaries. By merely glancing at this chapter, you now know enough about estate tax allocation to raise the subject with your lawyer as you establish your Living Trust.

Financial Advisor Alert

Not that impressing your clients is your predominant role as their financial advisor, but if you *really* want to impress your clients, say to them, "I want to take a look at the estate tax allocation provision of your Living Trust so I can see who pays the estate tax." *That* will do it! Then tell them what it says to see if it is comports with their understanding. However, since it is quite likely that they never before even thought about this issue, it becomes your function to map out the estate tax allocation arising from that provision and ascertain whether that result suits them. If the effect of that provision doesn't "fit" your clients, then you have to get them to their attorney so they can try on another one.

The Second Concept

The second concept is much more specific, and it is this: If your Living Trust leaves a specific bequest to a specific person, and your Living Trust contains an equal estate tax allocation provision, all hell will break loose among your Living Trust beneficiaries. You will have created a battle between the beneficiary who receives the specific gift and the rest of the beneficiaries who receive everything else.

Why this battle? Because the beneficiaries who receive everything else are now expected to bear the estate tax attributable to that specific gift.

You will more readily understand this conflict by reading the following example.

- You have four children—one daughter and three sons. You have a Living Trust that leaves your house to your daughter and all other Living Trust assets to your four children in equal shares.
- You die. Your after-death agent has valued your estate at $8 million. Of that $8 million, $2 million is attributable to your house.
- Your after-death agent determines that the estate tax due is $1 million.
- Your Living Trust includes an equal estate tax allocation provision, which states, in essence, that all four children shall bear the estate tax in equal shares.

Can you see where this is going?

Your daughter's specific bequest of your $2 million home constitutes 25 percent of your Living Trust assets. Fairness would seem to dictate that her share of the Living Trust assets should be reduced by 25 percent of the $1 million estate tax, which is $250,000. Instead, because of the equal estate tax allocation provision, the burden of paying the estate tax on your home falls upon all of your four children.

You want to see angry? Your three sons will be hopping mad! Not only did their sister get an extra gift, but they are responsible for three-quarters of the estate tax on that gift. That's a $62,500 reduction apiece.

Your three sons will argue that you did not intend to incorporate such an unfair estate tax allocation in your Living Trust, and they are probably right! In all likelihood, you would want your daughter to be responsible for the estate tax attributable to her specific bequest. But, because careful attention was not paid to this issue when you established your Living Trust, your document includes a general, boilerplate equal estate tax allocation provision, making your real intention irrelevant. As a result, your sons are stuck with the unfair and inequitable result.

The Third Concept

The third and final concept you must internalize is that you do not want your Living Trust beneficiaries to shoulder the estate tax burden that belongs to people who inherit your assets *outside* your Living Trust.

To illustrate this concept, let's think about the following scenario:

- You have a child from your first marriage.
- You have two children from your second marriage.
- You have a Living Trust that leaves all of your Living Trust assets to your two "second children."
- You love your one "first child." You do not want to leave him out of the inheritance arena. So, you buy an insurance policy that, on your death, pays out $500,000 to your first child.

- You die. Your after-death agent has ascertained that your Living Trust assets are worth $6 million. With your $500,000 insurance policy, your after-death agent determines your total net value at $6.5 million.
- Your after-death agent also determines that the estate tax on a $6.5 million estate is $450,000
- Your Living Trust provides that all estate taxes shall be borne by your Living Trust beneficiaries, in equal shares. This is the equal estate tax allocation provision.
- Your first child's $500,000 insurance proceeds pass to him outside of your Living Trust. All your first child needs to do is send a death certificate to the insurance company. The insurance company will then write a check to your first child for that amount.
- Your first child's $500,000 gift constitutes 7 percent (rounded) of your total estate. Ideally, your first child should be responsible for 7 percent of the $450,000 estate tax, which is $31,500. But, this is not the ideal world. Because your Living Trust provides that all estate taxes will be borne equally by your Living Trust beneficiaries, your non–Living Trust beneficiary—your first child—gets to skate away with his $500,000 without one penny of reduction.

Did you intend that your first child receive $500,000 without any reduction for the estate tax attributable to that gift? Probably not. If you had thought about it, you would have inserted a proportional estate tax provision that says, in essence, that all beneficiaries of your Living Trust assets and non–Living Trust assets shall bear their own burden of the estate tax and not shift the entire estate tax to the Living Trust assets.

But you didn't put in such a provision, because the issue of allocation was not brought to your attention.

Forewarned Is Forearmed

The allocation of the estate tax among the beneficiaries of your assets—whether they pass from or outside your Living Trust—is a very important issue that is almost always overlooked when a Living

Trust is established. But forewarned is forearmed! Now you are aware of the three most common types of estate tax allocation provisions, and that the wrong one in a Living Trust can have devastating unintended consequences among those beneficiaries.

So, now that you are armed with this advice from your Living Trust advisor, ask your Living Trust attorney this simple question at your next Living Trust review meeting—which, I assure you, he will never expect to hear from a client: "So, what type of estate tax allocation provision do you have in mind for our Living Trust?" I can almost promise you that his reaction will be to fall off his chair. After he picks himself up off the floor and dusts himself off, he will review his standard boilerplate estate tax allocation provision in the context of your particular set of circumstances.

And who knows? Perhaps he may conclude that his standard estate tax allocation provision may not be so applicable in your Living Trust.

POSTGAME

REVIEW AND LESSONS LEARNED

Y ou are now out of the Inheritance Arena. You established your Living Trust, lived with it, and died with it. Your lifetime of accumulations has been distributed to your children, grandchildren, charities, and other beneficiaries you have named in your Living Trust.

What happens now? Postgame review! This is when we play back the video of the game and learn from what went right . . . and what went wrong. Of course, since I have not had the pleasure of meeting you personally and getting to know your particular inheritance circumstances, it is impossible to review your game film to see how you did. Did your beneficiaries experience the smooth transfer of your Living Trust assets without diminishment from probate fees and estate taxes? Or did they engage in so much conflict that they had to resort to the televised court of Judge Joe Brown for resolution?

Since it is physically impossible for me to review your game film, I must resort to relaying the experiences I have had with various Living Trust scenarios from my 30 years of practicing in the area of inheritance planning. From the Q&A and the cautionary tales that are present in this cooling-down period, you may see yourself and be able to take away some valuable advice that you can incorporate into your Living Trust.

Your existence in the Living Trust world at all stages of the game is quite insular. You don't know anything about your neighbor's Living Trust. You probably don't know much about the Living Trusts of your closest friends and relatives, other than the fact that they have established them. The Living Trust is one of the most private matters that you will ever encounter. But when the inheritance instructions in Living Trusts are not carefully considered, the most private family matters explode into a public and legal forum where seemingly everyone knows your business. A lot of the game film you will now see in this part is just that. It is a display of previously private family matters that became public in a legal context because of Living Trusts that were not created using the wisdom of *The Living Trust Advisor.*

24

Question and Answer Time!

OR,

TAKE THE OPPORTUNITY TO ASK THIS EXPENSIVE LAWYER YOUR QUESTIONS . . . AT NO CHARGE

I always leave room at the end of my Living Trust seminars for Q&A, so I thought I would follow suit with the last section of this book, the Postgame Review.

Answering questions is my favorite thing to do as an inheritance planning attorney. Some people get their fun by hang gliding, making pottery, collecting coins, or watching flies getting killed by bug zappers. For me, fun is coaching girls' softball; hanging with my kids (whenever they are not embarrassed to be seen with me); dining with my amazing girlfriend, Kim; swimming and surfing; watching any movie that co-stars Eva Mendes (who I believe is the second coming of Raquel Welch); and answering inheritance planning questions—wherever and whenever. At my seminars. In newspaper columns. On radio and television call-in shows. At parties and restaurants. Over the phone, by e-mail, at the office, or at my home. It just makes me feel good to be able to respond to folks in a helpful and meaningful manner.

Whenever a question is posed, I get the opportunity to see how I perform with the answer. With so many questions being the same ("What is the Living Trust?"), I like to challenge myself by giving answers that deviate from the usual seminar script. Also, I want to see how well I fare with questions that deal with subjects for which I have only practical experience (as opposed to formal class training), which, for the most part, concern family and human dynamics in the inheritance arena that may best be answered by psychologists.

In all my previous books since *Beyond the Grave* was published in 1996, I invited readers to ask me any questions—for free—about the Living Trust or any matter in the inheritance arena that pertains to them. I would like to continue to extend that invitation to you, but please follow the guidelines I discuss at the end of this book in "About the Author." Here is my contact information:

Jeffrey L. Condon
Condon & Condon
3435 Ocean Park Boulevard
Suite 108
Santa Monica, CA 90405
Office: (310) 393-0701
Fax: (310) 394-3555
E-mail: jeff@condonandcondon.net

The Top Ten Questions I Receive from Real People

Without further ado and further revelation, here are variations of the most commonly asked questions I receive from my readers, seminar attendees, and clients about issues that arise in the inheritance arena. The process upon which I based my determination of most common is somewhat informal: just me sitting at my computer typing this chapter while trying to recall which questions seem to come repeatedly, and those that, I felt, would be of most interest to the reader. But I don't believe I'm too far off the track on what you, America, most want to ask about what I know about inheritance planning.

> **Q.** I have a Living Trust, but I still don't know what the heck it is. I don't want another review with my attorney, and I don't want to bother with any more reading. Can you just give me a really simple definition of the Living Trust so I can understand it once and for all?

A. Sure. Focus on this definition, and you will understand it for the rest of your life.

Your Living Trust is your after-death power of attorney. In your Living Trust, you appoint someone—your after-death agent—to sign your name to all the documents that are needed to transfer your assets after your death, such as the deed to your house.

Who will your after-death agent transfer your assets to? To the persons you've named in your Living Trust as the beneficiaries of those assets.

Who is your after-death agent? Whoever you named as your after-death agent in your Living Trust.

In its simplest form, that is the Living Trust.

Q. My daughter inherited $250,000 from her uncle. She is receiving Supplemental Security Income (SSI), which includes medical benefits. Won't this inheritance cause her to lose her government entitlements?

A. Yes. Ownership of money in excess of $2,000 will jeopardize her continued eligibility to receive SSI.

What can be done to ensure her continued receipt of those benefits from SSI?

She can disclaim the inheritance, which is the same thing as renouncing it. But, if more than nine months have passed since her uncle's death, she cannot make a valid disclaimer. Also, she may not want to give up the money.

She can give away the inheritance. But she will be ineligible to receive SSI for a number of years following her transfer of that money. And again, she may not like the idea of giving away $250,000.

Finally, she can transfer her inheritance to a Special Needs Trust. This is a trust that is established to hold and apply funds for her special needs that are not covered by the funds your daughter gets from SSI.

Specifically, SSI pays for your daughter's basic needs for food, clothing, shelter, and medical care. If your daughter's inheritance is used to pay for those basic needs, SSI is no longer needed. But if her inheritance is used to pay only for things that have nothing to do with those basic needs, such as travel and entertainment, then she can continue to be eligible to receive SSI.

Therefore, by placing her inheritance in a Special Needs Trust, those funds will only be used for her special needs, while SSI continues to pay for her basic needs.

Your daughter's uncle could have left her inheritance directly to a Special Needs Trust created in his Living Trust. But he didn't, so your daughter will have to establish her own Special Needs Trust. In such a case where a person establishes her own Special Needs Trust, she will likely have to hire an attorney to file the appropriate petition with the court to obtain an order consenting to the establishment of that Self-Settled Special Needs Trust.

Q. On my death, my son will inherit a substantial amount of money and property from my Living Trust. He's on his third marriage. I'm afraid the inheritance will end up with a new wife or girlfriend, and not my grandchildren. I know he will have a prenuptial agreement, but is that enough to prevent his inheritance from being siphoned off by his new significant other?

A. A prenuptial agreement between your son and his wife may not be a sufficient guarantee that your money and property will end up with your grandchildren. Once your son inherits your money and property, it's his to do what he wants with it, including putting his wife's name on the bank assets, brokerage assets, and real estate.

The only way you can obtain a 100 percent guarantee that your son will not divert his inheritance out of the bloodline is by leaving his inheritance to him in a protection trust, which I discuss in detail in Chapter 18.

The protection trust allows your son lifetime control of and access to his inheritance while preventing him from using the inheritance for improper purposes. What is an improper purpose? Anything that you say it is. You can put a provision in the protection trust that states your son is prohibited from transferring ownership of any inherited assets to any other person.

If your son is his own protection trust manager, you will be relying on him to police himself to not violate that restriction. If you don't trust your son to honor that restriction, you should name a professional fiduciary party as his protection trust manager, such as the trust department of a bank that will follow your instructions to the letter. Then, on your son's death, the manager of your son's protection trust will transfer the remaining inheritance to your grandchildren.

Q. My son is a drug addict. I love him, but I don't love what he does. I want to leave him an inheritance, but I just know it will end up spent on drugs. Shall I just cut him out and leave all of my Living Trust assets to my daughter?

A. Nobody wants to leave an inheritance to a child who you know will waste it. Your idea of leaving everything to your daughter is a natural and instinctual response to that concern.

But, if you cut out your son and leave it all to your daughter, bad things may happen.

If your son has a tendency to violence or rage, you or your daughter could become a victim of that physical aggression.

Your son may develop rancorous feelings toward his sister because he will believe (rightly or wrongly) that she is responsible for him being cut out of his inheritance.

Your son may believe that since his sister has his share of the inheritance, she has the duty to provide for his financial needs.

Your son may become a homeless or street person.

In other words, by dumping your son from your Living Trust, you may be dumping him into your daughter's life . . . and into the street.

Instead of cutting your son out of your Living Trust, perhaps it would be better to leave him his share of the inheritance, but in a protection trust where he has no control of or access to the funds. In this arrangement, you appoint a third party as the manager of your son's share who will apply the funds for his basic needs in life, such as food, clothing, shelter, and medical care. You can even provide that if your son somehow gets clean as measured by some objective standards, he can gain control and ownership of his funds. The "carrot" of gaining control could even conceivably be an incentive for him to shape up.

Q. My Living Trust says that $100,000 shall go to the YMCA. I want the YMCA to use the money for proper purposes, like buying new athletic equipment or sending underprivileged children to YMCA camp for the summer. How can I be certain that the funds will be used the way I want?

A. Since you will be dead, you will never know whether the money you leave to the YMCA will be used to assist children or applied toward the purchase of shrimp cocktail sauce for its next fund-raiser. However, you want to die confident that your gift will be used for the former.

There are four steps you can take to increase the odds that the charity you select to be a beneficiary of your Living Trust will use its gift in the manner you desire.

First, in your Living Trust, you must state how you want the YMCA to apply the gift. If you want the money to be spent on sports equipment or camp scholarships, put that instruction right in the bequest.

Second, also state in your Living Trust how you do not want the gift to be used. For example, in the Living Trust I would prepare for you, I would explicitly state this admonition: "The YMCA shall not use this bequest for any purpose that is not directly related to purchasing athletic equipment or providing camp scholarships for underprivileged youth. For example, the YMCA shall not use this bequest for the purchase of any item or service related to fund-raising, travel or entertainment of any board member or staff operative, or payment of any existing or future debt or tax."

Third, also state in your Living Trust that the president of the YMCA must enter into an agreement with your Living Trust's after-death agent that the funds will be used for the purposes specified by you. Add that if the president does not make such an agreement, the bequest to the YMCA shall be canceled and shall, instead, be given to a backup charity.

Fourth, let the fund-raising office of the YMCA know that your Living Trust includes a specific bequest to the YMCA that must be used for the purposes you set forth in your Living Trust.

Q. We have three children. Our daughter is a successful businessperson. Our two sons are nice guys, but not really financially oriented. When we establish our Living Trust, we want to appoint just our daughter as our Living Trust's after-death agent, because she is better equipped to deal with inheritance matters than our two other children. Don't you agree?

A. Not only no, but hell, no!

Do not make one child boss over your other children. Do not create a situation where you have one child in power and your other children on the outside looking in. This potentially creates a breeding ground for suspicion, resentment, and jealousy, which will result in rancor and divisiveness between your daughter and your sons.

Your after-death agent has a lot of power in the inheritance arena: the power to decide whether to liquidate real estate and stocks, the power to determine which attorney and accountant to use, the power to decide which assets will be distributed to the beneficiaries, the power to decide how and when the federal estate tax will be paid, and on and on.

While all these decisions are being made by your daughter, your other children are sitting on the sidelines, wondering what is going on, questioning whether their sister's decisions are prudent or self-serving, and asking why they have not been contacted for their input.

And fanning the flames are the feelings of your other children that you did not love them as much or trust them to do the job that your daughter has solely for herself.

If you want to name just one child as the after-death agent of your Living Trust, you have to sell me on the reason for doing so. If you tell me that your other children are drug addicts, mentally ill, permanently estranged, or missing, I will accept your decision and draft your Living Trust with that one child named as the sole after-death agent.

However, if you tell me that your other children do not financially measure up to your chosen child, or that your other children are located in faraway and exotic locales, or that all your children do not get along, or that you firmly believe that too many cooks spoil the broth, I will attempt to change your mind by asking you, and answering for you, this question:

Does your reason for appointing only one child as after-death agent outweigh the harm that will come to your family because only one child is named as your after-death agent?

Answer: No way! In my mind, your goal of an efficient Living Trust administration after your death never trumps the potential harm to your children's sibling relationships caused by your imposition of a power imbalance.

So, do not appoint just one of your children as your after-death agent. Appoint all your children. If one child elects not to serve, he can always resign or decline to act. The decision to serve is shifted to your children and imposed on them by you.

Q. I am a U.S. citizen. My wife is not. We have a Living Trust to which we transferred all of our joint assets. Are there any problems that will occur if I die before my wife?

A. Oh, yes!

There is something in the federal tax law called the marital deduction. This means that there is no estate tax on the transfer of assets from a deceased spouse to a surviving spouse. In other words, there is a dollar-for-dollar estate tax deduction for every dollar going from a dead spouse to a living spouse.

But, in order to get this estate tax break, the surviving spouse has to be a U.S. citizen. Even if your wife has a green card or permanent resident status, she will still not get that estate tax break, because she is not a U.S. citizen. Thus, if you die before your wife and your wife is not a U.S. citizen at the time, she will be required to pay an estate tax on every dollar she receives from your share of the Living Trust assets.

Why did Congress make this rule? Because Congress decided that your noncitizen wife is likely to return to her country of origin, taking the family wealth with her. If your wife takes such an action, she prevents the IRS from imposing an estate tax on those assets on her death.

What can be done to eliminate the estate tax if you die before your noncitizen wife? There are two solutions.

First, your wife can become a U.S. citizen before your death.

Second, in your Living Trust, you can provide that if you die before your wife, your half of the Living Trust assets will go to a special subtrust called a qualified domestic trust (QDOT). With the QDOT, you provide that your half will be held by your wife and a third-party U.S. citizen as co-managers of the assets. By appointing an American co-manager, you give the IRS assurance that sufficient controls are in place to prevent your wife from fleeing to her country of origin with the assets it wants to tax when your wife dies.

In the QDOT, the co-manager is instructed to pay to your wife income and additional funds that are necessary for her basic needs, such as food, clothing, housing, and medical. The QDOT further provides that if your wife becomes a U.S. citizen, the subtrust ends and your wife takes over control of the assets; but if not, then the QDOT assets pass to your children or other heirs on your wife's death.

Q. I know my parents have a substantial estate. I also know they have not done anything about establishing a Living Trust to avoid probate or putting together a plan to reduce estate taxes. How do I get them to do something without coming across to them like a greedy guy who can't wait for his parents to die?

A. I used to believe that people would jump at the opportunity to save probate fees and estate taxes for their family. I once believed that "cutting out probate fees and taxes" were magic words that would spirit people to my office to establish a Living Trust or other inheritance plan. As a result, I have spoken those words to tens of thousands of people during my 30-year practice at seminars, meetings, and consultations. If you count my radio and television appearances, the number of folks who have heard or watched me spread this gospel jumps to the hundreds of thousands.

Why, then, do I not have hundreds of thousands of Living Trust clients? Why do I not even have tens of thousands of Living Trust clients? Here's the truth I have gleaned after talking with so many client prospects during my practice: People do care about the loss of their money to probate and estate taxes after they are gone, but not enough to pay a lawyer to do something about it.

That's the truth, pure and simple. Paying a lawyer to do anything is out of the comfort zone for so many people, especially for those who have not had any prior dealings with lawyers.

People are not stupid. They recognize the benefits of the Living Trust and estate planning. But how much desire is there to pay for a product that produces a benefit that does not come into play until after their deaths? If your parents were to answer this question, they might answer, "Not a whole hell of a lot."

So, in the face of this "After me, who cares?" mind-set, what can you do to get your parents to do something? Forget about the former magic words of "avoiding probate" and "saving estate taxes." Your parents have already heard them ad nauseam and have done nothing. Instead, use this three-step plan of attack:

First, find a Living Trust lawyer and hire him or her to establish your own Living Trust. It does not matter whether you need one. That's not the point. The point is to be able to position yourself to say the words to your parents that appear in the third step.

Second, while you are in the process of establishing your Living Trust, go to your parents' house and show them a draft of the document. Do not send it to them. Do not leave it on their front porch. You have to physically drop it in their laps.

Third, while they are thumbing through the document, you say these words:

"Dad and Mom, as you can see, I'm in the process of establishing my Living Trust, and it's great. When I'm gone, it's going to make things a lot easier for my family. And you know what? If I have one, you should have one. Let me make an appointment for you to see my lawyer. He's terrific. And if you're happy with him, let him do a Living Trust for you, and I'll pay."

With these steps, you will have removed from their path two obstacles that prevented them from establishing their Living Trust: finding a lawyer and paying a lawyer.

If that doesn't help, I suppose you can try gunpoint.

Q. We do not have any real relationship with our daughter. We may speak with her a few times a year, but we do not feel like including her as a beneficiary in our Living Trust. Can we cut her out?

A. There is no law that says you have to leave anything to a child. It is your money. You can leave it to whomever and however you want. Leave more to one child and less to another, leave out one child entirely, or omit all your children. These are your decisions.

If you are going to cut out your daughter from your Living Trust, you have to do it right. If you do it wrong, you will leave a mess that your other children will have to clean up.

You must assume that when you die, your daughter will hire an attorney to prepare a lawsuit contesting your Living Trust. Your daughter needs a reason to support that contest, which she will find. Or if she cannot find a reason, she will make one up.

For example, did you know that your other children forced you into disinheriting her though duress or coercion? Were you aware that you did not have the requisite "testamentary capacity" when you signed your Living Trust? Don't you remember that you cut out your daughter by mistake? Well, you may not recall all of that, but your daughter and her lawyer certainly do, even though they were not on the scene at the time.

When your other children are faced with the lawsuit to overturn your Living Trust, they may find it cheaper to settle the case than pay a lawyer for the defense. Your daughter knows this; people often bring lawsuits for the sole purpose of extorting a settlement.

So, what you have to do is help out your other children by helping to prepare the defense of that after-death lawsuit before you die.

First, around the time you sign your Living Trust, visit your family doctor and get examined. Then, have your doctor write a letter on his letterhead, or a prescription pad, which says that, in the doctor's opinion, you are capable and competent to the extent that you can handle your own financial affairs and make your own financial decisions. Give that letter to your lawyer to be put in your file.

Second, write a letter to your daughter in your own handwriting that explains why you are cutting her out of your Living Trust. She will not be shown this letter. You will not send it to her. It will remain in your file in your lawyer's office, untouched and unseen.

Third, make an audiotape of your Living Trust's signing ceremony. On this tape, your lawyer will ask you to confirm that you are aware that you are cutting out your daughter.

Your answers must be in a tenor and tone that convey your understanding of your action and the strength of your conviction in taking that action. Once again, this item will stay with your lawyer in the file.

When you die, and your daughter announces that the lawsuit is forthcoming, your lawyer will send these three items to your daughter's lawyer. Upon receipt and review of the items, your daughter's lawyer will advise the client to drop the lawsuit. That will be the end of it. Your daughter will not be able to find any lawyer to take that case, even on a contingency basis. No lawyer wants to walk into the mouth of a cannon.

One last thing about cutting out a child: Even if it goes against your grain, you should tell your daughter you are leaving her out of your Living Trust. Why? Because, in my experience, I have found that greed may lead to family reconciliation.

I am talking about exactly what you think I am talking about. I want you to appeal to the greed in your daughter to motivate her to come back into the family fold. It takes whatever it takes to get estranged family members talking to each other; and if what it takes is the prospect of money, so be it. I have found that money can accomplish more than anything else to quiet the squeaky wheel of family estrangement.

In fact, the incidence of estrangement is so common, I created a standard form letter appealing to the greed in the child to be cut out. As it applies to you and your daughter, this is what my "greed letter" states to your daughter:

Dear Daughter of Clients:

Your parents have conferred with me about a Living Trust that, for now, excludes you as a beneficiary. Based on the estimated value of your parents' estate, this would result in a loss to you of $500,000. I understand that I am not your family advisor, priest, rabbi, mediator, or whichever facilitator you prefer. But, as your parents' attorney, I only want to say that while your parents are alive, there is a chance for reconciliation that could result in you receiving a share of their Living Trust assets. Obviously, that opportunity ends after your last parent dies.

Q. I change my mind all the time about who gets my personal property after I'm dead. But I'm sick of coming to you and paying a fee every time I want to make those changes in my Living Trust. What can I do to cut you out of the loop?

A. You are not the only one who is tired of making those types of changes to your Living Trust. I'm not crazy about them myself.

One of the simpler services I render is amending Living Trusts to accommodate changes in the disposition of personal property. Rings, antiques, cars, computers, clothes, dogs, cats, pictures, art—all the stuff that you have in your home, storage facility, or safe-deposit box. But do not equate simplicity with lack of effort. Like any amendment to a Living Trust, a personal property amendment still involves intake, attorney time, drafting, review, secretary time, and client time. While I don't charge for Living Trust consultations on the phone or in person, I do charge for work, which, of course, includes the preparation of the simple personal property amendment. As my father said, "Jeff, you can be the greatest estate planning attorney that ever lived, which you are not, but if you're not being paid for your work, you might as well be at the beach."

Still, I don't like drafting personal property amendments. The clients resent me because they feel the work is not enough to justify a charge. I resent the clients because they resent me, and because the personal property amendment takes me away from more pressing matters, more intellectually challenging pursuits, and, yes, more work that can result in higher billing.

So, to remove myself and the clients from this vicious circle of resentment, I now craft a standard provision in all of my Living Trusts called the "Personal Property

Memorandum." This provision states that the clients instruct that all of their personal property will be distributed by the after-death agent in accordance with their wishes as expressed in a separate Personal Property Memorandum ("PPM"). I supply clients with PPM forms on which they simply make their own instructions on who receives what. The PPM does not have to be on the form that I provide. It can be on any piece of paper the client titles "PPM."

The beauty of the PPM is that if the clients change their minds, they simply erase or cross out one instruction and fill in a new instruction . . . all without having to involve the lawyer! It does not matter if there are endless revisions to the PPM. It's still valid, and the instructions on the PPM are still valid. This isn't grade school where you get your grade marked down for neatness issues.

Certainly, the possibility looms that a PPM can be changed or altered by someone other than the client. To prevent that scenario from occurring, I instruct the client to send me a copy of the PPM each time he makes changes to it. Upon my receipt of the copy, I place it in the client's file. When the client dies, I will compare the copy of his original PPM to the copy in my file. If the original contains changes that are inconsistent with the copy, I will make further inquiry into the matter to determine if a "fast one" has been pulled. But, as a practical matter, I have not yet had such a scenario arise with any PPM, although there is always the proverbial first time.

What if clients do not include instructions in the PPM for the disposition of all their personal property items? For example, perhaps they used the PPM only to distribute their jewelry, piano, and gun collection, but did not mention who gets the clothes, furniture, or automobile. Or even more compelling, perhaps the clients did not complete any portion of the PPM. Who gets their personal property in that case?

To both concerns, fear not. In the PPM provision in the Living Trust, there is a backup plan that says what happens to items not described in the separate PPM, or in the event that the separate PPM does not exist at all. The backup plan can be whatever the client wants it to be. Perhaps it leaves the personal property to the client's children "as they so shall agree." Or perhaps it gives the after-death agent full discretion on selecting the recipients. Or perhaps it says that all personal property shall be sold, with the sale proceeds distributed in equal shares. When it comes to the backup plan, the possibilities are only limited by imagination.

The Top Five Questions I Receive from Financial People

Now and then, I conduct seminars about what every financial professional should know about inheritance planning. The following are five of the most common questions I receive at those sessions:

Q. What is most pressing and important issue that I should discuss with my clients about their Living Trust?

A. If your clients are married, and their combined net worth is less than $5 million, they *absolutely do not need* the provisions in their Living Trust that require that their trust estate "split" into an exemption trust/survivor's trust after the first spouse dies (sometimes known as the A/B trust split). Instead, after the first spouse dies, the surviving spouse will prepare and file the deceased spouse's federal estate tax return. When the Magic Box is checked off on that return, and the return is timely filed, the effect is the same as the A/B trust split, which is that the surviving spouse picks up the deceased spouse's lifetime exemption.

But, if the A/B trust split is mandated in the Living Trust, then the surviving spouse must still perform the A/B trust split and engage in the high-maintenance activities that Trust B requires—for the rest of the surviving spouse's life! Such a hassle that serves no purpose. Have your married clients amend their Living Trust to provide for an *optional* A/B trust split. While the surviving spouse will likely never have to use it, it's there if the need arises, such as a change in the estate tax law that lowers the lifetime exemption.

Q. Can a Living Trust be challenged?

A. Yes. While a Living Trust avoids the hassles and costs of probate and can be "built" with inheritance conflict-resolution provisions, any disgruntled heir can wage a court battle against it, just as a will can be challenged. The trick to preventing a challenge is to fill the client file with documents that establish that your clients were of "sound mind" when they signed their Living Trusts, such as letters from physicians that attest to their mental capacity and handwritten letters from your clients in which they state the reasons for their inheritance instructions. When your clients die and the unhappy heir announces that he has retained an attorney to challenge the trust, that lawyer will receive those documents . . . and that will be the end of the lawsuit.

Q. Will a Living Trust require a lot of additional work and cost if my clients add or delete property or investments?

A. No. Your clients' Living Trust does not have to change when their assets change. All they have to do is take title to assets in their names as trustees of their Living Trust, and transfer title to assets in their names as trustees of their Living Trust.

Q. You have directed me to look at my clients' Living Trust to see if it has certain provisions. I'm not a lawyer! Doesn't that constitute practicing law without a license?

A. Not a bit. I have not, and never will, direct you to draft anything or give legal advice. All you are doing is raising your clients' awareness on a particular Living Trust matter and advising them (sometimes strongly) to see their estate planning attorney for further review.

In my mind, it is the responsibility of the financial advisor to know when it is time to bring in the ancillary professional. I have coached you throughout this book to recognize when that time has come. Many of the Financial Advisor Alerts peppered throughout this book have pointed out how your clients' Living Trust could inadvertently cause family drama and economic loss after their deaths.

Let me put it another way. Your role as your clients' financial advisor involves recognizing money-related issues that are of great import to them. You perform that function when dispensing advice about their financial and investment activities. You give them options and point out the potential ramifications and effects. When you review your clients' Living Trust to examine a particular section (in the context of the Financial Advisor Alerts that you have read in this book), you fulfill that same vital function of issue-recognition. Once you have raised your clients' awareness about that matter-at-hand, you give them the opportunity to consider it further with their estate planning attorney.

Q. My client has named her daughter as the beneficiary of her IRA. But my client's daughter is nonstop "party girl." When my client dies, her daughter will take out the money to keep the party going. Can my client designate some type of trust as the IRA beneficiary to protect the funds for her daughter?

A. Yes. In fact, protecting the IRA funds from misuse is what the "IRA look-through trust" is all about, and that is the type of trust that should be named as the beneficiary of your client's IRA.

When inheriting an IRA, the beneficiary's main goal is to preserve the tax-advantaged status of the account for as long as possible. But if your client's daughter will likely cash out of the IRA and party down, then your client can force her daughter to comply with the IRA requirements by naming the look-through trust as the beneficiary. With that trust, the IRA account is preserved and protected from the daughter's vice . . . and the minimum required distributions are made, using the daughter's life expectancy as the measuring stick. When the distributions are made, they are made to the trust, not the daughter. As a result, your client will preserve for her daughter the ability to stretch the payment out over a long period of time.

In order for the look-through trust to qualify as a valid IRA beneficiary, there are four requirements that the trust must have:

1. It must be valid under your client's state law.
2. It must be irrevocable upon your client's death.
3. It must have an identifiable human beneficiary.
4. It must be delivered to the plan administrator or custodian by October 31 of the year following the year of your client's death.

A Random Sampling of Cautionary Tales from the Inheritance Arena

OR,

READ ABOUT, AND LEARN FROM, MY PREVIOUS MISTAKES AND THE MISTAKES OF MY CLIENTS

Legal knowledge about Living Trusts is not enough to prevent problems from occurring in the inheritance arena. Like the medical doctor who gains experience on the ills and bodies of patients, so it is with the Living Trust attorney who gains wisdom, understanding, and sensitivity to forecasting potential problems by seeing what happens when money and property pass from a deceased person to a spouse, children, grandchildren, and others.

The stories in this chapter are true. Each story is representative of things gone wrong because of the failure to foresee consequences in the process of money and property going from the dead to the living. They are incidents from which I gained experience to better advise clients on the right way of transferring money and property after death.

With these stories, you will gain invaluable information and insight about your own Living Trust or other inheritance plan that comes only from being there when assets go from the dead to the living.

With these stories, you will see that unintended consequences are common in the inheritance arena.

With these stories, you will benefit from my many years of observing the hurt that occurs when a mistake is made in the Living Trust or the inheritance arena.

Cautionary Tale 1: The Last One on the Scene Gets the Money

Lesson to be learned: If one of your children becomes your care-taker when you are elderly, that child might end up with a greater share of the Living Trust assets.

Mr. Washington's older daughter called me from Idaho, com-plaining that she had not been able to contact her father since her sister moved into his house to take care of him.

"I send him birthday cards, Christmas cards. No reply. When I call him, my sister always answers and says he isn't able to come to the phone. It's like she's afraid to let me contact him."

I recall saying, "That doesn't sound good. It's always the same. One of the children gets into control and ends up with the money." It is a scenario I had seen numerous times:

- A surviving parent becomes elderly and needs care.
- Some children are unable or unwilling to care for that par-ent, leaving a vacuum that is filled by a willing child, or imposed on that child because all of his siblings opted out of the burden.

Pretty soon, the child left holding the bag realizes that caring for the parent on a daily basis presents a significant imposition on his lifestyle, while the other siblings go on with their normal lives.

Eventually, the caretaker child thinks about being compensated for his services.

Mr. Washington was ultimately persuaded to see me about his Living Trust. The moment I saw him in his wheelchair being pushed into my office by his caretaker daughter, I just knew what

Mr. Washington was going to say to me, and he did not let me down: "Mr. Condon, I want an amendment to my Living Trust that leaves 80 percent to my daughter who lives with me. She deserves it for taking care of me. The other 20 percent can go my daughter who lives in Idaho."

You should have seen his daughter's face when I told Mr. Washington that I would not draft that amendment. With her mouth agape and complexion turning beet red, I said, "Mr. Washington, there is no way I am going to do that amendment. I've been through this too many times. When you die and your Idaho daughter finds out you left her only 20 percent, I'm the one she's going to scream at."

"What are you talking about?" Mr. Washington asked.

"I'm talking about why you are here. Who came up with the 80/20 split in the first place? You? I don't think so. It was your caretaker daughter, wasn't it?"

The caretaker daughter was silent. So was Mr. Washington. I took from their silence that I had hit the nail on the head. Since I was on a roll, I kept going.

"Listen, Mr. Washington. Take my advice. Leave your trust the way it is with all of your assets going to your two daughters equally. Just pay your caretaker daughter an agreed-upon rate per hour of service. Pay it as you go along. That's what your daughter would want if she had a job working for someone else. Instead, she's working for you, so you might as well pay her. Thanks for coming."

I did not have such a warm bedside manner, I admit. But sometimes I have to be abrupt in order to get my point across, especially to folks who come in thinking "A" and never before even considering "B."

When Mr. Washington and his caretaker daughter left my office (which was about five minutes after they arrived), I thought they would take my advice of pay-as-you-go-along. Until I received a call from the Idaho daughter, complaining that she still had no access to her father. During that call, I asked her whether she had ever heard from her sister or father about that payment plan.

The Idaho daughter responded that she did not know what I was talking about, which, to me, meant that the caretaker daughter had found another way to get paid. I instructed the Idaho daughter to check out title to her father's house and bank accounts. Why? Because I'd bet that the caretaker daughter convinced her father to put her name on those assets as a co-owner.

A few days later, the Idaho daughter called me back to tell me I had guessed correctly. The jaded attorney was right, but only because he had become so cynical through being a percipient witness to similar scenarios in the past. But the result is that when Mr. Washington dies, his caretaker daughter will own 100 percent of those assets, cutting out the Idaho daughter entirely.

So, what could the Idaho daughter do to remedy this situation, to remove her sister's name from those assets and transfer them back to her father's Living Trust? We discussed litigation to establish a conservatorship over her father. As conservator, she would have the power to cancel the joint ownership of her father and sister and return the assets to the Living Trust. However, to get to that point, the Idaho sister would have to prove that her father was influenced by his caretaker daughter into putting her name on title to his house and accounts and that he was unable to resist that influence. But the Idaho daughter was not desirous of spending her own money for what would be a never-ending pursuit involving a lot of expensive medical experts and testimony.

Finally, I said to the Idaho daughter, "If you don't want to sue, then there is only one solution. Get back into your father's life. You be the one to get his groceries, take him to the doctor, drive him everywhere, clean up after him, suffer through chemotherapy with him, get his medicine, and do all the other things your sister is doing for him, including watching him die. Can you leave your life in Idaho and do that?"

There was a long silence on the phone. I asked again, "Can you?"

The Idaho daughter timidly replied, "Thanks for your time." Then she hung up the phone.

Post–Cautionary Tale Comment: Whenever I get a call from one sibling saying that another sibling has taken over the surviving dependent parent, I automatically assume that the type of financial elder abuse described in this Cautionary Tale is taking place.

You should recognize that the child who takes care of you in your elder dependent years deserves, and is entitled to, compensation for services rendered and should be paid as you go along. In your Living Trust, you should have a specific provision that states that if you become incapacitated, your lifetime agent shall pay a salary to a caretaker child in an amount commensurate with the market rate for such services. This arrangement is preferable to your caretaker child simply helping himself to your assets because he thinks he deserves it.

The best advice I can give you to prevent such a takeover by one of your children is to not allow this situation to arise. Tell your children to stay connected. Tell them they cannot expect to receive a full share of the inheritance if the caregiving burden is shifted to, or assumed by, one of your children.

Cautionary Tale 2: A New Marriage Requires a New Living Trust

Lesson to be learned: If you are on your second spouse, your failure to update your Living Trust can give your second spouse inheritance rights to your Living Trust assets if you die first.

Mr. Gibson was about 85, but he didn't know his exact age. Born in Poland, he left to escape military conscription. He came to America, got married, and had a son named Sam. I met Mr. Gibson when I set up a Living Trust for him and his wife that said, in essence, that Sam would get all the Living Trust assets when his last parent died. Mrs. Gibson died a few years later, and Mr. Gibson moved into an assisted-living facility so he wouldn't be a burden to his son and his wife.

That sounds fairly conventional, doesn't it? But what is also somewhat typical for widowers is going a second time around. After only 10 days at the assisted-living facility, Mr. Gibson met a lady, somehow managed to travel to Las Vegas on a casino junket, and married her! No one knew of this plan. Who knows if even Mr. Gibson knew?

One thing was certain, though. As soon as Sam found out that he had a stepmother, he called my office to see me. When we met, he asked me, "Did my dad consult you before he got married?" I said, "Are you kidding? I only heard about it when you told me. But your dad should have talked to me before taking that plunge to do a prenuptial agreement."

I also told Sam that his dad had to amend his Living Trust to make sure that his new wife would not end up with up to one-half of the Living Trust assets if he died before she did. Why? Because under California law, his new wife would be entitled to one-half unless he signed an amendment specifically excluding her as a beneficiary. When I told Sam that he could lose a good part of his inheritance, he almost went apoplectic.

After that meeting, Sam went to his father and told him to see me. Mr. Gibson declined, supposedly saying, "Why? I've already spent a lot of money with Condon for my Living Trust leaving everything to you. Why spend more?"

Sam would not let it rest. He had me send a letter to his father that said, in essence: "Mr. Gibson, if you don't sign an amendment to your Living Trust excluding your new wife, she will end up with half of your estate. I'm sure you are fond of your new wife, but you have known her for only a few weeks. Would you rather your assets go to your lifelong son, or to an almost virtual stranger?"

Two weeks later, not having heard from Mr. Gibson, I called him at the assisted-living facility. Expecting to speak with a mentally addled, hard-of-hearing dependent adult, I shouted a monosyllabic recitation of the issue at hand into the telephone. I felt like an idiot when Mr. Gibson said in a clear-as-a-bell voice, "Mr. Condon, why the hell are you screaming? Do you think I'm a doddering old codger? I understood everything you said!"

Mr. Gibson said he would think about changing his Living Trust. I asked, "What is there to think about?" Then he and I had a brief exchange of words I have never been able to put out of mind:

Mr. Gibson: Yeah. I'll get back to you. It's time for lunch.

Me: Fine. Don't die in the meantime.

Why have those words resonated with me to this day? Because Mr. Gibson died the next day! He wasn't supposed to die until after I got him to sign an amendment cutting out his new wife. But he did.

Mr. Gibson's new wife hired an attorney who claimed one-half of his estate, and that's what she got. It was a big price for Sam to pay for his father's obstinacy.

Post–Cautionary Tale Comment: The force of circumstances or neglect may result in the failure to execute a prenuptial agreement or Living Trust amendment before or immediately after a new marriage. As a result, it is very common to rely on a previously established Living Trust to direct the flow of the inheritance. But, as seen with this Cautionary Tale, the effect is the unintended consequence of giving the new spouse certain inheritance rights in a Living Trust.

You can leave your new spouse whatever you like, even all of your Living Trust assets if that is your desire. It's your money and property, and you can leave it as you please. However, if you are on your second time around and it is *not* your intention to bestow a significant portion of your Living Trust assets to your new spouse, you must hightail it over to your lawyer's office for a very simple amendment that limits your new spouse's interest to those assets.

Cautionary Tale 3: Sometimes Having Too Much Money Can Be a Curse

Lesson to be learned: If you have been blessed with a fortune, you have to give some thought to whether the inheritance of that fortune will turn your children away from living a productive life.

Mr. Kendall was one of the nicest men I ever had the pleasure to meet. He was married, with two elementary schoolchildren, a beautiful home, and no debts; he had never been arrested for anything, and was active in local community affairs. That sounds like the life I want.

So what was the problem? Mr. Kendall was in his mid-40s and had never held a steady job in his whole life. He was a trust-fund baby. His grandparents, now deceased, established the trust in the late 1920s for the benefit of their children, grandchildren, and great-grandchildren. After his grandparents' deaths, the after-death agent (one of those stuffy East Coast banks that have been around since the beginning of time) started to send him $25,000 monthly, which would continue for the rest of his life.

Again, what a life! Can you imagine an existence where the only productive thing you have to do is wait by your mailbox once a month for the postal carrier to deliver your $25,000 monthly allowance?

When Mr. Kendall dies, the trust says his children will receive the entire principal of an estate worth approximately $25 million. They will receive it outright, as in "Here you go. Enjoy!"

The prospect of big and easy money deterred Mr. Kendall from any productive life. With the constant knowledge that he never had to worry, he barely finished high school, started college to follow his buddies but soon dropped out, and never had any really steady or gainful employment. Still, Mr. Kendall had enough self-awareness to know how easy access to funds ruined him. As he said to me, "I never really had the motivation to do anything productive. My parents gave up on expecting me to find a job. I guess they felt since I was never a problem to them, they'd just let me slide along; and here I am. But, Mr. Condon, even though it's too late for me, I don't want this happening to my children."

I'm sure that if his grandparents had been aware of the harm their trust could do to their grandson, they would never have signed the document that provided the impetus for his trust-fund-baby lifestyle. But, at least he was smart enough to know the downside of idleness and did not want to inflict that lifestyle on his own children.

And that's why he came to see me. He wanted to find a way to divert the trust money away from his children so they could lead more conventional lives.

I read the trust document. It allowed Mr. Kendall to divert the trust assets to a charitable, educational, or religious organization of his choice if he had no children. Of course, he had two children, so that alternative was a nonstarter. I had to find another way to rearrange the trust to accomplish Mr. Kendall's goal. So, I told him,

"Hey! That's what judges are for. Let's go to court and see if we can get a judge to change the terms of the trust. Maybe we can keep the money from going to your children outright when you die."

One court petition and $10,000 in attorneys' fees later, there we were in the probate division of the Los Angeles Superior Court to ask the judge to allow Mr. Kendall to "bust the trust"— meaning that the terms of a trust, even if they are irrevocable, can be changed if the proponent of those changes can convince a judge that the changes are in the beneficiaries' best interests. The parties were Mr. Kendall, the bank, Mr. Kendall's parents, and Mr. Kendall's children. All were represented by attorneys, each charging at least $350 an hour. I put Mr. Kendall on the stand, and the following exchange took place:

> **Me:** Mr. Kendall, are you a bum?
>
> **Mr. Kendall:** Heck, yeah!
>
> **Probate Judge:** I want to see all the lawyers in my chambers right now!

In chambers, the judge said, "In all my 25 years as a trial judge, I've never heard a lawyer ask his own client if he was a bum! And your client even seemed happy to say yes. What is going on here?" I explained how Mr. Kendall's inheritance led him by the nose to an unproductive life, and that he wanted to prevent his children from suffering the same fate by changing the trust so they would not have total access to their wealth on their father's death. The lawyer for Mr. Kendall's parents nodded his head in agreement. The lawyer for the bank said he did not care what the judge did.

All eyes then turned toward the lawyer for Mr. Kendall's children, who was appointed by the court to represent their interests. The judge asked, "Well, what is the position of the remaindermen?" (The remaindermen are the beneficiaries who receive the principal after the death of the income beneficiaries.) The lawyer said, "Just like I said in my opposition, Judge. We don't know anything. The children may turn out to be potheads, or they may use the funds to jump-start a company to create cold fusion in a kitchen sink. How can we be so presumptive as to automatically assume that great wealth will bring about wasted lives?"

The judge said, "We can't. Mr. Condon, what were you thinking in bringing this matter to court? Were you hurting for fees?"

I do not bring specious actions, and I do not churn clients for fees. I truly believed in the concept of Mr. Kendall's vision, so I took his case. Nonetheless, the judge chided me for taking on a cause that, according to him, I should have known would go nowhere. Then he went back on the bench and dismissed the petition. The trust remains as is. When Mr. Kendall dies, his children will receive great wealth without any controls.

Post–Cautionary Tale Comment: An unintended consequence of a trust for a child or grandchild is the diminishment, or removal, of the motivation for higher education or gainful employment. Why work when you can surf, play tennis, or engage in whatever other activity floats your boat?

So, the question becomes: how much inheritance is too much inheritance? One famous investor stated that he would leave his children enough so they will not go hungry, but not so much that they will feel they never have to work. That is a worthy ideal, but where does the rest of the money go? To a charity, perhaps?

Sarcastically speaking, yeah, right! Many of my moneyed clients tell me they wish they had the courage to minimize the amount of wealth to a child or grandchild, but they did not spend 50 or 60 years of their lives accumulating wealth just to see it removed from the family bloodline. However, there are solutions that can be incorporated into the trust that are designed to prevent a significant inheritance from undermining the desire to lead a productive life. I discuss these solutions, sometimes called incentive trusts, in Chapter 19.

Cautionary Tale 4: Keep Your Opinions to Yourself If You Want to Inherit from Your Gay Relative

Lesson to be learned: If you object to your family member's gay or lesbian lifestyle, you may find yourself cut out of the Living Trust.

I practice in Santa Monica, which is miles and worlds away from West Hollywood and Silverlake, two areas of Los Angeles County that have a significant gay population. Nevertheless, I seem to have attracted as clients a bevy of upscale and financially successful gay couples from those cities. Why? Because of this one exchange with my first gay clients many years ago:

> **Gay Couple:** Mr. Condon, do you get any gay couples in your office for Living Trusts?
>
> **Me:** No. I must admit, you are my first.
>
> **Gay Couple:** Are you bothered by the fact that we are a gay couple?
>
> **Me:** No. I say, live and let live—just as long as you don't smoke.

That one line sent them into hysterics. They became my clients and told their many friends in the gay community about the funny and nonjudgmental lawyer in Santa Monica.

Among those new clients were Robert and Tom.

Robert was a very successful real estate investor who, except for Tom, had no family—no children, parents, siblings, uncles, aunts, cousins . . . no one. Tom, by contrast, had two brothers and five nieces and nephews, all raised as Mormons in Salt Lake City.

When they first conferred with me about Living Trusts, Robert's net worth was about $10 million, with no one to leave it to except Tom, his longtime partner. Tom, in turn, wanted a Living Trust leaving his assets, which were nowhere near Robert's level, to Robert. All this was fine.

The discussion then turned to the backup beneficiaries. If Tom died first, Robert's assets would have to go to someone other than Tom, and vice versa.

In Tom's Living Trust, Tom could name his family as his back-ups if Robert died first—an easy choice.

But in Robert's Living Trust, who would Robert name as back-ups if Tom died before him? Since Robert was 10 years older than Tom, the naming of backups in Robert's Living Trust became a most compelling matter. I suggested charities as the backups, but that did not fly with Robert. Finally, Robert said he had a friendly relationship with Tom's siblings and their children, and he would name them as the backups.

Robert died about five years later, survived by Tom, who inherited Robert's assets. I attended Robert's funeral and was struck by the amazing turnout—which did *not* include any members of Tom's family.

A few years later, I had the occasion to run into Tom, who was now the owner of Robert's lifetime of accumulations. He seemed to be taking Robert's death pretty hard. Trying to make some attempt at conversation, I said to Tom that I could not help but be surprised that none of his family had attended Robert's funeral. For an estate planning attorney jaded from years of clients' deaths, that constitutes small talk.

With this one random statement, Tom seemed to change before my eyes, from depressed to livid. He then said, "Nope. None showed up. I was surprised, too. About nine months ago, I went home for a change of scenery and to visit my family. Do you know what they told me? They said they did not attend the funeral because they did not want to give their fellow Mormons the impression that they approved of gay couples or the gay lifestyle. Can you imagine that? They never told me anything like that before."

Tom added that running into me reminded him that he wanted to change his Living Trust to cut out his relatives, based solely on that slight. "Screw the whole bunch of them, Jeff. How fast can you change my Living Trust to leave everything to those charities you mentioned when Robert and I were first in your office?"

Years later, Tom died. After his funeral, which his relatives did attend, his brother called me, saying that he assumed he was named as a beneficiary in Tom's Living Trust and asking me how long it would take for him to receive his share. That's when I told him, "You got cut out after Robert's funeral. Your big no-show and your inability to keep your Mormon opinion to yourselves cost you and your family about $30 million in real estate."

Post–Cautionary Tale Comment: What comment can I make about this story other than the obvious? In terms of the size of the loss, the failure to tolerate an alternative lifestyle may have been the biggest mistake I have ever encountered in my practice.

Cautionary Tale 5: Don't Let the Law Write Your Inheritance Instructions

Lesson to be learned: Failing to execute a Living Trust, for whatever reason, may result in your money and property passing to persons you least intended.

After my first book, *Beyond the Grave,* was released in 1996, my father and co-author, Gerald, received a phone call from evangelist Pat Robertson to invite him to discuss family inheritance planning on his national cable show, *The 700 Club.* What a rush of excitement this call incited! My father and I practiced law together for 15 years, and the only time he yelled for me to run to his office was to take Pat Robertson's call on speakerphone.

Gerald told Mr. Robertson he would be delighted to travel to his studio in Virginia Beach and appear on the show. And in the interest of full disclosure, my father informed Mr. Robertson that he was Jewish and did not subscribe to any of Mr. Robertson's politics or religious beliefs. To his credit, Mr. Robertson did not hesitate in repeating his desire to have my father on his show.

After his *700 Club* appearance, Gerald returned to his office, where he received a call from a high school buddy who called himself the "Captain." I asked my father, "Why the 'Captain'?" He replied, "I think that it had something to do with his dad owning a fishing boat in the old Santa Monica Harbor."

The Captain and Gerald had last seen each other 20 years before when they ran into each other while surfing at Malibu's Surfrider Beach. Naturally, they did some catching up. While Gerald talked about his conventional societal roles as husband, father, and lawyer, the Captain talked about surfing. No marriage. No children. No steady or real employment. Just surfing.

The Captain's beach lifestyle kind of rankled my father, and he did not hesitate to tell this to the Captain. Gerald said, "Captain, you get up every morning and only have to worry about whether you are going to surf, swim, jog, or play tennis, while I have to put on the lawyer suit and go to an office and make enough money to support a wife, children, mortgage, office staff, overhead, and all that." To that the Captain replied, "That was a choice you made, Jerry."

Fast-forward 20 years with the Captain and my father on the phone. The Captain said, "Jerry, I just saw you on Pat Robertson's show. I didn't know you converted." My father and I laughed many times about that comment. Since the Captain had seen Gerald on that show discussing inheritance planning, my father mentioned that now would be as good a time as any to talk about doing a Living Trust for the Captain.

The Captain had a small house that he had bought in the early 1950s now worth at least $750,000, as well as stock and bank accounts of a few hundred thousand. He still had no wife or children. He was older, but he was still living the beach lifestyle.

My father reminded the Captain that if he did not choose who would get his house and money, it might go to the state of California. Why? Because if anyone dies without an inheritance plan, the law steps in to impose its own inheritance plan. And the law states that if a person dies without a testamentary document *and* with no blood relatives, all of that person's assets will escheat to the state.

The Captain said he did have relatives, two brothers living "somewhere back East" whom he had not seen for a long time. He also had a longtime girlfriend. Gerald told the Captain that if he did not have a will or Living Trust that named his girlfriend as a beneficiary, she would not receive one penny. The Captain responded, "Jerry, let's go surfing. It will be like old times. We can talk about that inheritance stuff then."

A week later, they were perched on boards at Surfrider, waiting for the next swell—just like the old days, except now they were kind of old. During a lull in the action, the Captain said, "Jerry, I hope to die on a day that's rainy and cloudy. I don't want to die when the sun is shining and the surf's up." Except for that comment, there was no other talk about death, dying, or inheritance planning. Who wants to talk about business at the beach?

The Captain did die on a bright, sunny day. It was a heart attack that hospitalized him, and eventually killed him. There was a surfer's burial. His body was cremated and buried at sea, surrounded by his surfing buddies on a small flotilla of surfboards.

About a week following the burial, the Captain's girlfriend visited Gerald, asking about his will. She had scoured the house looking for anything having the appearance of a testamentary document and found nothing. She came to my father assuming he had made a will and left it with us. But he hadn't. Even though Gerald had nagged him on and off for about a year, the Captain never got serious about doing one. It was always talk of "We'll get around to it."

The girlfriend had no standing as an heir. Unless she did something, she would get nothing. But what could she do? My father recommended she consider suing the Captain's estate by claiming that he promised to compensate her in a will for caretaking services; but it was just an idea. Gerald could not see suing his old surfing buddy, the Captain, even though the defendant would have only been his estate.

With no will or Living Trust, the law of the state dictated the recipients of the Captain's money and property, who were the Captain's brothers. My father hired an Internet investigator to locate the Captain's brothers. He found them. While figuratively holding his nose, my father called them with the news of their brother's death. Not only was this the first time they learned of their brother's death, but they also told my father that they had assumed he had died many years before.

Gerald also informed the brothers that the Captain's estate was worth about $1 million and, as the Captain's longtime friend, he would be honored to handle the estate administration for less than full charge.

My father never heard back from the brothers, other than receiving a letter from the brothers' new attorney saying that he had been retained by the brothers to probate the Captain's estate. The letter also requested that Gerald hand over any relevant files he had in his office. My father had no such files, because the Captain had resisted all entreaties to establish a will or Living Trust.

That was it. Near-strangers who had not seen or heard from their brother in over 50 years received the Captain's estate. I am certain they were the last persons the Captain would have wanted to receive his money and property. His girlfriend of over 20 years got nothing. And my father did not even get back the $100 he had paid to the Internet investigator.

Post–Cautionary Tale Comment: A piece of scratch paper could have prevented this disaster. In most states, a handwritten statement of testamentary wishes on any paper is sufficient to constitute a valid will. It does not have to be witnessed or notarized. It only has to be entirely in the handwriting of the person writing it. This is called a holographic will, and it is just as legal as any will drawn by an attorney.

This is exactly as it sounds. There is no catch. You could rip a page from this book and write your inheritance instructions in the margins. As long as the notations are entirely in your handwriting, those notations can serve as your holographic will.

No lawyers. Just you and a pen. Sure, there may not be any of the provisions we lawyers like to throw into a will to make it a complete document; but as long as you write down who gets what in your own handwriting, and as long as you sign and date it, you have a valid inheritance Band-Aid.

Cautionary Tale 6: Joint Tenancy Gone Wrong

Lesson to be learned: Don't place title to your house into co-ownership with your child just to avoid paying a lawyer to do your Living Trust. If your child gets into money problems, there goes your house.

She said, "Mr. Condon, I want to apologize about what I said to you." I responded, "I gladly accept your apology, but who the heck are you?"

I'm not very good at recalling names, but facts are my stock-in-trade. The more she talked about what happened, the more I recalled about her. It must have been about 10 years earlier when she first conferred with me. She owned a 10-unit apartment building in Santa Monica. Her husband had died and she had one child, a married daughter with an eight-year-old son.

I advised her to establish a Living Trust that would transfer her apartment building to her daughter after her death. She agreed. I then quoted her the fee to prepare her Living Trust. She was not happy. "Another money-grubbing attorney! she said. "What a surprise!"

There are three certainties in this life: death, taxes, and people who don't want to pay a lawyer a fair fee. My father said one thing to me about charging clients that I use as my standard to this day when I determine a fee: The fee has to be fair to both the client and the attorney.

Such is the truth. If the fee is not fair to the attorney, the attorney will perform the work grudgingly. If the fee is not fair to the attorney, the attorney will not bust his hump for the client to do the best work possible. If the fee is not fair to the attorney, the attorney may only want to do the minimum amount of work necessary to avoid a malpractice action.

You have every right to complain about what an attorney has charged you for services rendered. Heck, I complained a lot about the bills I received from my divorce attorney, because he charged me up the kazoo for very shoddy work that had to be redone by the attorney who replaced him. But when you speak with the attorney to discuss that bill, keep in mind this fairness standard and approach the discussion on that basis. It may save you a lot of wondering . . . and yelling and screaming.

In any event, the lady in my office 10 years earlier was not complaining about a bill for services performed, but rather my quote for a Living Trust yet to be performed. She said it was too high, and that the same probate-avoidance objective could be achieved at a fraction of the cost by putting her apartment building in joint tenancy with her daughter.

Of course, she was right. By signing a deed placing the property in her and her daughter's names as joint tenants, she could arrange that the daughter would end up with the entire property after the mother's death without any probate procedure. And compared to the Living Trust, the cost to prepare and record that deed was almost negligible.

When she mentioned the joint tenancy option, I immediately dove into my canned diatribe about the dangers of a parent and child as co-owners of real property, which is this: Your property becomes subject to your daughter's problems. If she gets into a divorce, if she or her husband files bankruptcy, or if she or her husband gets sued, there goes your house.

This was her response: "You did not talk about joint ownership until I raised it first. You don't fool me, Mr. Condon. It's a secret that you and all the other lawyers want to keep from people like me just to make more money." With that, she concluded our meeting with the "money-grubbing attorney" remark and walked out the door. I did not have any more contact with her until 10 years later with the call of apology.

So what happened? She hired another lawyer to prepare the joint tenancy deed, which put the apartment building in the names of her and her daughter as joint tenants. For about 10 years, nothing happened. She continued to collect rents and manage the building.

Then one day, her daughter sent a letter to each tenant telling them that she, the daughter, was a 50 percent owner and instructing each tenant to send her half the rent.

As soon as the mother found out, she confronted her daughter, who said, "My husband and I are having money troubles, and the only thing we could think of to help us out was use the apartment rents."

I had warned this lady 10 years before that making her daughter a joint tenant could lead to losing the building because of her daughter's problems. That the daughter might actually assert her right to receive 50 percent of the rent didn't come up. That was my mistake; but given her haughty "I don't need you" attitude, I doubt mentioning such a possibility would have had any effect.

I asked about what happened after she confronted her daughter. She said, "My grandson came into the room and chased me out. While I was running down the stairs, he said that he would hurt me if I ever came back and bothered his mother."

It is a sad story, but it ends with a halfway decent result.

The good half: The lady sued her daughter, which resulted in my client reclaiming her entire property.

The bad half: It took several years of litigation to achieve that result; the attorney fees and costs were 100 times more than what I had quoted her for a Living Trust; and she lost her daughter and grandson.

Post–Cautionary Tale Comment: Never put title to any real property in joint ownership with your child for the purpose of that child becoming the 100 percent owner if you die first. Yes, it is an inexpensive way of transferring ownership to your child after your death. Yes, it avoids the expense of a probate court procedure. Yes, it avoids the cost of a Living Trust. But, look at the downsides.

- It exposes your property to creditor problems of your child and your child's spouse.
- It exposes your property to the bankruptcies of your child and your child's spouse.
- It exposes your property to the IRS problems of your child and your child's spouse.
- It may give your child's spouse marital rights or claims in the event of a divorce.
- It will require you to get your child to sign deeds and other documents if you want to sell or refinance your property, and perhaps the signature of your child's spouse.
- It exposes your property to any malpractice and accident claims against your child or your child's spouse.
- It exposes your property to the risk that your child may attempt to sell or convey a share of the property to a third party.

There is also the remote possibility your child will die before you, which would put the property back in your name as a 100 percent owner, requiring you to start over with another transfer plan.

Cautionary Tale 7: When It Comes to Money, Family Loyalty Goes out the Window

Lesson to be learned: A senile surviving spouse + a little greed = zero protection for the surviving spouse.

No lawyer likes to be accused of not protecting a client. But there I was, standing so accused when Mrs. Ray said to me, "You didn't protect me."

How did I get there? How did it come to that point?

About eight years before that day, Mrs. Ray and her older son, David, arrived at my office. She appeared mentally alert and straightforward about what she wanted. She was weary and too old to continue to live alone in her Santa Monica home, which was the primary asset of her Living Trust. She wanted to move into an assisted-living facility that would cost about $5,000 per month. She would have to sell her house to pay for this.

Mrs. Ray relied on David for her daily needs, and now she wanted him to handle all aspects of the sale: hiring the listing agent, reviewing the offers, signing an acceptance, dealing with the escrow documents—all of that. The plan was that when the house was sold, David would place the funds in the bank and write the checks to pay the monthly assisted-living fee, as well as checks for whatever else she needed.

It was a decent plan, though a little unrealistic. A sale during her lifetime would generate an immediate capital gains tax; but that's what she insisted on, and she seemed clear-minded enough to know what she wanted.

The solution was simple enough. Mrs. Ray would resign as trustee of her Living Trust. With that act, the person named in her Living Trust as her after-death agent, David, would elevate to the position of lifetime agent. As lifetime agent, David would have the power to manage Mrs. Ray's Living Trust assets for her benefit and sign all documents (including checks) necessary to conduct business with the Living Trust assets.

I did not hear from Mrs. Ray until eight years later. Actually, the call came from one of the nurses in the nursing home section of the assisted-living facility, who said that Mrs. Ray wanted to see me. Putting aside my normal reluctance to visit this type of place (which always struck me as a storage facility for those waiting to die), I went.

In bed, and disheveled in appearance, it was fairly obvious that Mrs. Ray was suffering from some loss of mental acuity. She said, "I want to go home, but the nurse says I have no home to go to. What happened to my house?" I said, "Mrs. Ray, don't you remember?

You came to my office with your son and resigned as trustee. You put him in charge of your financial affairs. He followed your instructions to sell your house and use the money to pay the bill for the nursing home."

I knew there was going to be trouble when I heard her response: "I don't remember being in your office."

It seemed pointless to repeat what had happened. So I just sat there and took it when she pointed her finger at me and accused me of not protecting her. She felt cheated and taken advantage of, and, to her, I was to blame.

As she laid into me, for all the patients and staff to hear, I engaged in a series of mental gymnastics reliving the part I played. Eight years earlier, Mrs. Ray was fully aware of her action of resigning as trustee and appointing her son as lifetime agent to sell her home. That decision created a result that the client now did not want—the loss of her home. At the time, I gave her my usual written disclosure that a person who resigns as trustee surrenders management and control of the Living Trust assets to the new lifetime agent. But, should I have done more? Perhaps that disclosure works more to cover my backside than warn and protect the client. Should I have refused the client's instruction for her own safety and not taken that business?

With Mrs. Ray's accusation still ringing in my ears, I left the nursing home, went back to my office, and called David. I explained that I had visited his mother and she was wondering why she couldn't go home again. David responded, "Forget it, Jeff. She won't even remember you were there."

In light of Mrs. Ray's condition, I felt that David was probably right and I sighed a bit in relief. While I had David on the phone, I asked him about the sale price of his mother's home. David said, "Uhhhh . . . I didn't sell the house. My accountant told me that if I sold it, there would be a huge capital gains tax on it. He said that I could avoid that tax if I rented it out for two years and then exchanged it for another investment property. So, I did. I turned that house into an apartment building, and the rent goes for Mom's expenses."

That seemed like a good plan to avoid the tax. But then it dawned on me—that apartment building belonged to Mrs. Ray's Living Trust. I reminded David that as his mother's lifetime agent, he still had the duty to use that property for his mother's benefit only.

It was then that David casually pointed out that the property was now in the joint names of him and his wife. "Jeff, she's getting her rent paid. She doesn't know what's going on, so it just doesn't matter. It goes to me anyway after she's gone."

The hell it didn't matter. Mrs. Ray's Living Trust said that all of her Living Trust assets would pass to her two sons on her death. By taking that property out of his mother's Living Trust and giving it to himself and his wife, David stole his brother's half of that property. When I shouted this at David, he casually replied, "Calm down, Jeff. You'll blow a gasket. My brother died three years ago. It's just me. I get it all when Mom dies."

"David," I asked, "did your brother have any children?"

"Sure. He has three children."

"Well guess what, David? Your brother's children step into his shoes. They take his one-half share of your mother's Living Trust assets. You stole your brother's children's half of their inheritance."

David would not be fazed. To that he simply said, "Well, Jeff, they don't know anything about it. All they know is that my mother gave me the house in my name. So long as Mom is taken care of, I don't think they care."

"But David," I countered, "that's not what your mother's trust says. It says everything equally—one-half to you and one-half to your brother's kids if your brother dies before your mother. What part of that don't you understand?"

"Well, Jeff, maybe they will just never know."

For reasons dealing with attorney–client privilege, I could not notify anyone about this major breach of trust. Mrs. Ray was incompetent, so telling her would have no effect. I suppose I will have to deal with this situation when Mrs. Ray dies. But in the meantime, I cannot help but think of the Ray situation as another example of family loyalty having no meaning when it comes to dividing money in the inheritance arena.

Post–Cautionary Tale Comment: The Living Trust is not just a vehicle that contains your inheritance instructions. It also appoints a lifetime agent to manage your Living Trust assets for your benefit in the event of your incapacity. That is a terrific objective, but, as this tale has shown, one that clearly can be abused by your lifetime agent when you become incapacitated.

From an objective standpoint, I made no error with Mrs. Ray. I did what she instructed me to do, and I sent her a letter discussing the ramifications of that decision. She resigned as trustee, which brought in her son as the manager of her Living Trust assets with the instruction to sell her house.

But in hindsight, I now recognize that for some reason I failed to get the usual vibrations from my radar that something was up. There are times when you should say no to a client, and that was clearly such a time. Although she was fully capable of making that decision, I should have anticipated the possibility of her becoming senile, leaving her vulnerable to her son. But, with her so bright and vibrant in my office that day eight years ago, I did not consider it.

Should Mrs. Ray be responsible for her own actions? Should she have anticipated that she might someday be incapacitated to the extent that she would be unable to fathom or resist financial abuse perpetrated by her lifetime agent? Of course. We are all in charge of our own destinies. You reap what you sow.

Still, she came to me, the professional, for advice, and I should have been more vociferous in warning her about the possible negative wake created by her decision to resign as trustee. I will always believe that I should have jumped in to protect my client against herself, even if that meant refusing to do the work and not getting a fee.

Cautionary Tale 8: "Probate Is the Lawyer's Retirement Fund"

Lesson to be learned: If you have real estate, you need a Living Trust to transfer that real estate after your death.

Mr. Schultz was a cantankerous 80-year-old man who told me with pride, "Condon, I've always gotten along pretty good without having to pay a lawyer for anything."

So what brought Mr. Schultz to my office? He got remarried . . . and he was feeling the pressure from his new wife to go along with a new inheritance plan.

Mr. Schultz continued, "When my first wife died five years ago, I became the 100 percent owner of our house. When I remarried, I planned to keep it that way. But, my new wife wants us to sell our houses and pool all the money into a new house for the both of us. Since we're each putting up one-half of the cash, I want to keep one-half of the new house in my name."

Not such a great idea. To put it mildly, it's a tricky proposition for "second time around" spouses with children from their respective first marriages to own property jointly.

If Mr. and Mrs. Schultz take title to the new house as "tenants-in-common" (also known as "tenancy-by-the-entirety" in some states), the half of the first spouse to die will belong to whomever he or she leaves it. So . . . if the new Mrs. Schultz dies first and her inheritance plan leaves her half to her children from her first marriage, those children would be partners in the house with Mr. Schultz.

What's wrong with that? Because one co-owner (the new Mrs. Schultz's "first children") can always bring a legal action to boot the other co-owner (Mr. Schultz) out of occupancy and force a sale. If Mr. Schultz plans on staying in that house, this is not a pleasant scenario.

Of course, this is a goose/gander scenario, as Mr. Schultz's "first children" could do the booting to the new Mrs. Schultz if he dies first. Still . . . doesn't Mr. Schultz want the relief of knowing that he won't get the boot from the house if he is the survivor? And doesn't Mr. Schultz want to have the satisfaction of knowing that his new wife will be able to live in the house for the rest of her life if he dies first?

These are not rhetorical or academic questions. This is real life . . . with real-life consequences. I put these questions to Mr. Schultz and he responded, "Do I look like an idiot, Condon? Do I want to get evicted by my new wife's kids? No! And do I want to be sure that my kids won't kick out my new wife if I die first? No! So . . . what else is there we can do?"

I then told Mr. Schulz about another "joint owner" option . . . which was for them to take title to their new house as "joint tenants with right of survivorship." With this method, the surviving spouse automatically inherits the half of the first spouse to die. That surviving spouse then owns the entire house and will be free to leave it all to his or her "first children" . . . completely cutting out the "first children" of the one who died first.

In the context of "second time around" spouses, this is also not such a great way to take title to property. The spouse who dies last ""wins" the entire property. And so do the children of the spouse who dies last. Not exactly a pleasant prospect for both spouses.

In any event, after my little speech about these downsides of joint ownership, I started my usual spiel of how a Living Trust could be used to prevent those problems while avoiding the probate process, but Mr. Schultz interrupted me with the usual exasperated client refrain: "Sounds too complicated. I'll just do the tenants-in-common thing that you talked about first."

"Okay," I replied. "I'm not sure that's the best thing for both of you. But, if that's what you want, then just tell the escrow that you want to take title in your names as tenants-in-common. But, since you'll own your share in your sole name, you must have a will or a Living Trust that says who gets your half of the house on your death, and your new wife needs to do the same." But, when I quoted him the fees for the Living Trust packages, he muttered aloud something about a will being cheaper, stood up, thanked me for my time, and left.

I get that a lot after my price quotes—the "thanks-for-your-time-I'll-get-back-to-you-but-not-really" routine. I'm used to it. Still . . . I could do without the muttering aloud, which I have always found more-than-slightly grating.

Mr. Schultz never got back to me . . . but his second wife called on me after he died. At our meeting, Mrs. Schultz presented me with a page torn out of a letter-size notebook. This page, according to her, was in his handwriting. It had words sounding like a will, which said, in essence, that it was his wish that his share of the house would go to Mrs. Schultz.

"Is this valid?" she asked me with a quiet sense of desperation. To her great relief, I informed her that it was a valid California holographic will—written, signed and dated entirely in the handwriting of her husband. But, this will was not self-executing. In order to carry out Mr. Schultz's wishes, the will had to be submitted to court for *probate*, which, in a nutshell, is the court-supervised process of transferring assets from the dead to the living. The probate process took about 13 months and about $12,000 in court costs and attorney fees—but she ultimately ended up with the entire house.

End of a fairly dry story? Not quite. At some point during the probate process, I advised Mrs. Schultz that now that she owned the entire house, she should have a Living Trust. With a Living Trust, she retains ownership and control of the house during her life. On her death, the Living Trust then transfers the ownership of the house to her children without that probate court nonsense. But like her husband, Mrs. Schultz did not warm too kindly to my price quote: Actually, her reaction was somewhat aghast: "Mr. Condon, I can get that same Living Trust for half the price from one of those outfits that advertises in the *Los Angeles Times*. You just got thousands of dollars from me from probate . . . and now you want more money from me for my Living Trust? You should do it for free!"

A frustrated client insisting that I should do free legal work? I think I would have preferred the muttering aloud.

But, as with her husband, Mrs. Schultz left my office . . . never to return. But whom did I see about a year later? Mrs. Schultz's children! Who informed me that their mother died before completing her Living Trust . . . and who hired me to engage in yet *another* probate process to transfer the house from their deceased mother to them.

More fees for me? Of course! Another probate equals more attorney services equals more money for the attorney. If I'm not getting paid, I might as well be at the beach.

But this time . . . the fees would be double! Why? Because the probate fees are based on a percentage of the value of the assets going through the probate process. The $12,000 I received from Mr. Schultz's probate was based on the value of half the house, because it was only his half that went through probate. Now, with Mrs. Schultz being the owner of the *whole* house—and with the *whole* house now subject to the probate process—my fees would be based on the value of the *whole* house!

Silently, I thanked my deceased clients for not doing a Living Trust and unwittingly contributing to my retirement fund.

Post–Cautionary Tale Comment: There are actually two points to take from this Cautionary Tale. Call it a bonus for getting through this really dry stuff.

First, and quite simply, if you own real estate and don't use a Living Trust to transfer that real estate after your death, you will have diminished your assets by the amount of money consumed by probate costs and fees.

Could you avoid the Living Trust and probate by adding your children on title to your real property as joint tenants with right of survivorship? Sure! They would automatically receive ownership after you die. However, by putting your children on title to your house, you subject your house to your children's problems. Your children file bankruptcy? Your children get a divorce? Your children cause an accident and have insufficient insurance? Your children have tax problems? Your children pile up the creditors? Quite possibly, your house can be sold during your life to resolve those problems.

Bonus Second Point . . . as Promised! In these "new start" situations, where remarried spouses sell their respective houses and pool the funds for a new house, a Living Trust is essential to ensure that the survivor can remain in the home until the survivor's death without the fear of getting the boot from the family of the first spouse to die.

If title is held as "joint tenancy, with right of survivorship" (or as a "tenancy in the entirety"), the survivor will be the 100 percent owner and the survivor can direct who shall receive the entire property—such as children from a prior marriage . . . or even a new spouse.

In a community property state, such as California, taking title as "community property" or as "tenants-in-common" gives the first spouse to die the power to bequeath by will or trust his or her one-half share directly to that spouse's "side." However, the "side" of that deceased spouse becomes "partners" with the survivor . . . and any partner can always force the end of that partnership by forcing a sale of that house, which potentially puts the survivor out on the proverbial street.

The only solution? The newlyweds should establish a Living Trust, put title to the new house in the Living Trust, and put instructions in the Living Trust that say, in essence, the survivor is in control of the entire property for the rest of his or her life, and the house (or the sale proceeds) shall be distributed equally to each "side" after the survivor dies.

Cautionary Tale 9: "I Don't Want to Be a Weekend Father"

Lesson to be learned: Never leave an inheritance outright to a child.

"If I sign a Living Trust that leaves my inherited house to my kids, my wife will divorce me!" In all the excuses I've heard to justify not establishing a Living Trust, this one from Daniel Slosberg was the topper.

Daniel was in his early forties, married with two daughters, ages 3 and 5. He and his wife lived in a 50-year-old home he inherited from his mother. His parents bought the house in 1952 for $20,000 with the help of the G.I. Bill, which, 50 years later, was worth over $1,000,000 due to inflation . . . and being in the prime residential area within walking distance of the beach.

I established Daniel's parents' Living Trust, which said, in essence, that Daniel (their only child) would inherit the house after both died. Daniel's father died first . . . and now Daniel was in my office to confer with me shortly after his mother's death.

At first, Daniel lauded the services I rendered for his parents. He was delighted that the Living Trust would avoid a costly and time-consuming probate process. All Daniel had do to receive ownership of the house was to sign a deed in which Daniel, as the successor trustee of his parents' Living Trust, transfers the house to Daniel, in his individual capacity.

If this transfer had taken place in a probate context, it would have taken nine months and cost thousands of dollars. With the Living Trust, it would take just $750 and the time necessary to prepare the transfer deed—about 20 minutes.

As my secretary typed the deed, I casually mentioned to Daniel that he should have his own Living Trust to leave his inherited house to his children. With that, Daniel stopped singing my praises and berated me for what he perceived to be a money grab: "Some racket you have going on here, Condon! You charged my parents for their Living Trust to transfer their house to me. How come I now have to pay you another fee for doing the same kind of Living Trust for the same house?"

I'm only human. I can only take so much from people taking umbrage at paying me for my services without responding adversely. So . . . I kind of lost it. I stood up and said (yelled, actually), "We're starting over, Daniel! That was your parents' Living Trust! Now we're talking about *your* Living Trust! A new Living Trust means a new fee! What part of that don't you understand?!"

I fully expected Daniel to run from the room, but to my surprise, he stayed put. Too shocked to move from being witness to such unprofessional conduct? Perhaps, but he was also one of those types who admired people who had the temerity to tell him off. Daniel then hired me to prepare his Living Trust. Maybe I should yell at my clients more often.

After our meeting (shouting contest?), I prepared Daniel's Living Trust, which provided that his inherited house would, on his death, be distributed to his two daughters. I met with Daniel a few weeks later so he could review the first draft . . . and to schedule the signing appointment for the following week. This is the usual Living Trust process: the first meeting to order it . . . the second meeting to review it . . . the third meeting to sign it.

During the review appointment, Daniel asked whether he should leave the house to his wife instead of his children. I replied,

"Daniel . . . if you leave it to her, there is no guarantee that she'll leave it your children. Just do this my way."

Do you take issue with your doctor when he gives you medical advice? Probably not—and you probably comply as well with the advice your lawyer bestows upon you . . . as did Daniel. He left his Living Trust the way I drafted it, and we scheduled the date for the signing appointment.

The day of the signing meeting came . . . but no Daniel. My secretary called him to reschedule. We rescheduled; but, another no-show. Another call . . . another reschedule . . . another no-show. This routine went on about three more times. During each rescheduling call my secretary made to him, he came up with the same excuse: "family problems."

Daniel finally showed up for the signing appointment on the sixth go-round. He looked drawn, tired, exasperated. "What's bothering you?" I asked him.

And he sure told me . . . with that same antagonism as before.

"You almost destroyed my marriage, Condon! I brought the draft home and my wife saw it. She picked it up and read the part about the house going to our children instead of her. She started hyperventilating. I thought she was going to have a heart attack. She gave me the look of death and said, 'I always thought I would get the house if you die. Looks like I won't. I may as well as divorce you now!'"

"Listen, Daniel," I said. "Your wife has no right to that house. It's not community property—it's separate property. It's *your* separate property. There is no rule that says you have to leave it to your wife. You can leave it to whomever you want. And I'm sure that your parents didn't intend to have the family home end up out of the bloodline."

To that, Daniel yelled, "It's my life, Condon! Not yours! I'm not signing. I know my wife, and she'll do just what she says. I am not going to be one of those guys who sees his kids every other weekend! So &#! your Living Trust . . . and @#&! you while you're at it!"

Needless to add . . . but I'm adding it anyway . . . he got up and stormed out, never to come back . . . and never to pay me for any of the services I rendered in preparing the final draft.

Was I a bit brazen about dismissing Daniel's slight initial suggestion to initially leave the house to his wife? Sure. But . . . I was also in the right. If Daniel died first, and his wife remarried, it is entirely possible that his parents' house could end up with their ex-daughter-in-law's children from her new husband's first marriage. Hey . . . don't laugh! This has happened more times than you'll ever know!

Somehow, I did find out later that Daniel complied with his wife's wishes by signing a deed that transferred the house from his parents' Living Trust to himself as his separate property . . . and then signing another deed, which transferred the house to him and his wife as their community property. If he dies first, she gets the whole thing.

Post–Cautionary Tale Comment: Even though I believe my advice to Daniel during the signing appointment was right, Daniel was also right. I could not live his life for him. His parents were dead, the house was his to do with as he pleased, and he had the absolute right to do what he needed to do to keep his family together.

And on sober second thought, I was really bothered by the fact that the advice that I had given so casually almost caused a divorce.

You live, you learn. I now prevent that marriage-destruction scenario by not giving people who inherit (like Daniel) the choice of whether to leave the inherited house to their children or their spouses. I now leave that choice with their parents.

Specifically, if I was drafting Daniel's parents' Living Trust now, I would provide that when the last parent dies, the family home would stays in the parents' Living Trust in a subtrust that I call the *protection trust*. This protection trust would act just like the Living Trust that I prepared for Daniel that he never signed. By leaving the house to Daniel in the protection trust, Daniel would own and control the house. And when Daniel dies, the terms of his protection trust would state that the house must go to Daniel's daughters.

The use of this subtrust (which I discuss at greater length in Chapter 18) is like getting two Living Trusts for the price of one. The first one is Daniel's parents' Living Trust, which transfers the house to him. The second one is the protection trust, which leaves the house to Daniel's children.

And even more important . . . the decision of ultimately leaving the house to Daniel's children would have been made by Daniel's parents . . . not Daniel. So when Daniel's wife would shimmy up to her husband and "suggest" that he leave the house to her, he could retort with something like, "Honey, you know I would love to. But my hands are tied. My parents left it to me in trust for the kids."

Cautionary Tale 10: "It's Just a Piece of Paper"

Lesson to be learned: Just because you leave an equal inheritance to your children does not necessarily mean that you have treated them equally.

During the Korean War, the Gilfords started an airplane parts sales business, acting as intermediary between buyer and manufacturer. When they started, they were barely able to afford the lease on the building that housed their business. However, their devotion to their business caused it to become a great financial success. After 10 years, they were able to buy that building and lease it to their business. When they first visited me, their assets consisted of that building, a large home, and a significant stock and cash-based investment portfolio. Their total worth was about $5 million. Only in America!

The Gilfords had a son and a daughter. Their son worked for them part-time while in high school and college and, ultimately, ran the business full-time after his parents retired from day-to-day operations. Their daughter had absolutely nothing to do with the business . . . save for the occasional drop by to see if she could get a check for some recreational endeavor.

Mr. Gilford saved me from having to give my "treat your children equally" speech . . . because that is the first thing he said he wanted to accomplish in their inheritance plan. However, he also wanted to leave the business equally to his two children. As he said, "Sure, Mr. Condon. We acknowledge that the business's value has increased under our son's watch. But he received a salary for that. He's been well compensated for his efforts. So we want to leave the business to our two kids equally."

With all the gravitas that I could summon (so as to give the impression of the all-knowing, "seen-it-all" attorney), I told the Gilfords this plan would not fly with their son. After devoting his entire professional life to the business and almost single-handedly increasing the business's value, he would, to put it mildly, be somewhat miffed that he would have to share that business . . . and the appreciation that came from his efforts . . . with his sister. Unless they left their son a significant "something extra" that recognized his contribution to the business's increased value, he could become upset to the point of quitting and starting another business on his own.

The Gilfords didn't see it that way. The wanted an equal value division between their two children of everything they owned—the house, stocks, cash, business and business property . . . would be split between them. Mr. Gilford then said, "You don't know our kids, Mr. Condon. They'll get along just fine."

Certainly, my clients know their children better than I do. How could I possibly know them when I have never met or spoken with them? But after having been in the inheritance business for quite some time, I know my clients' children better than they do in the inheritance arena. Family loyalty goes out the window when the inheritance happens. And my clients will never know that . . . because they'll be dead.

Still, with my brilliant admonition still ringing in my ears . . . not their ears . . . I took their "order" for financial equality between their two children. It seemed fair on paper—and that's all that mattered to Mr. and Mrs. Gilford. The only deviation they made from a true 50/50 split of each asset was leaving their son slightly more business stock as a tribute to his fine efforts in keeping the business going, but they made up the difference with their daughter by leaving her with a little more cash. The end result—a pinpoint-accurate equal financial division.

Fast-forward 15 years. Both Mr. and Mrs. Gilford were dead . . . and their son and daughter received equal shares of their parents' assets. And a mere 6 months after that, their daughter came to the realization that her equity stock in the business became worthless. Just a piece of paper. Why? Because her brother had the majority interest of the stock. As the majority shareholder, her brother was still the boss . . . still had control . . . and was still able to determine his salary and expense account that left little to zero corporate profits.

When his sister complained and threatened a lawsuit for corporate malfeasance, her brother informed her that what he was doing was "perfectly legal." Later consulting with an attorney, she was told that she could bring a lawsuit to dissolve the corporation and liquidate the assets, but that would be akin to cutting her throat to spite her face.

Ultimately, she got her revenge . . . in her capacity as a co-owner of the real estate that was leased to the business.

When the Gilfords were alive, they gave their son a "sweetheart" deal on the leasing arrangement between themselves as the land owners and their son as the business head. The rent was only 25 percent of the fair market rental value. So after her parents died and she got the bum's rush from her brother, she bumped up the rent on her one-half ownership of the real estate—to 10 times the current rate!

Her brother screamed! Like a little girl! He also threatened a lawsuit . . . and threatened to abandon the business. His sister said she would back off . . . but only if he kept his salary and expenses in check.

The Gilfords' children finally had the good sense to involve me to help them resolve this Mexican standoff. At some point, after long (and billable) discussions and negotiations, I was able to placate them with a deal. But, their once-close relationship was never the same. In fact, it was nonexistent. Their parents' hope of preserving a good relationship between their children . . . and grandchildren . . . with equal division of the inheritance had failed.

Post–Cautionary Tale Comment: Clients often accuse me of being dogmatic with my advice, which I often convey in a "my-way-or-the-highway" tone. Well . . . if that's true, it's scenarios such as the Gilford family saga that got me to that point. I've been a percipient witness to the "bad" that arises in the intergenerational transfer of wealth so often that I can project with utmost certainty the family fallout that will take place. In other words, you have to take my advice because I've been there and lived it hundreds of times. And you haven't.

If you don't want the blame . . . treat your children financially the same. This is a fundamental rule of family inheritance planning Sure, there is no law compelling you to leave your children equal shares. And if you are you one of "those people" who take the "After Me, Who Cares What Happens" approach, you will disregard this basic tenet of equalization. If that sounds like you, please recall the biblical story of Jacob, who gave his son, Joseph, the "Coat of Many Colors." What did Joseph's brothers do? They were so angry and jealous at not being treated the same that they sold Joseph into slavery.

If you are like most of my clients, you, like the Gilfords, do not need to be sold on equalization between your children, but the nature of the equal gifting makes one child "more equal." The Gilford family saga illustrates but one example, but there are numerous others, including:

- Gifting of stock of equal value at the time the inheritance is received, but the value of one child's shares surpasses the shares of the other children.
- Gifting income property, usually apartment properties, having equal value when received, but for certain reasons, one property escalates in value over the other.
- Gifting a commercial property in equal shares to your children but the property is subject to a long-term "sweetheart lease" in favor of the business given to one child as part of an inheritance plan.

The lesson to be learned is not to select a specific asset for a child. Do not control from the grave. Give each child an equal asset and let your children "sort it out." Let each child make his or her own decision about what is personally best.

Cautionary Tale 11: I Don't Want Him!"

Lesson to be learned: You have to predict the future about the nature of the relationship between trustee and beneficiary.

I've heard a lot of grumbling from my colleagues about having to make "field trips" to meet with clients. This has always mystified me. It almost goes without saying that an integral part of this job is meeting with elderly and infirm people in their homes.

Besides . . . who doesn't relish the opportunity to get out of the office during the workday for a few hours? One can't make a quick trip to Wild Oats for their incredible oatmeal-chocolate chip cookies while chained to a desk.

It was on such a "house-call" that I came upon Mrs. Clancy. Her caretaker opened the front door and ushered me into the main bedroom, where Mrs. Clancy was propped up in her bed. I started to introduce myself, but Mrs. Clancy appeared to be in no mood for pleasantries, as she shouted, "I don't want him! Get rid of him!"

I stopped in my tracks. Already, this was not the typical house call where I encounter a docile and infirm elderly person. Though 87 and bedridden, Mrs. Clancy appeared to have a residue of strength and full mental acuity. And I'm not usually greeted by the occupant with a loud demand to do something.

"Who don't you want, and why don't you want him?" I asked Mrs. Clancy who then proceeded to enlighten me. Her husband died a few months prior to my visit. They established their Living Trust some years ago with another attorney. She didn't pay much attention to the documents. Her husband hired the attorney. He made the arrangements. She went were he went. She signed what he signed.

Now that she was alone, the words in that Living Trust came to reality. Their Living Trust provided that if Mr. Clancy died first, a third party would be in charge of their assets in the Living Trust— their money and property . . . for the rest of her life. This shocked Mrs. Clancy to her core . . . as she had no idea that this was the plan that her husband had arranged.

I don't think that Mr. Clancy was attempting to "get" his wife by removing her from control of the family assets if he died first. In light of his wife's physical infirmity, I am reasonably certain that he was looking out for her best interest by arranging for a third-party trustee to manage their assets for her benefit . . . which would leave her free to focus solely on her health.

Eventually, Mrs. Clancy did come around to that line of thought. The big problem that she had—and the reason for my being summoned to her bedside—was that she hated, nay, *loathed* the person her husband had selected as the trustee: the attorney who drafted their Living Trust.

I knew this attorney—somewhat of an abrupt, impatient, "no bedside manner" type. The first time Mrs. Clancy learned of the attorney's new role in her life was when he showed up for the funeral. As Mrs. Clancy said, "It went downhill from there."

I suppose Mr. Clancy must have had faith in his attorney. But, it is unusual for the drafting attorney to want this "job" because it is often difficult to sustain a law practice while engaging in the daily rigors of managing, administering, and distributing the assets of someone else. I figured that the attorney accepted this responsibility for the obvious reason . . . fees. Their Living Trust said that the attorney would get a yearly salary of 2 percent of the value of the trust estate for his trustee services. Which is way more than the usual and customary trustee fee of 1 percent!

"I feel like a beggar asking him for my money," Mrs. Clancy continued. "It's like it's his money. One time I said I needed one of those automatic pillows that you can adjust with buttons. He said that I could make do with the pillows that I have. But it hurts when I move, and I told him that. But that son-of-a-bitch didn't care!. I want him out, Condon! I'll take anyone else . . . but I want him gone."

This wasn't my first rodeo with a beneficiary and a trustee not seeing eye-to-eye. Usually I can smooth out the conflicts by calling a meeting to bring both parties in the same room where each side has the opportunity to "air" their differences . . . which I can then resolve with old-fashioned problem resolution. But, when the trustee–beneficiary relationship turns poisonous and, for whatever reasons, cannot be paved over with my skill set, the trustee typically resigns . . . often graciously . . . sometimes grudgingly.

But, in this case, the attorney refused to resign. I called him after my meeting with Mrs. Clancy. I explained how displeased she was with his curt and "know-it-all" manner . . . how she adamantly believed he was not responsive to her most basic needs . . . and how vehement she was in ridding herself of his control over her and her assets.

I then said something that, upon reflection, must have come across as patronizing, especially to a fellow professional: "C'mon, buddy. I can't see how you would want to keep being trustee in such a poisonous atmosphere. If I was in your shoes, I wouldn't want to wake up every single day with the knowledge that I have to deal with someone that hates me. Life is so short . . . too short to be around such negative energy. So what do you say? Let's give both of you and Mrs. Clancy a break from each other and each of you will live a happier life."

Well . . . whether he was a control freak . . . or whether he wanted to maintain his trustee fees . . . or whether he was miffed by my borderline-insulting commentary, he declined, mumbling something about "loyalty to the husband."

When I gave the bad news to Mrs. Clancy, she wanted to know what else could be done to bounce him as trustee. I told her that she could bring an action in court to have him removed, but that there was little chance of success. Why? Because being a jerk is not enough to get a trustee booted. If we could prove that he embezzled or mismanaged the trust estate, then sure . . . he would certainly get the court-ordered removal. But, without those facts, there was nothing Mrs. Clancy could do.

Or was there? "%$#! Him!" she said to me. "He doesn't give one %$#! about my husband or his wishes. He just wants money. So that's what I'll do. I'll just offer that piece of @$%! some money to resign."

So, Mrs. Clancy offered him money to resign . . . something that I did not even consider. Did he take it? You bet he did! He took that $25,000 and signed the resignation documents so quickly that I conjectured that he must have had creditors chasing after him.

Post–Cautionary Tale Comment: Two comments, actually.

First, if you signed your Living Trust without reading it because you had faith in your spouse to make the right decisions, you should really take a look at the "who-gets-what" and "how-they-get-it" sections before the first one of you dies. If you don't, you, like

Mrs. Clancy, may be shocked to find yourself in a situation that was unimaginable to her.

Second, getting the right trustee to manage the family money and property for the surviving spouse's benefit is a very important choice. If surviving spouse and the trustee can't get along, problems and unhappiness will arise.

Putting a private person in charge of one's money and property is dangerous. Sometimes "faith" is not enough. The private person is not bonded. There is no policeman looking over that person's shoulder. There is no one around to say no. The money and property go into that person's name, which empowers that person to do what he/she wishes with the assets. The private person will charge the same, if not more, than the bank or corporate trustee and may not do as good a job.

My personal preference is the professional trustee, which is contrary to most clients' decisions. If a personality or management-driven conflict arises between the beneficiary and the individual assigned by the bank or other institutional trustee to interact with the beneficiary, a different person can be assigned. However, if a private person is chosen as trustee after the first spouse dies, and that choice causes great stress to the surviving spouse, it will be more difficult to substitute that trustee without court involvement . . . if at all.

Cautionary Tale 12: "*Si, Si!* Community Property!"

Lesson to be learned: Terminate the economic connection between your first children and your second spouse.

After Boyd's wife died, and whenever I saw him at Santa Monica Chamber of Commerce mixers, he always made a point of telling me that poor South American women are so much more compliant than American women . . . and that his next wife would definitely be a peasant girl from South America.

We all thought Boyd was full of bluster. At age 65, he was the model of the conventional family man, with a successful building contracting business, two children, and a long-standing reputation for civic and community service. Sure, his business often took him to South America where he picked up some Spanish and, maybe, a good time with the locals. But . . . marry a peasant girl from South America? Yeah, Boyd, I thought. I'll believe it when I see it.

Well, he sure showed me . . . when he came to my office and introduced me to his new wife, Carmen, a 35-year-old woman from Costa Rica, who was holding their 1-year-old baby girl. After my initial incredulousness dissipated, I quietly snickered at Boyd for having to struggle with the installation and use of baby car seats and strollers at age 65.

My silent insults, however, turned into quiet admiration for Boyd as I engaged in light banter with Carmen, who was just learning to speak English. She was charming, and her affection for Boyd seemed sincere. Carmen was a blessing to Boyd, because I never saw him look so good and have so much energy.

What brought them to my office was the baby. Boyd wanted a plan that would leave something for his "first children" and also take care of his new wife and child.

The "first children–second wife" scenario is a most difficult one to handle . . . unless there is great wealth to satisfy and placate both "sides." Boyd did not have great wealth and, thus, could not accomplish the goal of making everyone happy. Still, Boyd was insistent that his "first children" and new family each receive an inheritance in a way that would satisfy all concerned.

I advised Boyd that he could achieve that end by giving money to his "first children" to purchase an insurance policy on his life, with Boyd continuing to give his children money for the annual premium payments. By doing this, his children would receive the insurance proceeds on his death with no tax obligation. Also, Boyd could put provisions in his Living Trust that establish a subtrust for Carmen where she would have the use of his assets for the rest of her life, which, upon her death, would be distributed to their new daughter.

Boyd then insisted I explain this plan to Carmen in a way that she could understand. In my best Spanglish, I explained that if Boyd dies first, his money and property would provide for her and her child. She stared at me blankly and said, "Si, Si, community property."

Well . . . that response was inaccurate and irrelevant . . . and compelled me to somehow convey that Boyd's assets were the separate property of Boyd . . . not the community property of Boyd and Carmen. In my best broken Spanish, I said, "*Lo siento, Carmen. La casa de Boyd. Y el dinero de Boyd. Solamente the separada propiedad de Boyd.*" (Don't laugh! With four years of high school Spanish being a distant memory, I thought that was a fairly decent stab at it.)

After my explanation, I asked her if she understood ("*Tu entiendas?*") to which she responded in heavy-accented but clear English, "*Si.* Boyd's property is our community property." Eh . . . not quite. I explained it again to which she said, "*Si claro! Entiendo.* Boyd's property is our community property."

I think "community property" was the first thing she learned in English.

In any event, her misunderstanding of the character of Boyd's property did not make any difference. It was his separate property and his Living Trust—and he could leave his assets however he desired.

Boyd liked the plan I suggested . . . and that's what he did. He gifted the money to his "first children" for them to purchase a $1,000,000 life insurance policy on his life and additional funds each year for the premium payments. He also amended his Living Trust to provide the subtrust for Carmen and their daughter.

A few times over the next 15 years, Boyd stopped by to see me and make slight trust revisions. Carmen's English became much better, if not profoundly so. Their daughter was growing up as a California surfing girl, and it was easy to see she was Boyd's delight.

I heard nothing further about his "first children" . . . nor did I see them, until it became apparent that Boyd's illness was terminal. They came to my office to see me to find out if they would receive any inheritance from their father. Of course, as Boyd's attorney, I could not disclose that privileged information. I asked them if they had been to see their father, and one of them said, "No. We just want to know about the money."

I was a bit taken aback by the boldness of their statement. Usually when I meet the estranged children of my clients, there is some attempt to summon a modicum of sincere concern for their parents . . . even though everyone in room knows that the inheritance (or lack thereof) is the main motivation for their visit. But with Boyd's "first children," there was no such attempt at disguise. Nonetheless, being unable to give them the response they had sought, I simply told them, "I'm sure your ailing father would like to see you. Have a nice day." They shuffled silently out of my office.

From time to time, Carmen called to apprise me of Boyd's condition. I'm sure it wasn't easy for her to take care of Boyd through the periods of chemotherapy; the radiation, the weight loss, and changing of diapers. "Not once," she said, "did his sons come and see him."

How ironic. Boyd's friends and associates (including myself) initially condemned his "May–December" marriage as a stereotypical old-man fantasy arrangement. While his "first children" couldn't give a damn about their father, Carmen and their daughter turned out to be the best things that ever happened to him . . . and gave him life's greatest joy.

Post–Cautionary Tale Comment: To arrange the insurance policy for his "first children," Boyd and his "first children" must have had, at least, some basic communication with each other. Therefore, those children would have some knowledge and expectation about their windfall prior to their father's death. So when they came to my office, they must have been aware of their expected insurance windfall—and they still were asking me about the money. Apparently, the $1,000,000 policy was not satisfactory to them. Personally, in light of how happy his new family made him, I think those "first children" were lucky to get anything.

Still, the point of this story is that a client with two families used an insurance policy to provide a monetary inheritance for his "first children" . . . and you can, too, if you are on your "second time around" and you want to ensure that both sides are taken care of in the inheritance arena.

I know—just the word *insurance* makes your eyes (and mine) glaze over in boredom . . . and conjures an image of a sleep-inducing insurance agent presentation in your living room. But . . . keep it simple. When you purchase a policy as a device to provide an inheritance for both your "first children" and second family, you don't need to know about cash value or where you fall in the actuarial tables. All you are thinking is how much that policy will cost to provide one side (either the "first children" or the second spouse) with an amount that is reasonably comparable to the inheritance that the other side will receive.

Cautionary Tale 13: "He's Got Too Many Friends"

Lesson to be learned: Not every child can handle money. Sometimes the inherited money must be controlled by a third party.

"My son is a Good-Time Charlie to his so-called friends, Mr. Condon. When my wife and I are dead, he's going to throw it all away." This was how Mr. Evans described his son, Blake, to me. Midforties, divorced, no children. Blake was gainfully employed, but never seemed to be able to hold on to his earnings. And when Blake inherited some money from his grandmother, he blew it all on good times for him and his buddies.

In his parents' mind, their son lived for today with no thought whatsoever about the future. In my mind, he was yet another child of a client counting on his inheritance as a fallback.

The Evanses also had a daughter, Evelyn, whom they described as completely opposite of their son . . . an industrious working mother with two children and a solid marriage. They had no concern about leaving Evelyn her inheritance outright without any controls. But, they felt that some control was needed for their son's share to prevent him from plowing through it.

So, the burning question was, how do they leave their daughter an outright share while tying up their son's share, which would be doled out to him on a defined basis?

As a sweeping generalization, I am philosophically against treating children differently with respect to how they inherit their shares. Of course, there are situations where it is painfully obvious that a child's share requires third-party control to protect the assets from that child—and for that child—such as when there is present a significant prospect of the inheritance ending up with that child's drug pusher. But, when the main difference between children is the degree of their financial maturity, the usual result is the "controlled child" does not feel the control is justified and harbors jealously and resentment toward the "free child." And most clients don't want to die knowing their children are in conflict . . . and angry with their parents for creating that conflict.

Oftentimes my advice to clients is not really optional . . . it's "my-way-or-the-highway." Call it arrogance . . . call it avoidance of being caught up in the family problems that I just know will arise when the clients die . . . whatever. In situations when I perceive that a child's inheritance *must* be controlled because that child poses a palpable risk of loss to his inheritance, the clients *must* accept third-party control . . . or I don't take the case. But in cases like the Evanses', where the risk of loss is posed by financial immaturity, their perceptions of the "realness" of that risk are quite material. As a result, I left the decision of third-party control to them.

To have third-party control over Blake's share or not . . . that is the question I presented to the Evanses. And Mrs. Evans answered, "We don't know. What do you think, Mr. Condon?" Not exactly that emphatic statement I was seeking.

I then made the observation that in the ordinary and statistical course of events, Mr. Evans would die first and Mrs. Evans would die later, in her late eighties or early nineties. At that time, Blake would be in his midsixties and, perhaps, a more mature and concerned man with respect to money issues. If the Evanses appointed a third party—a trustee—to control his share, that person would be involved in Blake's life . . . in perpetuity. And if Blake somehow "straightened out," that control would serve no purpose other than to force him to go through the hassle of approaching the third party every time he needed funds for his day-to-day needs.

Further, if they went ahead with the third-party control approach, they would have to pick a third party. Who would that be? Mr. Evans did not hesitate. "Our daughter, of course. She's super-responsible."

"No," I advised. "You don't want Evelyn to be Blake's moneyholder. You don't want to put that stress and burden on her . . .

even if she agrees to take the job. And even if she's a responsible person, there is no policeman looking over her shoulder. Blake's share will be in her control, and sometimes faith is not enough when it comes to holding someone else's money. That leaves the bank or other institutional trustee who is bonded and highly regulated, and who will do a professional job of managing and investing Blake's money."

After a bit more back-and-forth of this scintillating discussion, the Evanses decided that each child would get their inheritance share outright. What was the deciding factor? Money! As Mr. Evans said, "We don't want to pay a place just to watch Blake's money and write checks."

Well . . . whatever. It's hard to talk folks out of tightly held preconceived notions . . . even if they are inaccurate. And besides, with my forecast of Blake being in his midsixties when his last parent died, I further surmised that he would inherit at a point in his life when he would have attained some financial maturity. So with these suppositions in mind, I drafted their Living Trust with each child receiving their shares outright.

Fast forward two years. Mrs. Evans died shortly after she was diagnosed with ovarian cancer at age 72. Mr. Evans died two years after that. Blake was 50 when he inherited his share . . . still on the track to financial maturity, not yet arrived at the right station. Stated less diplomatically . . . he was still young enough to be Good-Time Charlie, primed to blow it all.

After estate taxes and expenses of administration, Blake received a check for $780,000. When I handed him the check, I said, "Blake, let me take you and introduce you to some really nice guys at the bank down the street. They have a really good trust department and will help you take care of the money so you'll have it when you really need it." Granted, this was not very strongly worded. What I *really* wanted to say was, "Blake, I'm going to drag your ass to some folks who will save you from yourself and make sure you don't piss the money away!" But, decorum and sugarcoating were needed to convey lawyer-like wisdom to him . . . and to not scare him off from the goal at hand.

My offer to Blake was an attempt to get him to self-impose a monthly limit on his spending—to give him help with investments and to provide him with an excuse to tell his buddies that he didn't have any money because it was in a trust. I felt a sense of having failed his parents by my casual dismissal of my "highway" approach. I made an assumption, and it didn't pan out. This was my way of trying to make things right.

But Blake was deaf to my offer. He didn't want anyone telling him what he could or could not do with his money.

The next time I heard from Blake was when he called me about a year later . . . at 3:00 a.m. from jail. Arrested for driving under the influence of drugs, he needed someone to bail him out. Going to a bail bondsman and the police station in the middle of the night to get my deceased clients' son out of jail is not part of my job description. But, still feeling somewhat responsible for his plight, I got in my car (still in my pajamas) and bailed him out. He eventually pleaded guilty and got six months' probation.

I engaged in a bit of wishful thinking that that was a one-time occurrence . . . until six months later, when I received a call from an attorney in Normal, Illinois (the home of Beer Nuts), who informed me that Blake was arrested for a similar offense. He was fined and put on probation with the promise he would return to California and stay out of Illinois.

It keeps going. I saw Blake about a year after that, when he came to my office to have me prepare the lease and other paperwork necessary to—get this—open a nightclub. Yes, a nightclub . . . where the pervasive presence and scent of spirits easily lends itself to allowing his addiction to continue . . . and run rampant.

Did I lambaste Blake for such a foolhardy plan that may fuel his destruction? I was about to—and then I recalled the character of Sam Malone on *Cheers* . . . a recovering alcoholic who owned a bar. Whenever Sam was met with the inquiry of why he established a business selling a product that led to his destruction and ouster from professional sports, he replied that his experience in drinking, partying, and hanging with his friends gave him enough working knowledge about bars and nightclubs to make a successful venture. So, with a fictional television character as my guide and moral compass, I withheld the self-righteous speech and dramatic refusal to get involved and did the work.

Of course, the nightclub failed, and Blake got me involved to negotiate a buyout of the lease to avoid litigation.

Blake was out of cash . . . and down to the valuable house he inherited from his parents. At one point I told him, "Blake, let's do something to remove the house from your failures. It's the last thing you've got, and if you lose it, you'll be homeless." Again, he refused—and it wasn't long after that that he was homeless. He mortgaged the house several times and lost the money on drugs, alcohol, and stupid "deals" touted by his friends.

I see Blake once in a while. He's homeless and hangs around at the beach. We don't speak anymore so I don't know if he has any source of support, although I suppose he gets some money from his sister from time to time. I still feel some sense of guilt, but I somehow manage to tell myself that his downward spiral was not my fault.

This experience continues to resonate in my head to the point where it sometimes interferes with sleep. Now, when my clients tell me they have some concern about a child's ability to handle money, we'll do it my way with corporate trustee third-party control . . . or it's the highway. If they react negatively to the concept of the corporate trustee holding and managing the family money, I relate to them the Evans family saga, which usually gets them on board.

Post–Cautionary Tale Comment: The need to have a third-party control is readily apparent and implicitly understood when dealing with an inheritance for a minor child, a physically disabled child, a mentally deficient child, an emotionally disturbed child, or an addicted child. And because of my experience with the Evans family, I now throw in "financially immature child" into that mix.

Still, caution must be taken to prevent the unjustifiable and unnecessary use of third-party inheritance control. Oftentimes, clients describe their children as wasteful spendthrifts who need third-party inheritance protection when, in reality, they have conventional intelligence and generally normal attributes. As one client said, "My son has a good job and a good education, but he throws his money away on computers and other electronic junk instead of saving it for the future." Or as another client put it, "My wife and I didn't get our first new car until we were married 20 years, but our daughter just got a new car a few months after she got married." And another client said, "Our daughter spends everything she earns on clothes and doesn't know how to save a dime." And so on and so on.

This is a true gap in generational perspective. Parents often feel the inheritance must be preserved and protected from their children's folly. But from their children's perspective, there is no folly. Their parents may misconceive or disapprove of their children's exercise of spending power, but the spending is consistent with the norms of their generation. Thus, it sometimes falls to the inheritance lawyer . . . which would be me . . . to show that their labeling of their children as "wasteful" is unrealistic.

But keeping the Evanses in mind during that process, and after factoring in the conventional life expectancies of the parents and the age of their children when the last parent dies, I may elect to err on the side of caution and advise that third-party inheritance control be instituted in their Living Trust.

Cautionary Tale 14: "We Were Cheated!"

Lesson to be learned: You have to ask yourself if your children will carry out your Living Trust's inheritance instructions.

I don't see too many teenagers in my office. But if they're sitting in front of me, it's usually because they feel they got a raw deal with an inheritance issue. Victor and Melinda did not disappoint my expectation.

They were in their teens, the young man about 19 and his sister about 17. They were quite animated and spoke at a rapid rate . . . almost simultaneously. Not because rapid overlapping speech is a stereotypical trapping of youth . . . but from the agitation having been cheated and finally getting their story out to someone who could possibly help them. After I told them to slow down to hear from just one of them, Victor told me what happened.

Victor and Melinda were preteens when their parents divorced and they went to live with their mother in Los Angeles. When their mother died of brain cancer a year later, they moved in with their father in New York City. Before they relocated, they enjoyed a close relationship with their mother's family . . . their grandparents, uncles, aunts, cousins. But with 3,000 miles distance between them, that closeness gradually dissipated and became superseded by their relationship with their father's family . . . his parents, siblings, and cousins.

I had prepared a Living Trust for Victor and Melinda's maternal grandparents, Mr. and Mrs. Debevic. As Victor spoke, my secretary brought their file and I perused the document I had prepared. The Debevics' inheritance instructions were quite conventional. Three children. One-third to each of them when the last spouse died.

Their Living Trust also contained typical "backup" beneficiary provisions that say who gets a child's share if that child dies before their parents. Specifically, if any of the Debevics' three children died before both Mr. and Ms. Debevic were gone, that deceased child's children . . . the Debevics' grandchildren . . . would "step into" the inheritance shoes of that deceased child.

Mr. Debevic died first. Mrs. Debevic died about 10 years later, with a daughter, Victor and Melinda's mother, dying before her. Victor and Melinda stepped into the inheritance shoes of their mother and were entitled to receive one-third of their maternal grandparents' assets. The other two-thirds would go to their grandparents' two other children, their uncle and aunt.

Okay. Melinda and Victor inherit one-third. So why did they feel cheated? Because of the action (or should I say, inactions) of the persons in charge of carrying out the terms of the Debevics' Living Trust—Melinda and Victor's uncle and aunt.

The Debevics' Living Trust appointed all three of their children as the successor co-trustees . . . the ones who carry out the inheritance instructions . . . after both Mr. and Mrs. Debevic were dead. But, it also provided that if any child is "unable or unwilling" to act as a successor co-trustee, the remaining two children will act as successor co-trustees. Again, pretty typical backup stuff. So . . . the two other children were in charge.

And then I understood why Victor and Melina felt cheated . . . to the point where I could finish Victor's story for him. Which I did. "Victor, let me guess. You approached your uncle and aunt about getting your mother's share of the trust estate. And they told you to buzz off. No wonder they didn't come to see me after your grandmother died. If they involved an attorney, they knew they could not get away with cutting you out of your one-third."

But why did Victor and Melinda wait two years after their grandmother's death to complain? In all my years of practice, I have *never* once encountered someone who had to be notified to learn he has inherited. I've had situations where people in the deepest part of Africa somehow find out about an inheritance and show up to make the claim. The beat of the inner tom-tom inheritance drum is a loud one.

So what happened with Melinda and Victor? They were not indifferent . . . just living in a different world. Their mother died when they were young and they became ensconced and engrossed in their new surroundings across the country. They were generally aware of their California relatives but did not have any contact with them. And when their grandmother died, they were 17 and 15 . . . , too young to think about such things as a possible inheritance.

A few days before this meeting with me, they left New York to accompany their father on a business trip to Los Angeles. After their arrival, they were invited to a cousin's house for dinner to meet or get reacquainted with "long-lost" relatives. It was at that occasion that they began thinking, "Hey . . . is it possible that we get Mom's share of Grandpa and Grandma's money?" At the dinner, they meekly approached the successor co-trustees—their uncle and aunt, whom they barely knew—with that inquiry. Their response was an evasive, "We'll check it out and get back to you."

Later that evening, a helpful cousin who overheard that exchange gave Victor and Melinda the idea of checking with the attorney who drafted their grandparents' inheritance plan. Victor and Melinda again brushed up to their uncle and aunt and asked for the name of that attorney, but they claimed ignorance.

The next day, with that cousin's assistance, they were able to track a copy of the Debevics' Living Trust. Even though they were teenagers without any kind of business sophistication, and although that Trust was 60 pages chock-full of beyond-tedious legal gobbledigook, they were able to decipher the "who gets what" part. And there they discovered for the first time that their uncle and aunt cheated them out of their one-third share—which would have been about $350,000 for each of them.

And now Victor and Melinda were sitting in my office . . . angry and dumbfounded. I was angry, too. Although I have become somewhat jaded to the high-pitched emotions and situations that play out before me, I still get riled up big-time when kids get screwed out of something that could help them get a leg up in life. So I didn't hold back when I said, "Let's sue those bastards!" (Yes. I literally said that.) That really pumped them up, as Victor said, "Yes, Mr. Condon! Yes! That's just want we want! Now *that's* a lawyer!"

But ultimately, the emotions subsided and calmer and more professional minds prevailed. "Let's hold off on any litigation until I have had a chance to speak with your uncle and aunt," I advised as I felt my lawyer-like demeanor returning. "Let's find out what happened."

I called the phone number of their aunt. When the aunt answered, I introduced myself, informed her that her niece and nephew were present in my office, and suggested that she and her brother meet with me about their parents' Living Trust. "Why?" she asked. I cryptically responded, "I think you know. And I also think that in the long run, you will find that meeting me is the wise thing to do."

I'm not used to making veiled threats . . . but this one worked. The next day, the uncle and aunt were in my office and singing like canaries. They hated their deceased sister's husband. They felt he was responsible, at least in part, for their sister's death. They were distressed when their deceased sister's children went to live with their father. An attorney advised them there was no use in fighting for custody because there was no evidence their father was an unsuitable parent. So they devised a way to "get" Victor and Melinda's dad . . . by keeping their deceased sister's share of the inheritance.

Of course, that made no sense, and no one bought it. How does depriving their deceased sister's children of their rightful one-third share achieve "noble" revenge against the man they felt was responsible for their deceased sister's death? It doesn't! Taking Melinda and Victor's share doesn't "get" their father . . . it only "gets" their deceased sister and her children.

The uncle and aunt's decision to take their deceased sister's share was simply about getting more of their parents' estate for themselves . . . and then justifying and becoming more comfortable with that decision with their tale of revenge. Their niece and nephew? Out of sight, out of mind.

In any event, the aunt and uncle were caught. They gave Victor and Melinda their rightful share . . . plus interest. And each received $50,000 extra as a punitive measure.

People do sometimes "go crazy" in the inheritance arena. When faced with an opportunity for further enrichment, it's very tempting to set aside common sense and family loyalty and follow that path and see where it leads. Hence, my old adage, "There is no such thing as family loyalty when it comes to dividing money."

Post–Cautionary Tale Comment: My clients almost always designate their children as their successor co-trustees in their Living Trust. As successor co-trustees, they have the legal responsibility to carry out the terms of their parents' inheritance plan as stated in their Living Trust.

Still—will those appointed children do the right . . . and legal . . . thing and carry out those wishes? When I pose that question to my clients, they invariably respond with some form of, "Of course! How dare you even ask!" That is my cue to regale them with a few stories of how my clients' children have casually disregarded their parents' inheritance instructions . . . with the Debevic family saga being the centerpiece—followed by my canned (but still sage) advice: "No one knows for certain whether your children will do the right thing. But the fact remains that they have the ability to deviate from your inheritance instructions. If your children want to do it their way, who is around to say no? Not you!"

After my clients hear me read from this script, they respond by summarily dismissing my admonition without another thought . . . or by voicing this refrain: "Gee, Mr. Condon. I never thought about that before. Maybe we should consider this further." When I hear that second type of response, I know I've done my job in helping my clients recognize the problem . . . because 95 percent of the solution to any problem is recognizing that problem in the first place.

Once this issue of inheritance plan diversion has been raised, we can then embark on a discussion of whether appointing persons or an entity other than the clients' children as successor co-trustees is appropriate.

Cautionary Tale 15: "Am I My Brother's Keeper?"

Lesson to be learned: Cutting out the "bad child" and leaving it all to the "good child" may make the "good child" the financial keeper of the "bad child."

If I think a client's inheritance instructions are going to throw the family into a world of chaos, I will decline to prepare that Living Trust. As I've said several times elsewhere in this book, the drafting attorney often gets caught up in the post–death family drama . . . being sued, harassed, hassled . . . and I just don't want that trouble interfering with my beach time. Still, there are clients who are persistent, such as Mr. and Mrs. Floyd, in doing it their way and attempt to prevail upon me to comply . . . even if I've summoned all my lawyer smarts to convince them otherwise.

When I first met Mr. and Mrs. Floyd, each was in their midseventies. They had two children—a "normal" daughter and a son with a lifelong drug addiction. At age 53, he was the same he had been at age 15 . . . and his parents felt a moral compunction to support him all the while. They tried everything to help him overcome his addition. Counseling. Psychiatrist. Voluntary and involuntary placement. Nothing really worked. While their son did have some months of sobriety that Mrs. Floyd described as "Heaven on earth," he would always fall back. Mrs. Floyd said to me, "God must have been punishing us by giving us an irreversible addict for a son!"

Their plan was to establish a Living Trust that cut out their son and left everything to their daughter. They loved their son, but they were not going to reward him for the mess he made of his life . . . and theirs..

As you may have gathered from my previous discussions of disinheriting a "problem child," I react instinctively against clients' cutting out an addicted child. Of course, the clients are concerned with the addicted child using his inheritance to fuel his destruction. But, an additional concern is the impact of cutting out the addicted child on the clients' other children. By dumping the addicted child out of inheritance, they dump him into the life of his siblings who received "his share." And that addicted child will make his siblings' lives miserable with incessant calls, e-mails, and unannounced visits at work and home, saying, in essence, "You got my share, and now I'm your responsibility."

They don't teach you about this ramification in wills and trusts class at law school. My knowledge stems from the Law School of Hard Knocks—the many times I have seen this "dance" happen before. Clients cut out a child . . . the clients die . . . and the cut-out child does the "you've-got-my-money" routine with his siblings. The better solution is to leave the addicted child his share in a protection trust with third-party control to protect the inheritance for him . . . and from his vice.

But, notwithstanding that excellent advice, the Floyds mounted the protest that clients usually give me when I tell them no: "Condon, this is our money. It's our plan. We can do it any way we want!" I responded, "Of course it is! But you haven't seen what I've seen in these situations. The outcome will be just as I told you. A bad one. Tell you what. Go ask your daughter what she thinks of your plan, and don't leave out the part where the lawyer predicted that her brother will frequently intrude on her life. If she says okay, I'll do what you want."

The Floyd left and came back a week later . . . with their daughter in tow. She was in her forties, married, with two children. She seemed like a sensible woman. "Explain to our daughter what you explained to us, Mr. Condon," instructed her parents. So I did. Particularly the unintended consequence of her brother's intrusive behavior that lay in store for her.

Their daughter liked the idea of inheriting her parents' entire estate. Who wouldn't? But, did she truly appreciate the Parade of Horribles that I laid out for her? Perhaps. But she saw an economic opportunity . . . and grabbed it. She accompanied her parents to tell me to my face that she could handle whatever her brother might happen to throw at her . . . and to reinforce their decision to leave everything to her.

Fast-forward seven years. Mr. Floyd died, and Mrs. Floyd and her daughter met with me for the "what happens now" discussion. I recalled her son's addiction and wondered aloud how he was faring. Mrs. Floyd regretfully informed me any change in his addiction was for the worse.

With the Floyds' Living Trust before me, I pointed out that Mrs. Floyd has now sole control of the trust estate . . . which includes the power to amend the inheritance instructions to incorporate a protection trust for her son to provide him with funds for his personal and medical needs. As I made that statement, my peripheral vision caught the sight of their daughter flinching as if she had been punched in the shoulder. Clearly, this was not a question the daughter wanted to hear. But to the daughter's great relief, Mrs. Floyd said that she would go on with the plan as she and her husband intended.

Mrs. Floyd died about five years after that meeting, and the daughter was in my office yet again. Her parents' Living Trust left everything to her. With the house, the two apartment buildings, the brokerage account, certificates of deposit, household furniture, and all contents, she inherited about $3 million. She signed the transfer documents . . . and away she went.

I never saw the daughter again . . . but I did hear from her again. Many times! Why? Because she called me nearly every time her brother intruded in her life. For some reason, I became the person she complained to . . . like a substitute father. Her brother's calls and e-mails came every few weeks, demanding money for rent, food, automotive repairs, phone, medicine, and even bail. Each of those calls begat wrestling matches she had with her conscience: "I feel so much pressure to cave in to his money demands. I know it's my money . . . but he's my brother. I had no idea I would feel this way. I have to give him what he asks for, or he'll probably end up dead on the streets!"

And each time she called me, I gave her the same advice: "You have no legal obligation to give him anything. A moral obligation . . . that's another question. You have to do what you think is best. But keep in mind that your parents gave everything to you because of their concern that any money to your brother would just go up his nose. They didn't want their money to kill him."

Eventually, the daughter stopped calling me, but her plight was never too far from my mind. I sympathized with her. No amount of money was worth having to endure being caught in the vortex of her brother's world of addiction. And with her being unable to resist that unexpected moral dilemma she described to me, I suspected that she acceded to all of her brother's demands for money.

Then one day a well-dressed, well-groomed, physically fit man in his early sixties came to my office. To my abject surprise, it was the Floyds' addict son . . . the one who had been a curse to his parents.

I couldn't believe it! It never dawned on me that this transformation could happen. Once an actively using addict, always an actively using addict. I presumed that he would die on some street looking for the next score. But this? He could have been the model for the image that the Santa Monica Chamber of Commerce wants to project to the public.

Naturally, I asked him, "What happened?" He said, "I begged my sister to pay for one of those expensive Betty Ford rehab-type places. It cost $300 a day . . . about a hundred grand a year. It got me off the streets for a year. She paid and I went." Not only had he been off the drugs for about a year, he had a clothing sales job, an apartment, a car . . . and a wife whom he had met at the rehabilitation facility. All in all . . . he was leading a normal, conventional life.

But the next thing he said hurt a bit—and made me rethink my view on addiction and recovery: "You know, Mr. Condon, I don't blame you for my parents' cutting me out of their Trust. That was their decision. But, you should have told them that miracles can happen. And maybe they would have set aside my half just in case that happened."

Post–Cautionary Tale Comment: By the time parents confer with me about their "bad child," their pain is so pronounced and engraved that I have great difficulty in getting them to consider alternatives, such as a protection trust, that offer protection of that child's inheritance share from his vice. As a result, they don't want to hear about any alternatives and instruct me to simply draft provisions in their Living Trust that cut out that "bad child."

A problem that exists between a parent and child typically stays between that parent and child. But, if that problem causes the parent to disinherit that child, the parents unintentionally shift that problem . . . and the burden of support . . . to their other children. And ultimately, the cut-out child will engage in a campaign of harassment and vexation against his inheriting siblings.

The frequency of clients desiring to cut out a child's inheritance plan has led me to create what I call "the Greed Letter." With my clients' permission, I prepare this letter, which advises the prospective "cut-out" child that his parents have conferred with me for the purpose of disinheriting him, discusses the reasons for that decision, and points out the amount that he is losing because of being disinherited.

And most important, the letter informs the child that it is entirely possible that his parents could change their mind if he changes his ways.

Obviously, this is an appeal to that child's greed. Losing big inheritance bucks is a powerful motivation to make amends or conform to conduct, which would find his parents' approval. Whether this meets with societal approval or not, the question invariably asked is, "Does the Greed Letter work?" If success is measured by invitations to birthday functions, Thanksgiving dinner, Super Bowl Sunday, Christmas Eve, Christmas Day, and the first night of Hanukkah, I have about a 50 percent success rate.

So what if it's greed that is the grease for the squeaky wheel? Clients are so happy to see a "bad child" mend his ways, they heartily welcome him back into the fold. As one client said to me, "My son was wasting his life. Partying all the time. I didn't speak to him for 10 years. Then he got your Greed Letter . . . and he shaped up. I know it's the money talking, but I don't care. I've got my son back."

Cautionary Tale 16: "I Don't Want to Die with My Daughters Mad at Each Other"

Lesson to be learned: Conflict and jealousy may ensue by leaving an inheritance gift to one family member to the exclusion of your other family members.

Mr. and Mrs. Adair had two daughters, Bonnie and Michelle. I prepared their Living Trust, which left everything equally to their daughters. But, Mrs. Adair was still concerned that their daughters will be mad at each other when their inheritance is divided. Why? Because Mrs. Adair's brother, Clay, left his house entirely to his favorite niece, Bonnie, and nothing to Michelle.

"My brother never married and had no children, Mr. Condon. Clay treated my daughters as his own. He bought them both cars. Contributed to their education. Helped pay for their weddings. He kind of favored Bonnie, but he didn't want them to think he played favorites so he pretty much treated them the same. But when he died, he left his house to Bonnie alone and nothing to Michelle. It's worth $550,000! Then the fight started. Michelle accused Bonnie of doing something fishy to get Clay's house, and she demanded that we leave her an extra $550,000! We don't even have enough assets to leave Michelle that extra amount. Then

Bonnie flipped out and screamed at her sister to shut up and that her inheritance from her uncle is none of our business."

At first, I kind of agreed with Bonnie. Uncle Clay's inheritance plan should have no bearing on the Adairs' Living Trust, and the Adairs should just keep their inheritance instructions as a 50/50 split. But then Mrs. Adair said something else that got me thinking in the other direction: "I don't want to die knowing that my daughters are mad at each other. If they're not talking to each other, then *their* children will never talk to each other. Everything we built up for our children will be meaningless if our family is split apart."

I am a firm believer in my clients' children receiving an equal inheritance to avoid the conflicts and jealousies in the inheritance arena that can tear families apart. And as I pontificate previously in this book, equal treatment in the Living Trust does not mean that children have received an equal inheritance if the **parents** have treated their children financially unequally during their **parents'** lifetimes. Indeed, when **parents** make a lifetime gift to a child, they usually do so without keeping an economic scorecard to keep track of how much each child received. But . . . their children *are* keeping a scorecard, and if the end-of-life tally shows a substantial inequality of gifts made by their **parents**, they will not consider themselves to have received an equal inheritance . . . even if their **parents'** Living Trust provides for an equal split. And as hard as it is to believe, that inequality can bring an otherwise peaceful and close family relationship to its knees. So, in every first-time client meeting, I bring this issue of unequal lifetime gifts to the fore so **parents** are aware of the potential family fallout that it can trigger, and then bring to their attention any number of techniques that they can incorporate in their inheritance plan to resolve this inheritance problem.

Notice how I bolded the word "parents" in that last paragraph? I do so to emphasize that I look upon this unequal treatment problem exclusively in the context of the parent–child relationship. But, with the Adairs before me, I had to ask myself whether I need be concerned about this problem in the entirely different realm of unequal financial treatment by nonparents.

Well, I must admit, what Mrs. Adair said about not wanting to die with her children mad at each other got me. Though the Adairs' unequal inheritance problem arose in a different context, the heavy emotions of family estrangement were the same. They were almost medically depressed over the fighting between their daughters and the prospect of conflict infecting their descending generations.

I agreed strongly with the Adairs' goal of keeping their family intact in the face of Bonnie's inheritance of a valuable home from her uncle. Now all I had to do was think of a way to accomplish it. That's why this is called the "practice" of law. We get to practice this stuff until we get it right.

A week later, I called for an Adair family meeting at my office. I wanted everyone there and they all showed up. Mrs. and Mrs. Adair. Bonnie. Michelle. The husbands of Bonnie and Michelle. The tension was thick. The room was silent. All eyes were fixed upon me at the head of the table, ready to play Solomon and reunite the family.

I didn't have any brilliant, complex, or mathematical solution up my sleeve. What I had to do was level this problem up from a money concern to a family concern that they, Michelle and Bonnie, felt pressure to resolve themselves. Why? Since the Adairs did not have sufficient assets to leave Michelle an extra $550,000, the equalization problem was not resolvable. And pressure for a resolution from "The Lawyer" during a family meeting in a formal office setting can only go so far. All I could do was push the right emotional buttons to engender within them the motivation to resolve this issue in a manner they could both live with.

I looked at Bonnie and Michelle and said, "Do you want your parents to die knowing their only two children are fighting with each other?" Of course, they said, "No." So far, so good. The rest of my sermon focused on getting them to agree that after everything their parents did for them, they didn't want their parents to die knowing their girls and their grandchildren were split up over money. And then my dramatic conclusion: "You are the only ones who can help your parents. No one else can do it."

Ultimately, we worked out some minor compromise that resulted in amending the Adairs' Living Trust to leave Michelle a small but "symbolic" extra amount. Mr. and Mrs. Adair were happy because the shouting matches had stopped. Bonnie and Michelle were, however, anything but happy, as anyone looking closely could easily see that they still harbored resentment, suspicion, and ill-will toward each other. But, for their parents' sake, they did appear on the surface to be satisfied.

Now their parents could die in peace

Post–Cautionary Tale Comment: One of my most popular (or threadbare) mantras is . . . if you don't want the blame, treat your children the same. In the inheritance arena, treating children the same not only means leaving them equal shares in the Living Trust, but finding a way to equalize lifetime gifts.

But now, because of my brush with the Adair family saga, I ask clients whether any of their children have received an inheritance from any other source and, if so, whether that inheritance was shared equally. If that "outside inheritance" was exclusive to one child, I relate my experience with the Adairs and advise that such a disparity could result in feelings of resentment and jealousy by the child who got the short end of the stick against his inheriting sibling.

Of course, my clients invariably say, "My kids' inheritance from their dead [fill in family member here] has no relationship to what we leave to our children. Why should we try to resolve that inequality in our Living Trust when we had nothing to do with it?"

To that, I simply ask, "How would you feel if your sibling received an expensive gift and you didn't? And how would you feel if I could resurrect you from the grave so you could see your children squabbling because of that?" Those questions really do more than anything to bring this problem home. Everyone can relate to exclusion and being made to feel less-than-special.

Parents may not care how their children feel toward each other or toward themselves. However, most do care, because they don't want to run the risk of their children—their most precious "possessions" in this world—ending up in conflict. But even the most concerned parent may not feel that spending extra time and energy to come up with a plan to equalize "outside inheritances" is justified.

And that's fine by me. This situation is not one where I refuse to do the work if my advice is disregarded. Nonetheless, I still raise the issue, which allows the parents to adopt or disregard the advice as they please.

Cautionary Tale 17: "I Lost the Bet"

Lesson to be learned: Even if you own your home with your spouse as "joint tenants with right of survivorship," don't presume that you will own the whole house if you outlive your spouse.

I didn't mean to be flippant with Mrs. Barber. But, when she told me her husband "screwed her," I said "I hope so!" I know. Very unprofessional. But, the opportunity to use that line was served up to me like a tennis lob, and I just couldn't resist the smash. I don't think Mrs. Barber noticed, though. She was too involved with her own thought process to notice my lack of decorum.

Mrs. Barber was in her midseventies. Married twice. She had two children from her first marriage, which ended in divorce.

Mrs. Barber's second marriage was to a man 10 years older than her with a son from his first marriage. She was the housewife with little business knowledge. He was one of those business executive types. Her second marriage lasted for 20 years until her second husband's recent death. There were no children from that second marriage.

Shortly after Mrs. Barber entered her second marriage, they sold their separate houses and combined the funds into one new home to get a fresh start. When it came to deciding how to take title to their new home, the escrow lady suggested "joint tenancy with right of survivorship." Sounded good to her. With her second husband being 10 years older, and with women statistically having a longer life expectancy than men, she assumed that he would die first and then she would own the entire house.

Later, they bought an apartment building together and took title the same way . . . joint tenancy with right of survivorship. As Mrs. Barber said, "We talked it over and he agreed that if he died first, the house and the apartment building would be mine; and the apartment building would throw off enough rents to take care of me."

Just as Mrs. Barber assumed, her second husband died first. But contrary to her expectation of receiving her second husband's half of the house and apartment building, his shares went to someone else. That's why she was meeting with me . . . and why she said she got screwed.

I had a fairly decent idea of what happened. After I checked out the title to the properties at the county recorder's office, it turned out that I was right. A few months before Mrs. Barber's second husband died, he terminated the "right of survivorship." This was easy to do. He simply signed a deed that severed the joint tenancy by transferring his half from himself as a joint tenant to himself as a tenant-in-common. As a result, the second husband was free to leave his half to anyone he wanted.

And he sure did. The second husband transferred his halves of the properties to a separate Living Trust that Mrs. Barber never knew existed. After his death, Mrs. Barber discovered this Living Trust, and that left those halves to . . . here it comes—his secretary!

The second husband's secretary and Mrs. Barber were now equal co-owners of the properties. Partners! Like out of a movie, yes? Shocking . . . but true!

What a shock this was to Mrs. Barber. A triple shock, actually. Her second husband dies unexpectedly. She discovers he has a longtime mistress. Then she learns that the mistress would be getting what she assumed she would get.

Then the fourth shock arrived in the form of a letter from the mistress's lawyer. To paraphrase the contents: "Mrs. Barber, my client is now the co-owner of the house and the building. She offers to sell you her half of those properties at fair market value. If you don't elect to purchase those halves, we will go to court to get an order forcing you to join in with my client to list those properties on the market for sale."

"Can she do that, Mr. Condon? Can she force me to sell them if I don't buy her out?" I felt like the doctor who faced the task of telling his patient he had a life-threatening sickness. "Yes," I said mournfully. "She can."

Sometimes the doctor can offer the hope of a possible cure. But there was no cure for Mrs. Barber's "condition." She made the fatal mistake of assuming joint tenancy would protect her . . . and she was wrong.

Mrs. Barber did not want to lose her home or the rents from the apartment building, but she didn't have the resources to buy the secretary's half. So she was forced to sell. Today, Mrs. Barber resides with one of her children in another state, a far cry from the social and financial independent life she envisioned.

Maybe Mrs. Barber's second husband loved her. After all, their marriage lasted for 20 years. And in light of his extravagant gift to his secretary, I figure he must have loved his secretary equally. Or more. But being a sophisticated business type, Mrs. Barber's second husband must have known that such a gift would make his wife and his mistress partners in the same assets. How can a man possess such love toward two women and still intentionally create a chain of events that places those mortal combatants in the same plane?

I still have not reconciled that one.

Post–Cautionary Tale Comment: Actually . . . more of a warning than a comment.

Husbands and wives commonly take title to real estate as joint tenants with right of survivorship. With joint tenancy, the expectation is that the surviving joint tenant will be the 100 percent owner . . . and life goes on.

But, as seen with the Barber family saga, that expectation can be a fallacy. Any joint tenant can terminate the joint tenancy, which leaves each former joint tenant with the power to leave his share to anyone he desires—without the knowledge or consent of the other former joint tenant.

The solution is for husbands and wives to own real estate in a Living Trust. If a spouse desires to move half of the property out of the Living Trust, this cannot be done without first obtaining the knowledge, consent, and signature of the other spouse.

Cautionary Tale 18: "I Only Have the Children I Choose to Tell You About"

Lesson to be learned: A child whom you want to exclude from an inheritance may still be able to inherit from you.

When I realized that I had screwed up, I must not have been able to disguise the fear of failure—and of being sued—on my face. Because Josh reassuringly said to me, "Don't worry, Mr. Condon. I'm not planning to make any claim."

I could have been in significant difficulty. But fortunately for me, Josh was not the litigious type.

I had established a Living Trust for my client, Mr. Warburton. About 20 years later, Mr. Warburton died, and about two months after that, Josh introduced himself to me as Mr. Warburton's son.

As Josh and I met, I perused the Warburton file and saw my handwritten notes next to the usual litany of questions an inheritance lawyer asks a first-time client. One of those standard questions was: Do you have any children of your current marriage or prior marriage? My note next to this question recorded Mr. Warburton's response: "Two children from marriage, Henry and Denise. No prior marriages. No other children."

I assumed Josh was one of those two children who was here for advice on the administration of the Warburtons' Living Trust . . . until I noticed that Josh wasn't Henry or Denise. "Josh," I asked, "Do you also go by 'Henry'? To that Josh replied, "No, Mr. Condon. My name is Josh, and I just found out a few months ago that Warburton was my biological father."

It was dislike of math that drove me to law school, but I now had to engage in some math to process the information that Josh just presented to me. Mr. Warburton was married for 55 years before his death at age 82. Josh was 63. Which means that Mr. Warburton would have been around 19 when Josh was born, years before he married. In light of what I remembered about Mr. Warburton, an unassuming and conventional business-and-family type, I was surprised that he had sired a child out of wedlock while still a teenager.

The stuff of cinema, yes? Well . . . it can also be the stuff of real life, as Josh so informed me.

"That's about it, Mr. Condon. It was at the beginning of World War II. Warburton was in the Navy. About to go overseas. Met my mother, who was only 18. Had their fling. He left. She never saw him again. After I was born, my mother met and married a guy named Dan Balter. I thought Dan was my father. He and my mom raised me. Dan died about a month ago. And for whatever reason, my mom felt compelled to tell me that Dan was not my biological father."

As much as I would like to delve into the soap-opera aspect of this story, I must focus on its less-compelling legal side. Here was Josh—Mr. Warburton's unacknowledged yet biological child. And here was Mr. Warburton's Living Trust . . . which made no mention of Josh. With these two elements present, Josh could make a claim against Mr. Warburton's estate to receive an equal share.

Why was Josh entitled to an equal share? Most states have certain laws that state, in effect, that if a parent has a child at the time that person executes his inheritance plan . . . *and that child is not expressly omitted as a beneficiary* . . . then that child *still* gets a piece of that parent's estate. Even if the parent did not intend to leave any piece to that child! This is the law of *pretermission,* which states, in effect: If your inheritance plan fails to mention or make any reference to your child, we shall presume that failure was accidental . . . and the child should not be penalized because of that inadvertent omission.

However, there is a way around this law: If a parent wants to cut out a child, the parent merely has to state in the Living Trust that the child is cut out. It's that simple.

This is why I felt myself becoming warm with fear when Josh told me his soap-opera story. Mr. Warburton's Living Trust made no mention of Josh . . . or cutting out Josh. As a result, Josh could file a claim demanding one-third of Mr. Warburton's estate. It matters not whether Mr. Warburton knew about Josh's existence at the time he established his Living Trust. The law is the law. And as the attorney who drafted that document, Mr. Warburton's two other children could come after me for failing to include a provision cutting out Josh.

Sure, I relied on the response of Mr. Warburton when he said that he had no children other than Henry and Denise. But, since when has common sense stopped anyone from suing the "deep-pockets" attorney?

Well . . . it turns out Josh was a good guy who had no interest in creating any trouble for anyone. Josh was a physician with his own family . . . a wife and two children. He didn't want to meet his two half-siblings . . . and he didn't want to make any claim against Mr. Warburton's estate as an "accidentally cut-out child." (Besides, Josh had twice the money that Mr. Warburton had.) When Josh's mother told him the truth about Mr. Warburton being his biological father, Josh just wanted to find out more about him.

When Josh finally tracked him down, he found that he had died about a month before. Bad timing. So Josh was left with talking with his father's old "cronies" to discover more about that man. And that's why Josh came to my office. Not for money . . . but for memories.

Post–Cautionary Tale Comment: A physician cannot fully or accurately diagnose and treat a patient who is less than forthcoming about his medical history. The same holds true in the context of attorneys and their clients. In order for attorneys to give the best and most salient advice possible, they have to know everything relevant about that client. And there is nothing more relevant in the inheritance planning field than the existence of a child.

If a child was born before the parent executed an inheritance plan that does not mention that child, then that "omitted child" may be entitled to take a portion of that parent's estate. The underlying legal philosophy is that failing to mention the "omitted child" must have been an oversight . . . and the law will correct that oversight by treating that "omitted child," for inheritance purposes, as a child who is entitled to participate equally with the decedent's other legitimate children.

However, if the parent signs an inheritance plan after the birth of the "omitted child" and mentions or specifically disinherits the child, the child has no inheritance rights.

Cautionary Tale 19: "I Want My Money . . . So Hurry Up and Die!"

Lesson to be learned: If you hate your second wife, put her in a situation where your first children have to wait for her to die to get their inheritance.

The four daughters of Carlos Medina were crowded around the meeting table in my office's small conference room. The oldest daughter, Vera, was elected spokesperson and told me the story.

Their 92-year-old father married his 40-year-old housekeeper. After they married, he redrafted his Living Trust so his second wife could live in his house for the rest of her life . . . with Carlos's children inheriting the house after the second wife's death. Because of the second wife's young age, they might not get that house for 40 or 50 years—assuming she didn't outlive them. Vera then asked, "What can we do about this?"

Whenever I hear the story of an elderly man marrying a significantly younger woman, the first thought that enters my mind is "undue influence." Maybe he became dependent on her and couldn't live without her . . . and she threatened to leave unless she received assurances that she had a place to live for the rest of her life. Then I commence my silent judgment passing, such as, "If the old guy's kids had bothered to take care of their father, this probably wouldn't have happened to begin with."

Or, maybe their father was senile and didn't know what he was doing when he signed that Living Trust redraft. Or, perhaps he was still "with it," but so lonely that he felt it worthy to bypass his children in favor of the woman who kept him company.

Nonetheless, whatever the reason, his children wanted a remedy in order to prevent "this stranger" from inheriting that house after their father's death.

"There's the easy way and the hard way," I told them. "The easy way is to talk it over with your father and convince him to change his mind." They said they tried, but he warned them that he would give the second wife the house *now* if they tried to interfere.

So what was the hard way? Having to fight their father . . . in court. "You will have to pay me thousands of dollars to prove to the probate judge that your father does not have the capacity to make financial decisions or tend to his day-to-day needs. That means getting his doctors involved to declare he is incapacitated. If you win on that issue, one of you will be appointed as your father's conservator. Then you will have to pay me more money to get the probate judge to rescind your father's Living Trust."

Vera asked me about the downsides of this plan. Besides the drama of being involved in litigation, there are two painful repercussions. One, they will have to pay me a lot of money to embark on, and travel down, that road of litigation. Vera said that wasn't a problem, as she and her sisters would share the expenses. But it was the second downside that gave them the most pause: If the Medina children are not successful in securing the conservatorship over their father, he will undoubtedly retaliate by cutting them out completely.

Even with the likely cloud of disinheritance looming overhead, I'm sure there are other lawyers who would "egg on" and sign up Vera and her siblings right then and there for that fight. But that's not the kind of matter I like to take . . . no matter how much I could bill.

Establishing an involuntary conservatorship over a parent is the most labor-intensive aspect of an inheritance planning practice. When a child asks the court to make health and financial decisions for her parent, she is really asking the court to allow her to restrict that parent's decision-making liberties. It's a true "takeover" of that parent . . . and the probate judge does not look upon such an endeavor lightly or casually. The probate judge demands a ton of proof that shows with absolute certainly that the parent cannot take care of his health and medical affairs, and that the person requesting to be that parent's conservator is one who will do an effective—and honest—job of tending to her parent. Believe me—this is an all-consuming "clear-the-decks" job that lays waste to any other work in my office.

I can handle the work. Of course I can. The involuntary conservatorship is often a necessary part of practicing in the inheritance arena. But, then there are the heightened and unhinged emotions that are ever-present in this process. Not my emotions . . . but those of the "taking over children" who will make dozens of highly charged calls to me, which are absolutely enervating. And of course, there is the inevitable end result of the parent and children becoming permanently estranged . . . a result that I simply loathe having a hand in.

Sure, I would miss those fees. Because those fees help keep my kids happy, maintain my beach lifestyle, and stoke the fire in my relationship with my extravagant girlfriend. But at what cost? Having to steel myself for another draining phone call? Being a participant and percipient witness to family destruction? No . . . I like my peace of mind.

So notwithstanding the nice payday, I'm always on the lookout for a solution to this problem other than involuntary conservatorship, which I attempted with Mr. Medina's children. After I told them about the downsides of that process, I said, "Listen. Before you further consider the conservatorship, I'd like to meet your father. Is there some way you could arrange a meeting? Maybe he would be more attuned to your concern about the house if he hears it from the lawyer."

I don't know what they said to him, but a few days later, he and his children were in my office. Mr. Medina may have been 92, but he did not look or act like 92. He walked tall, and had a full head of gray hair. He was totally and completely alert. Perhaps the smartest one in the room. When we exchanged pleasantries, I learned he was a first-generation American who served in an army hospital throughout WWII.

Long story short. Mr. Medina was just fine . . . and absolutely capable of handling his own affairs. Second wife was not taking advantage of him. He left his house to his second wife for her life because he loved her. It was that simple. Did she love him? Who knows? But she stuck around, and her mere presence made him happy and gave him purpose.

Mr. Medina's children stayed in my office after Mr. Medina left, and I told them it would be a waste of their money to pursue conservatorship litigation. At that time, the probate judge who would hear the case was around 75 . . . which placed him somewhat close to Mr. Medina's peer group. If that probate judge heard Mr. Medina clearly and lucidly speak about his military service, his second wife, and why he left his house to the second wife for her life, the Medina children wouldn't stand a chance to "win" the conservatorship.

Would Mr. Medina's children have had a shot at a success if the probate judge was in his forties? Probably. A younger judge faced with a 92-year-old man marrying a 40-year-old woman would probably presume something sinister was afoot. But, that was conjecture . . . and the Medina children were stuck with an older judge who would be more sympathetic to their father.

In any event, Mr. Medina died about 2 years later and his second wife just stayed in the house—as was her right under his Living Trust. But, it wasn't a free ride. Under California law, a "life tenant" in a residence must pay all expenses of maintenance and property taxes, insurance, repairs . . . or she forfeits the property. Second wife did none of those . . . and the Medina children hired me to seek that forfeiture. Just before I could file the lawsuit, she managed to come up with the money to bring all those expenses and taxes current.

This dance repeated itself numerous times. Second wife got behind. We prepared a lawsuit. Second wife paid all arrearages at the last minute. Finally, I told the Medina children, "Let's see if we can make a deal to buy her out. Cash money to her now instead of nothing when she dies might look good to her—and you'll get your house now to sell and divvy up between all four of you."

At first, Vera and her siblings rejected this proposal out of hand. As Vera said, "How appalling, Mr. Condon! You dare even suggest that we buy our own inheritance?" But eventually, cooler heads prevailed and they determined that this proposal made sense from a business point of view. So, I negotiated a buyout amount with the second wife's lawyer. The second wife moved on with some cash in her pocket, which was way more than she had when she first met Mr. Medina.

Post–Cautionary Tale Comment: The Medina children got their inheritance—but they were unhappy. Well, that's part of the deal when "first children" must contend with their stepparent while attempting to secure at least a portion of their inheritance at a time when they can best use and enjoy it the most, which is during their life. It's tough to spend money when deceased.

Remarriage is common. Having children of a prior marriage is common. Conflict between "first children" and "second spouse" is inevitable. The "second spouse" usually has only an economic relationship with the "first children" . . . who are waiting for "this stranger" to die to get their inheritance. This is not a healthy scenario for either party. The economic connection between them often leads to animosity, lawsuits over investment strategy, allocation of income, and asset maintenance.

The preferable, if obtainable, goal is economic separation between them in the form of assets left outright to each of them. No "first children" hovering over the "second spouse" to see if she's still breathing. And each can go on their merry way with their separate and disconnected inheritances.

About the Author

OR,

AN INVITATION FROM THE AUTHOR
TO CONTACT HIM AT NO CHARGE

Jeffrey L. Condon is an attorney who has practiced in the field of trusts and estates since 1987. He received his bachelor of arts in English literature at UCLA (class of 1983) and his law degree from Whittier College School of Law in 1987. He practices at the law offices of Condon & Condon in Santa Monica, California.

With his late father, Gerald M. Condon, Jeffrey is the co-author of *Beyond the Grave: The Right Way and the Wrong Way of Leaving Money to Your Children (and Others)*, published in 1996 and revised in 2001 and 2014 (HarperCollins). The *Wall Street Journal* has called Jeffrey's first book "the best estate planning book in America."

Jeffrey has been cited as a source for over 200 newspaper and magazine articles discussing inheritance planning in publications including the *New York Times, Los Angeles Times, Washington Post, Wall Street Journal, Time, Kiplinger's,* and *BusinessWeek*. The topics in this area are so many and so diverse, he has been quoted in periodicals ranging from *Fortune* to *DogWorld*.

Jeffrey has discussed various inheritance planning issues on more than 70 radio call-in shows throughout the United States, and on numerous television programs including *The Money Club* (CNBC), *Primetime News* (CNN), *The 700 Club* (CBN), *One on One with John McLaughlin* (NBC), and *The Dr. Laura Show* (CBS).

Jeffrey has conducted more than 300 talks and seminars on the Living Trust and family inheritance planning throughout the

United States, which have been presented by businesses, banks, insurance companies, charities, civic groups, service clubs, real estate companies, trust companies, and conventions. For information about retaining Jeffrey's speaking services, you can contact him (see contact information that follows) or consult his speaker's Internet site at www.harpercollinsspeakersbureau.com/speaker/jeffrey-l-condon.

When *The Living Trust Advisor* was first published in 2008, Jeffrey, in an attempt to be different and clever when writing this *About the Author* section, asked his then 10-year-old daughter, Carly, what his interests were outside of his law practice. In Carly's response, which was printed verbatim, she stated that her father is (1) bald; (2) an ineffective coach of her softball team; (3) a good swimmer; and (4) a fan of Adam Sandler movies. With eight years having passed since Carly uttered that nonfiltered response, Jeffrey approached the now-18-year-old Carly about her present perception of her father's outside-the-office interests. As before, here is Carly's word-for-word response:

> Since I was last asked, my dad has lost more hair, which he whines about every time he looks in a mirror. He hasn't coached my teams for a long time because he only knows enough about softball to coach seven- and eight-year-old girls who are just beginning. So now he only coaches the little girl beginners. He still swims every single day because he's obsessed about not getting fat from all the cookies he eats. He's still a pretty good swimmer for an old man. He spends a lot of time doing nothing with his girlfriend, Kim, but they seem to really enjoy doing nothing together. And they both like Adam Sandler movies, so that's good. And he just bought me a car. so he's a pretty good dad.

Jeffrey welcomes your comments or questions about any information in *The Living Trust Advisor* and is pleased to, without charge, respond to brief general questions you may have. The contact information is:

Jeffrey L. Condon, Esq.

3435 Ocean Park Boulevard

Suite 108

Santa Monica, CA 90405

Telephone: (310) 393-0701

Fax: (310) 394-3555

Web site: www.condonandcondon.net

E-mail: jeff@condonandcondon.net

When communicating with Jeffrey, please follow these five guidelines:

1. For the most immediate response, your questions or comments should be made by telephone. When calling, please state that you are making a "book call."
2. If Jeffrey is unavailable to speak with you, you may leave your name and telephone number to receive a return call.
3. Jeffrey will most likely respond to all fax and e-mail communications by telephone. Therefore, all communications to him should include a telephone number for a return call.
4. All communications from Jeffrey are made with the understanding that he is not engaged in rendering legal, accounting, or other professional service by responding to your comments or questions. If you need legal assistance, you are required to (1) retain Jeffrey as your attorney or (2) retain the services of other competent attorneys who emphasize a practice in estate and/or inheritance planning.

Index